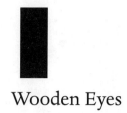

Wooden Eyes

EUROPEAN PERSPECTIVES

EUROPEAN PERSPECTIVES

A Series in Social Thought and Cultural Criticism

Lawrence D. Kritzman, Editor

European Perspectives presents outstanding books by leading European thinkers. With both classic and contemporary works, the series aims to shape the major intellectual controversies of our day and to facilitate the tasks of historical understanding.

For a complete list of books in the series, see pages 263–264.

Wooden Eyes

NINE REFLECTIONS ON DISTANCE

Carlo Ginzburg

Translated by Martin Ryle and Kate Soper

COLUMBIA UNIVERSITY PRESS

New York

Columbia University Press

Publishers Since 1893

New York   Chichester, West Sussex

Translation copyright © 2001

Columbia University Press

Occhiacci di Legno © 1998

Giangiacomo Feltrinelli Editore Milano

All rights reserved

Library of Congress Cataloging-in-Publication Data

Ginzburg, Carlo.

[Occhiacci di legno. English]

Wooden eyes : nine reflections on distance /

Carlo Ginzburg.

p. cm. — (European perspectives)

Includes bibliographical references and index.

ISBN 0–231–11960–7

1. Perspective (Philosophy) 2. Culture—Philosophy.

3. Aesthetic distance. I. Ryle, Martin H. II. Soper, Kate.

III. Title. IV. Series.

BD348 .G5613   2001

195—dc21   2001017407

Casebound editions of Columbia University Press books
are printed on permanent and durable acid-free paper.

Printed in the United States of America

Designed by Audrey Smith

c 10 9 8 7 6 5 4 3 2 1

Wooden eyes, why are you looking at me?

—Collodi, *Pinocchio*

To Amos Funkenstein

CONTENTS

PLATES

PREFACE

The reader will find here nine essays, three of them previously unpublished, that I have written during the last decade. The "distance" referred to in the book's subtitle is both literal and metaphorical. Since 1998, I have been teaching in Los Angeles. Conversation with students such as those who attend UCLA, whose intellectual background is quite unlike my own and who are ethnically and culturally diverse, has obliged me to look afresh at research themes and topics on which I have long been working. My sense of their importance has not lessened, but that importance has become less self-evident. I have come to understand better something that I thought I already knew: that familiarity, which is in the last analysis bound up with cultural belonging, cannot be a criterion of what is relevant. To say that every place in the world is like our place does not mean that everything is the same; it means that we all find ourselves astray, out of place, vis-à-vis some things and some people.

I know that I am saying nothing new, but perhaps it is worth pausing to reflect on the intellectual fecundity of this condition. This is what I have tried to do in the essay that opens the collection. Even the first written, however, on representation (chapter 3), was animated by a wish to awaken in the reader (and first of all, in the writer) this sense of being astray, by compressing a vast topic into a few pages and by setting Europe and Italy in a very wide chronological and spatial framework. In it, I engaged with a double ambiguity: the ambiguity of images, which are simultaneously presences and surrogates for what is not present; and the ambiguity of the relationship between Jews and Christians, in which closeness and distance have been interlaced, often with fatal consequences, for two millennia. These ambiguities come together in the theme of idolatry, which is alluded to in the title of the book and discussed in the essay on idols and images. This ends abruptly, in a juxtaposition of the first two commandments: "You shall not make a carved image for yourself nor the likeness of anything" and "You shall not make wrong use of the name of the Lord." I return to the contiguity of the word and the image in my inquiry into myth. The Greeks both depicted their gods and spoke their names; and they reasoned on the nature of images and of words. However, this apparent contrast between the Greeks and the Jews perhaps conceals a hidden symmetry: both the Greek reflection on myth and the Jewish prohibition of idolatry are instruments of distantiation. Greeks and Jews, in their different ways, sought to develop tools that would allow them to cast a critical gaze on reality without becoming submerged in it. Christianity set itself against them both, and learned from them both.

I am a Jew who was born and grew up in a Catholic country; I never received any religious education; my Jewish identity is to a large degree the result of persecution. It was almost unawares that I began to reflect on the multiple tradition to which I belong, seeking to cast a distanced and if possible critical gaze upon it. I was, and am, only too aware that I am less well prepared than I might be for such a task. Following the chain of scriptural quotations in the Gospels, I reached a position from which I was able to read them, and indeed to interpret the figure of Jesus, from a viewpoint that I myself had not anticipated. Here again I encountered the opposition between showing and telling, morphology and history—an inexhaustible theme and one that has long fascinated me. It is the theme on which I reason, from various angles, in the second, fourth, fifth, and sixth essays. A practice of reflection inaugurated by the Greeks has allowed us to discover what image, name, and myth, despite their diversity, have in common: the fact that they all lie beyond truth and falsehood. In our culture we attribute this character to art in general. Yet artistic fictions, like the fictions of the law, speak of reality. This is what I show in the essay on defamiliarization (the first), and also in a somewhat inverted way in the reflections of the eighth, on the Chinese mandarin: in one place the right distance, in the other too much; here absence of empathy, leading to critical distance, there lack of empathy leading to dehumanization. And now distance, which had prompted my reflections, became their theme—distance itself, historical perspective (the seventh essay): and I realized I had written this book.

Many people have helped me. Apart from those mentioned in connection with the individual essays (where I trust I have omitted no one), I must thank Giovanna Ferrari, whose professionalism contributed greatly to the preparation of the manuscript. Here I name those with whom I have had especially intense and rewarding conversations: Perry Anderson, Pier Cesare Bori, Saul Friedländer, Alberto Gajano, Stefano Levi Della Torre, and Franco Moretti.

I would never have written this book had I not met Amos Funkenstein and become his friend. It is with great affection and gratitude that I mention him here.

As I bid these pages farewell, my thoughts turn to Adriano Sofri, closest and distant friend; and to Ovidio Bompressi and Giorgio Pietrostefani, with the hope that their innocence will soon be finally acknowledged.

BOLOGNA, DECEMBER 1997

I finished writing this book in Berlin, at the Wissenschaftskolleg, during a year of intense, peaceful work. I thank everyone who made this possible.

The first essay appeared in *Representations*, 1996; the second in *I Greci*, vol. 1, *Noi e i greci*, ed. S. Settis (Turin, 1996); the third in *Annales*, 1991; the fifth in *Sight and Insight: Essays in Art and Culture in Honour of E. H. Gombrich*, ed. J. Onians (London, 1994); the eighth in *Historical Change and Human Rights: The Amnesty Lectures 1994*, ed. O. Hufton (New York, 1995); the ninth in *La Repubblica* (October 1997). All—especially the third—were revised for their publication in book form as *Occhiacci di legno* (Milan, 1998), and the present translation in based on that text.

Wooden Eyes

Making It Strange

THE PREHISTORY OF A LITERARY DEVICE

I

1. In 1922, the Russian critic Viktor Shklovsky, in a letter
to Roman Jakobson, exclaimed cheerfully: "We know how
life is made, and how *Don Quixote* and the car are made
too."[1] The characteristic note of early Russian formalism is
very audible in this—its conception of literary criticism as
a rigorous form of knowledge, and of art as an assemblage
or device. The friendship between the two men, both of
them in their twenties when the letter was written, was not
to last, but their names would remain indissolubly linked
with the formalist movement.[2] Shklovsky's *Theory of Prose*,
published a few years earlier (in 1917), included chapters
titled "The Making of Don Quixote" and "Art as Device."
Shklovsky embarks, before long, on a discussion of human
psychology:

If we examine the general laws of perception, we see that as it becomes habitual, it also becomes automatic. So eventually all our skills and experiences function unconsciously—automatically. If someone were to compare the sensation of holding a pen in his hand or speaking a foreign tongue for the very first time with the sensation of performing this same operation for the ten thousandth time, then he would no doubt agree with us. It is this process of automatization that explains the laws of our prose speech with its fragmentary phrases and half-articulated words.

So heavily do unconscious habits weigh on us, Shklovsky goes on to write, that "life fades into nothingness. Automatization eats away at things, at clothes, at furniture, at our wives, and at our fear of war."

At this point, a definition of art in general is introduced:

And so, in order to return sensation to our limbs, in order to make us feel objects, to make a stone feel stony, man has been given the tool of art. The purpose of art, then, is to lead us to a knowledge of a thing through the organ of sight instead of recognition. By "estranging" or "de-familiarizing" objects and complicating form, the device of art makes perception long and "laborious." The perceptual process in art has a purpose all its own and ought to be extended to the fullest. *Art is a means of experiencing the process of creativity. The artifact itself is quite unimportant.*[3]

Shklovsky's notion that art is an instrument for revitalizing our perceptions, which habit has made dull, at once reminds us of the role played by involuntary memory in Marcel Proust's work. In 1917, only the first volume of *À la recherche du temps perdu, Du côté de chez Swann*, had appeared. Proust's name, moreover, is nowhere mentioned in Shklovsky's analysis of "art as device." For examples of *ostranienie*—"de-familiarization" or "making it strange"—he turns above all to Tolstoy. In Tolstoy's short story "Kholstomer," Shklovsky points out that as "the story is told from the point of view of a horse," this defamiliarization is mediated "not by our perception but by that of the horse."

This is how the horse sees the rights of property:

Many of the people . . . who call me their horse did not ride me. Others did. These same people never fed me. Others did. Once again, I was shown many kindnesses, but not by those who called me their horse. No, by coachmen, veterinarians and strangers of all sorts. As my observations grew, though, I became increasingly convinced that this concept of *mine* was invalid not only for us horses but also for human folk, i.e., that it represents nothing more than man's base and beastly instinct to claim property for himself. A landlord, for instance, says "my house" but never lives in it, concerning himself only with the structure and maintenance of the house. A merchant says "my shop," "my clothing shop," yet he himself does not wear any clothes made from the fine material displayed in it.

. . . I am now convinced that what distinguishes us from human beings and gives us the right to claim a higher place on the ladder of living creatures is simply this: that the human species is guided, above all, by *words*, while ours is guided by *deeds*.[4]

As well as analyzing a number of passages from Tolstoy, Shklovsky considers examples of a completely different literary genre, namely, riddles with erotic undertones. In one example, the wife of the hero of the *bylina*, Stavyor, appears before him in disguise. He does not recognize her. She sets him this riddle:

"Don't you remember, Stavyor, don't you recall
How we learned our alphabet together:
Mine was the silver inkwell, and your pen was golden?
I moistened your pen then and there,
Yes, I moistened it all right, then and there."

However, Shklovsky observes, defamiliarization "is not a device limited to the erotic riddle—a euphemism of sorts. It is also the foundation of all riddles: every riddle"—except those based on a kind of auditory mimicry—"defines and illustrates its object in words which seem inappropriate during the telling of it."[5]

Here, Shklovsky is echoing the general point that he has made earlier, in reference to the way in which "the removal of [objects] from the sphere of automatized perception is accomplished in art."[6]

2. Shklovsky's essay retains all its fascination, and all its youthful arrogance. Apart from one brief reference that I will discuss later, it shows a deliberate lack of historical perspective. To ignore history in this way is typical of the Russian formalists, and this attitude strengthened their view that art can be seen as a "device." If art is an assemblage, we need to know how it works, not how it came into being. The idea of "de-familiarization" (*ostranienie*) has deep resonances in twentieth-century literary theory, of course: Brecht's "alienation" is a well-known instance.[7] Their very success, however, has helped shield Shklovsky's ideas from scrutiny. We might ask why (beyond the obvious practical reasons) he placed such emphasis on Russian texts. We might ask, too, what kind of connection exists between riddles, as a literary genre, and the sophisticated uses to which Tolstoy puts *ostranienie*. Finally and above all, is "de-familiarization" to be considered as coterminous with artistic practice in general, as Shklovsky suggested, or should we understand it as a procedure bound up with a particular literary tradition? In seeking to answer these questions, I shall be led to consider the notion of "making it strange" from a perspective that is, unless I am mistaken, rather different from that usually adopted nowadays.

3. The path that I shall follow is somewhat tortuous. It begins with the reflections that the emperor Marcus Aurelius wrote in Greek in the second century B.C. Various names—*To Myself, Memoirs, Thoughts,* and so forth—have been given to these reflections.[8] The first book is a kind of autobiography, composed in the form of a catalog of the people, whether relatives, teachers, or friends, to whom Marcus Aurelius felt morally or intellectually indebted. The other eleven books consist of a series of fragmentary passages, of varying length, and in an apparently haphazard order. Some were written during Marcus Aurelius's military campaigns, as a means to moral self-education, drawing on the vocabulary of the Stoic philosophy in which he had been trained. The work was not intended for publication, a fact that influenced not only its form but also, as I shall show, its fate after the author's death.

Marcus Aurelius was interested in self-education rather than introspection. The imperative was his preferred mode. "Wipe away the impress of imagination," he wrote ever more frequently, employing a term—*"phantasia"*—from the technical terminology of the Stoics. Epictetus, the philosopher-slave whose ideas profoundly influenced Marcus Aurelius, maintained that this striking out or erasure of imaginary representations was a necessary step in the quest for an exact perception of things, and thus in the attainment of virtue.[9] This is how Marcus Aurelius describes the successive stages:

> Wipe away the impress of imagination. Stay the impulse which is drawing you like a puppet. Define the time which is present. Recognize what is happening to yourself or another. Divide and separate the event into its causal and material aspects. Dwell in thought upon your last hour. *(7.29)*

Each of these injunctions required the adoption of a specific moral technique aimed at acquiring mastery over the passions, which reduce us to puppets (this was a favorite simile of Marcus Aurelius). First of all, we must pause and take stock. That which is dear to us must be broken down into its component parts. For example, the "tuneful phrase" of a song must be subdivided "into every one of its notes": "ask yourself about each whether you are its servant."

All things, virtue excepted, must be subjected to this treatment:

> Generally then, excepting virtue and its effects, remember to have recourse to the several parts and by analysis to go on to despise them, and to apply the same process to life as a whole. *(11.2)*

However, it is not sufficient just to break things down into their simplest elements. We must also learn to view them as from a distance:

> Asia and Europe are corners in the Universe; every sea, a drop in the Universe; Mount Athos, a clod of earth in the Universe; every instant of time, a pin-prick of eternity. All things are petty, easily changed, vanishing away. *(6.36)*

If we appraise it across this immensity of time, amid this multiplicity of individuals, we come to understand that our own existence has no importance whatever:

Ponder . . . the life led by others long ago, the life that will be led after you, the life being led in barbarian races; how many do not even know your name, how many will very soon forget it and how many who praise you perhaps now will very soon blame you; and that neither memorial nor fame nor anything else at all is worth a thought. *(9.30)*

This cosmic perspective clarifies the meaning of the injunction quoted above: "Dwell in thought upon your last hour." Everything, our death included, must be seen as part of a general process of transformation and change:

Dwell upon everything that exists and reflect that it is already in process of dissolution and coming into being by change and a kind of decay or dispersion, or in what way it is born to die, in a manner of speaking. *(10.18)*

The search for the first cause is itself part of the Stoic technique whose aim is to attain an exact perception of things:

Surely it is an excellent plan, when you are seated before delicacies and choice foods, to impress upon your imagination [*phantasia*] that this is the dead body of a fish, that the dead body of a bird or a pig; and again, that the Falernian wine is grape juice and that robe of purple a lamb's fleece dipped in a shell-fish's blood; and in matters of sex intercourse, that it is attrition of an entrail and a convulsive expulsion of mere mucus. Surely these are excellent imaginations [*phantasiai*], going to the heart of actual facts and penetrating them so as to see what kind of things they really are. You should adopt this practice all through your life, and where things make an impression which is very plausible, uncover their nakedness, see into their cheapness, strip off the profession on which they vaunt themselves. *(6.13)*[10]

4. To a twentieth-century reader, this extraordinary passage must inevitably seem like an anticipation of the technique of "making it strange." There are some grounds for using the term. Tolstoy deeply admired Marcus Aurelius, and more than fifty extracts from the

emperor's writings were included in the calendrical anthology of universal wisdom that the novelist compiled in his old age.[11] Moreover, Tolstoy's radical attitudes toward law, ambition, war, and love were profoundly influenced by Marcus Aurelius's reflections. Tolstoy regarded human conventions and institutions with the eyes of a horse or a child: as strange, opaque phenomena, devoid of the significance generally attributed to them. To his gaze, at once impassioned and detached, things revealed themselves "as they really are," to use Marcus Aurelius's words.

This reading of Marcus Aurelius, which is indebted to two memorable essays by Pierre Hadot, adds a fresh dimension to Shklovsky's discussion of "art as device." Moreover, it confirms the parallel between the technique of estrangement and that of riddles: we can imagine Marcus Aurelius asking himself, for instance, "What is a lamb's fleece dipped in a shell-fish's blood?" In order to give their proper weight to human honorific insignia such as those that denote membership of the Senate, we must take our distance from the object and seek its cause, asking a question such as riddles pose. Moral self-education requires of us above all that we erase mistaken representations, reject seemingly obvious postulates, and refuse the familiar recognitions that have become trite through repetition, thanks to our habits of perception. In order to *see* things, we must first of all look at them as if they had no meaning, as if they were a riddle.

II

1. Riddles are found in the most diverse cultures—perhaps in all cultures.[12] The possibility that Marcus Aurelius drew inspiration from a popular genre such as the riddle accords with a cherished view of mine that a circular relation is often found between learned culture and popular culture. This kind of circularity is also involved, in a way that I believe has not previously been noted, in the singular fate that befell Marcus Aurelius's reflections after their author's death. To make this point clearly, I shall have to make a considerable detour, in order to show *how* Tolstoy read Marcus Aurelius. We shall see that he found in the Roman writer's thoughts the confirmation of an attitude acquired earlier in his intellectual and moral development, which is why they affected him so deeply.

Marcus Aurelius's reflections were known to exist in late antiquity, because they are referred to and quoted in writings by various learned Greeks and Byzantines. The text has come down to us by way of just two more or less complete manuscripts. One of these, on which the *editio princeps* was based, is now lost. This scarcity of manuscripts undoubtedly reflects the unusual nature of Marcus Aurelius's works, written as these were as a series of scattered reflections, vividly phrased, fleeting and fragmentary.[13] Some years before the *editio princeps* appeared (in 1558), however, the life and letters of Marcus Aurelius became familiar to the learned public of Europe in the form of a fictitious travesty. This fake was the work of a Franciscan friar, Antonio de Guevara, bishop of Mondoñedo and court preacher to Charles V. Guevara's work was published in Valladolid, in 1529, and bore the title *Libro del emperador Marco Aurelio con relox de principes* (The Book of the Emperor Marcus Aurelius, with the Dial of Princes). In the preface to the first printing, Guevara claimed that he had brought back from Florence a Greek manuscript by Marcus Aurelius and that some of his friends had subsequently translated it for him. The book Guevara claimed to have translated, however, bore no relation to the text of Marcus Aurelius's reflections, which was first to appear in print some thirty years later. Guevara mixes a modicum of history with a deal of imagination, inventing letters by Marcus Aurelius, dialogues between him and his wife, and so forth. This admixture enjoyed a remarkable success. Often known as the *Golden Book of Marcus Aurelius*, it was translated into many languages, among them Armenian (Venice, 1738), and went on being reprinted for decades. In 1643, the English philologist Meric Casaubon remarked disdainfully, in the introduction to his own edition of Marcus Aurelius's reflections, that the success of Guevara's forgery could be compared only to that enjoyed by the Bible.[14] However, Guevara's reputation was already set on a swift downward course. Bayle's cutting entry in the *Dictionnaire historique et critique* portrays him as a forger.[15] Only a very small part of Guevara's book was destined to survive. This is a speech supposedly addressed to Marcus Aurelius and the Roman Senate by one Milenus, a peasant from the Danube region. More than a century later, these pages were to inspire a famous poem by La Fontaine, "Le paysan du Danube." A brief excerpt from this speech is enough to show that it is an eloquent denunciation of Roman imperialism:

So greedy have you been for the goods of others, and so great has been your arrogance in seeking to rule over foreign lands, that the sea with all its deeps has not sufficed you and the land with its broad fields has not satisfied you . . . for you Romans pay no heed to others, except to trouble peaceful folk and rob the fruits of other people's toil.[16]

To a sixteenth-century reader such as Vasco de Quiroga, we know it would have been clear that the true target of this speech was the Spanish conquest of the New World. The *Golden Book of Marcus Aurelius* can be read as a lengthy sermon addressed to Emperor Charles V by the court preacher Antonio de Guevara in order to make some sharp criticisms of the Spanish conquest and its horrors. This applies especially to the group of chapters that became familiar in court circles, before their inclusion in the book, as the separate work titled *The Peasant of the Danube*.[17] Milenus's speech made a powerful contribution to the myth of the noble savage, giving it currency across Europe:

If you say that we deserve to be slaves, because we have no Princes to command us, nor Senators to govern us, nor army to defend us, then I reply that as we have no enemies we have no need of an army; and as each of us was happy with his lot, we needed no proud Senators to govern us, and being all equal we were unwilling to have any Princes among us, whose office is to put down tyrants and to preserve the people in peace. If you say, that in our land we have neither a Republic nor a civil order, and that we live like brute beasts in the mountains, you are wrong in both points, for we allow to live in our country neither liars, not disturbers of the peace, nor men who might bring to us from foreign parts such things as might corrupt us or enfeeble us: inasmuch as just as our dress was decent, so too our diet was plain.[18]

This idyllic description, it has long been recognized, was largely inspired by the *Germania* of Tacitus. The attack on the misdeeds of Roman imperialism also draws on a well-known passage in Tacitus, the powerful speech in the *Agricola* in which the Caledonian chief Calgacus accuses the Romans of "making a desert and calling it peace" (*"atque ubi solitudinem faciant, pacem appellant"*). Calgacus is no more than a name, however, whereas Milenus, the peasant of the Danube, is a thoroughly concrete individual. This is how Antonio de Guevara describes him:

> This peasant was small-featured, but large-lipped, his eyes were deep-set, his color was sere, his hair bristled up, he was bare-headed and wore shoes of porcupine's hide and carried a goatskin bag, his belt was made of seaweed, his beard was long and thick, his eyelashes covered his eyes, his breast and his neck were as hairy as bearskin, and in his hand he bore a spear.[19]

Marcus Aurelius (in other words, Guevara) comments, "When I saw him enter the Senate, I thought he was some animal in human form." Who, though, is this peasant, bold enough to denounce the crimes of the Roman emperor? A preliminary draft of Guevara's text, never printed, portrays the Danube peasant as beardless, and it has been thought that this detail marks him out as a Native American.[20] However, his monstrous, animal-like physiognomy also suggests a different origin. He is a close relative of the peasant Marcolphus or Marcolfo or Morolf, who in the famous medieval text speaks so boldly to King Solomon:

> Marcolphus was a small-built man but tall in height; he had a large head, a broad forehead, ruddy and wrinkled, his ears were hairy and hung halfway down his jaws; he had large squinting eyes, his lower lip hung down like a horse's, his beard was filthy and adorned with hideous thick hairs like a goat's, his hands were short and with short thick fingers, his feet were round and swollen, his nose was thick and crooked, his lips big and thick, he had the aspect of an ass and his hair was like a he-goat's. His shoes were of the most rustic fashion, and his flesh was spotted with divers stains and heavy with mud and mire.[21]

A tiny detail confirms that these two texts are closely connected. Guevara's odd reference to "shoes of porcupine's hide" ("*zapatos de un cuero de puerco espín,*" in the Spanish) is due to his having absentmindedly run together two phrases in the Latin version of the *Dialogue of Solomon and Marcolphus,* where Marcolphus's shoes are mentioned immediately after a comparison between his hair and the quills of a porcupine: *"capillos veluti spin-ule ericiorum; calciamenta pedum."*[22] Guevara's veiled criticism of Spanish policy in the New World was thus based on a curious mixture—on Tacitus, but also on what the twelfth-century historian William of Tyre had called "fabulous popular narratives," stories in which Marcolphus "alternately solved the riddles which Solomon set him, and set new ones of his own."[23] Both traditions, classical and medieval, could be drawn on for the purpose of defying the established powers.

The popularizing tradition of the Middle Ages depicted the king as challenged by a peasant whose grotesque physical appearance went along with an unexpected sharpness and wisdom. In the most famous reworking of the *Dialogue of Solomon and Marcolphus*, Giulio Cesare Croce's *Sottilissime astuzie di Bertoldo*, King Alboinus proudly exclaims: "See how many Lords and Barons stand about me to obey me and do me honor." Bertoldo promptly replies: "Just as big ants stand about a rowan-tree and gnaw away at its bark."[24] Animal similes of this kind express a tendency to make little of the king's authority—a theme of which Bakhtin gives a profound analysis in his great work on the popular culture of the Renaissance.[25] From a subjective point of view, the innocence of the animal strips the veil from the hidden reality of social relations, as in the case of Tolstoy's story of the horse Kholstomer, which Shklovsky analyzed. The Danube peasant, an "animal in human form," undoes the pretenses of Roman (and Spanish) imperial ideology, comparing the conquering powers to brigands who rob and kill innocent peoples. Marcus Aurelius (the historical Marcus Aurelius), who was the most powerful man in the world, had reached a similar conclusion after considering himself in the light of a series of belittling and degrading parallels:

> A spider is proud when he traps a fly, a man when he snares a leveret, another when he nets a sprat, another boars, another bears, another Sarmatian prisoners. If you test their sentiments, are they not bandits? *(10.10)*[26]

2. Guevara was probably not telling the truth when he claimed to have had access to a translation of Marcus Aurelius's reflections. Nonetheless, he undeniably succeeded, in the forgery that he com-

piled, in capturing a faint echo of the melancholy tone in Marcus
Aurelius's then unpublished text. I do not intend by this to claim

that Guevara can be enumerated among the precursors of literary
defamiliarization. When the Danube peasant concludes his speech
by announcing that "empire is nothing but robbery," this is presented as something evident; it does not emerge out of an
antecedent moment of opacity or misunderstanding. However,
Guevara's text left an indelible mark on the subsequent development of defamiliarization as a literary technique. Ever since its publication, the savage, the peasant, and the animal, together or singly,
have offered a viewpoint from which it is possible to turn upon society a distanced, estranged, and critical gaze.

I shall cite just a few examples, beginning with a famous text by
Montaigne. Montaigne undoubtedly knew Guevara's *Marcus Aurelius*, since it was among his father's favorite books.[27] In his essay
"On the Cannibals" Montaigne writes with incredulous amaze-
ment about the tales told of the natives of Brazil, whose peaceful
and innocent life seemed to evoke the classical myths of the
golden age. The essay's conclusion, however, returns the reader
abruptly to Europe. Here Montaigne tells the story of three
Brazilian natives brought into France. Asked what had most
struck them there, they mentioned two things. First of all, they
were amazed to see grown men in arms (the Swiss guards) obeying the orders of a child (the king of France) instead of choosing
a proper leader. Second—here Montaigne explains that they use
an idiom by which men are called the "halves" of one another—
they had

> noticed that there were men among us fully bloated with all sorts
> of comforts while their halves were begging at their doors, ema-
> ciated with poverty and hunger: they found it odd that those des-
> titute halves should put up with such injustice and did not take
> them by the throat or set fire to their houses.[28]

The Brazilian natives, incapable of perceiving the obvious, had
seen something normally concealed by habit and convention. Montaigne delighted in this inability to take reality for granted. He was
ready to question himself about everything, from the foundations of
our social life to the smallest details of daily existence. The surprise

of the natives of Brazil showed the distance that European society, marked as it was by political and economic inequality, had traveled from what Montaigne called *naïveté originelle* ("original naivety").[29] "*Naïf*," "*nativus*": Montaigne's love of this term, and his corresponding disgust with the artificial, takes us to the heart of the notion of defamiliarization. To understand less, to be ingenuous, to remain stupefied: these are reactions that may lead us to see more, and to take account of what lies deeper, what is closer to nature.

3. The French moralists of the seventeenth century transformed the essay, as it had been developed by Montaigne, into independent and separate fragments or aphorisms. One of these fragments, included in the 1689 edition of La Bruyère's *Caractères*, illustrates how the full corrosive power of defamiliarization was emerging:

A number of wild animals are to be seen, both male and female, scattered over the country. They are blackened, livid, all burned by the sun, and fixed to the earth, which they rummage and work away at with invincible obstinacy: they have, as it were, articulate voices, and when they stand up on their feet they have human faces, and indeed they are human beings; they retire at night into dens where they live upon black bread, water and roots; they spare other men the labor of sowing, ploughing, and harvesting in order to live, and thus they deserve not to go short of the bread that they have sown.[30]

This passage is extraordinary both for its content, which departs markedly from La Bruyère's usual support for the dominant ideology, and in the way it is constructed. An initial misunderstanding ("a number of wild animals") is followed by an observation that contradicts this, and that has a note of perplexity: "they have, as it were, articulate voices." Then comes a sudden enlightenment, like the moment in which a riddle is solved: "when they stand up on their feet they have human faces, and indeed"—*en effet*—"they are human beings."

The expression "indeed" introduces a factual description ("they retire at night into dens," and so forth), which leads into the ironic observation "thus they deserve not to go short of the bread that they have sown." The apparent social and moral equity of this conclusion is implicitly denounced as hypocrisy, given what has been said earlier. "They" deserve to survive, and no more than that. "They" are never named.

In the earlier examples analyzed here, those compared with animals were people at the top of the human social scale. Here, there is a similar comparison, but with reference to those at the bottom, and with equally degrading implications. The reader might have expected a direct affirmation: "peasants live like animals," or "peasants live in inhuman conditions." La Bruyère chooses rather to put a number of obstacles in our way: the initial misunderstanding, the unnamed subject, the ironic conclusion. The reader is drawn into a cognitive struggle that transforms the implicit conclusion into a kind of reward. The effect is incomparably more powerful, in both artistic and rhetorical terms.

4. In 1765 Voltaire, writing under the easily recognizable pseudonym of "l'abbé Bazin," published a short *Philosophy of History*. It included a chapter titled "Des sauvages" (Of savages), which began with a lengthy rhetorical question:

By the term "savages," do you understand peasants, living in huts with their women and a few animals, exposed at all times to the rigors of the season, knowing nothing beyond the land on which they live and the marketplace to which they occasionally travel to sell their produce and buy rude garments; speaking a jargon never heard in towns; short of ideas, and consequently of expressions; in subjection, without knowing why, to some jack in office, to whom they must give each year half what they have produced in the sweat of their brows; gathering together on certain established days in a barnlike building to celebrate ceremonies of which they understand nothing and to listen to a man dressed in clothes unlike theirs, saying words that mean nothing to them; sometimes leaving their cottages at the sound of the drum, and undertaking to go and get themselves killed in a foreign land, and to kill people like themselves, for a quarter of what they could earn by staying at home and working?

This splendid passage was clearly inspired by the fragment by La Bruyère that I have just analyzed. In both cases, the periphrastic style sets up a cognitive tension in the reader as the surprisingly *strange* features of a familiar object are gradually revealed. There is, however, a difference. La Bruyère does not name the object of his discourse. Voltaire, in a stroke of genius, begins by giving it a mistaken name, and then gradually reveals this to be the right name. Here is how Voltaire replies to his own rhetorical question:

> Savages like this can be found everywhere in Europe. Let us be quite clear that the people of Canada and the Kaffirs, whom we are pleased to term savages, are infinitely superior to our own. The Huron, the Algonquin, the Illinois, the Kaffir, and the Hottentot know how to make for themselves everything that they need, while our peasants lack that art. The peoples of America and Africa are free, while our savages do not even have the idea of freedom.
>
> The savages (as they are called) of America . . . know honor, of which our European savages have never heard a word. They have a fatherland that they love and will defend; they make treaties; they fight bravely, and often speak with heroic energy.[31]

The Jesuits called the fields of Europe—the theater of their missionary enterprise—the Indies *"de por acá"*: the Indies in this world.[32] It is well known that the Jesuits had a markedly open-minded attitude toward extra-European cultures. Voltaire had had a Jesuit education; when he identifies the real savages as those who inhabit our continent, he echoes the attitude of his masters, pushing it to the point of paradox.[33] He looks at the lives of European peasants from an infinite distance, like the giant from the star Syrius who is one of the protagonists of his tale *Micromegas*. His intentionally opaque and astonished gaze transforms taxes, war, the Mass into so many senseless performances, absurd and lacking legitimacy.

5. In a chapter of *The Theory of Prose* titled "The Structure of Fiction," Shklovsky returns to the notion of defamiliarization, remarking that Tolstoy had presumably encountered it in "French literature, perhaps in Voltaire's Huron, nicknamed 'l'Ingénu,' or perhaps in the description of the French court made by Chateaubriand's 'Savage.'"[34] The texts I have cited in the course of this digression

belong to a longer tradition, and one which Tolstoy greatly
admired.[35] Tolstoy's work recalls in particular the chapter "Des

sauvages," taken from the *Philosophy of History*, which Voltaire had
originally dedicated to Catherine II, empress of Russia, and subsequently republished as the introduction ("Discours préliminaire") to
the *Essai sur les moeurs*.[36] When the horse Kholstomer denounces the
animal-like ways of human beings, we seem to hear an echo of
Voltaire's denunciation of European peasants as the real savages.
Shklovsky's general reference to French literature as providing
precedents for Tolstoyan defamiliarization needs to be made more
specific; it is the literature of the French *Enlightenment*, and first of all
Voltaire, that we must note.[37] Above all, a purely formalistic assessment cannot grasp what Tolstoy learned from Voltaire, namely the
use of defamiliarization as a delegitimizing device at every level—
political, social, religious. Voltaire had written of peasants "gathering together on certain established days in a barn-like building to
celebrate ceremonies of which they understand nothing and to listen to a man dressed in clothes unlike theirs, saying words that mean
nothing to them." Tolstoy developed this passage when he came to
write about the Mass in *Resurrection*, in a passage that the Russian
Synod took as proof of the author's blasphemous attitude, expelling
him from the Orthodox Church:

The service began.

It consisted of the following. The priest, having dressed himself up in a strange and very inconvenient garb of gold cloth, cut
and arranged little bits of bread on a saucer and then put them
into a cup of wine, repeating at the same time different names
and prayers.[38]

His early immersion in the tradition of the Enlightenment deeply
influenced the way Tolstoy later came to read Marcus Aurelius. This
double influence explains why Tolstoy never used defamiliarization
merely as a literary technique. For him it was a means (as Marcus
Aurelius had written) for "going to the heart of actual facts and penetrating them so as to see what kind of things they really are," a way
to "uncover their nakedness, see into their cheapness, strip off the
profession on which they vaunt themselves." For Marcus Aurelius
and equally for Tolstoy, to see things "as they really are" meant to

free oneself from false ideas and images; meant, in the last analysis, to accept transience and death. A revealing anecdote is told by one of Tolstoy's daughters, Alexandra Lvovna. One day, she told an old peasant woman who used to help her in the house that she was in a bad humor. "If you read Marcus Aurelius," the old woman replied, "all your sadness would disappear." "Who is this Marcus Aurelius?" asked Alexandra Lvovna, "and why should I read him?" "To be sure, the Count gave me his book," explained the old woman. "It is written there that we shall all die. And if death lies before us, then all our sorrows are nothing. Just think of death, and your heart will grow lighter. Whenever some grief troubles me, I say: 'Come on, boys, read Marcus Aurelius to me!'"[39]

This story delighted Tolstoy. No doubt it confirmed his deep conviction that peasants, because of their distance from modern life and its artifice, were closer to the truth. Montaigne (another writer whom Tolstoy greatly admired) based his attitude toward the natives of Brazil on similar grounds. There was nothing paternalistic about Tolstoy's populism: he saw the old peasant woman as perfectly capable of understanding Marcus Aurelius. In this, he was probably right—partly because some of Marcus Aurelius's reflections drew inspiration from the popular literary form of the riddle.

III

1. At this point the circle might seem to be closed. However, the reconstruction I have offered so far is incomplete. As I noted, Shklovsky's chapter "Art as Device" makes no mention of Marcel Proust. Proust, though, does develop a rather different notion of defamiliarization, analyzing it explicitly (though under another name), and in *À la recherche du temps perdu* this plays an important and arguably a crucial role.

The narrator's much-loved grandmother is among the most important characters in *À l'ombre des jeunes filles en fleur*, the second novel in the sequence. Every reader of Proust will remember that she has a passion for the letters of Madame de Sévigné:

> But my grandmother . . . had taught me to admire their true
> beauties. . . . Before long, I was to be still more forcibly struck by

them, since Madame de Sévigné belongs to the same artistic family as a painter, Elstir, whom I was to meet at Balbec and who was to have such a deep influence on the way I saw things. I realized at Balbec that she, like him, had a way of presenting things in the order of our perception of them, rather than explaining them by their cause. But already that afternoon, in that carriage, as I read again that letter where the moonlight appears—"I could not resist the temptation, I put on all my unnecessary caps and jackets, I went out into that alley where the air was as gentle as the air in my room; I came across a thousand chimeras, *white monks and black monks, linen thrown here and there, men buried upright against tree-trunks*, and so on"—I was delighted by what I would have called, a little later, the Dostoevskyan side of the *Letters of Madame de Sévigné* (for does she not depict landscapes in just the same way as he depicts characters?).[40]

Madame de Sévigné, Elstir, Dostoesvky: what do they have in common? This question comes to the surface, implicitly or explicitly, in four different passages in *À la recherche*, passages that (unless I am mistaken) have not been analyzed together.[41] In the first, which I have just quoted, Madame de Sévigné is praised because she "[presents] things in the order of our perception of them, rather than explaining them by their cause." This at once brings to mind the definition of Tolstoy's *ostranienie* that Shklovsky had given a few years after the publication of *Du côté de chez Swann*: describing things as if one were seeing them for the first time.[42] Closer analysis, however, shows that Proust proceeds somewhat differently.

I have sought to demonstrate that the intellectual tradition behind Tolstoy's work can be ideally connected with Marcus Aurelius's quest for true causal principles as an antidote to false images. Thus to describe peasants as if they were animals or savages, as La Bruyère and Voltaire respectively did, is not so different from seeing choice dishes as if they were (to use Marcus Aurelius's words) "the dead body of a fish . . . the dead body of a bird or a pig." Defamiliarization, in this tradition, is the means by which we overcome appearances and arrive at a deeper understanding of reality. Proust seems in some ways to have the opposite end in view—to be trying to preserve the freshness of appearances against the intrusion of ideas, by presenting things "in the order of perception" and still uncontaminated by causal explanations. Tolstoyan defamiliarization can be exemplified by La Bruyère's account of the peasants; Proustian defamiliarization by Madame de Sévigné's letter about the moonlight, written a few years earlier. In both cases there is an attempt to present things as if they were being seen for the first time. The results, however, are quite different: in the first case, social and moral critique, and in the second an impressionistic immediacy.

Such a conclusion would seem to be supported by the second of the passages I intend to examine, in which Proust gives a very detailed description of Elstir's paintings. Elstir is usually regarded as a kind of ideal portrait, referring simultaneously to various artists who practiced or were close to impressionism: Manet above all, perhaps Monet, and even Degas.[43] Here, Proust implicitly throws light on the parallel with Madame de Sévigné that the passage cited above had suggested:

> Now Elstir's quest to show things not as he knew they were, but in accordance with the optical illusions that determine how we first see them, had indeed led him to highlight certain of these laws of perspective, which were the more striking at that time because it was art which first revealed them. A river, because of a bend in its course, or a bay, because of the way the cliffs appeared to draw closer together, would seem to hollow out, in the midst of the plain or the mountains, a lake completely closed off on all sides. In a painting of Balbec made on a hot summer day, a sea-channel shut between walls of pink granite seemed not to be part of the sea, which began further away. The continuity of the ocean was suggested only by some gulls, hovering above what looked to the viewer like stone, but actually breathing the dampness of the waves.[44]

This, clearly, is an experiment in the tradition of *ekphrasis*, going back to antiquity, in which writers have made extremely elaborate attempts to produce verbal transcriptions of nonexistent, but plausible, pictures. Proust's writing also has a theoretical implication, however, which Maurice Merleau-Ponty drew out many years later in his essay on Cézanne.[45] Elstir, Proust tells us, tries to show things "not as he knew they were," and this remark is linked to his usual tendency to play down the importance of the intelligence and to insist on the primacy of lived experience as against preconstituted formulae, rigid habit, and "knowledge."[46]

Modern urban living brings with it a huge intensification of sensory life, and this phenomenon was a central concern of the experimentalism of the twentieth-century literary and artistic avant-garde.[47] It was also, as has often been stressed, the cause of a qualitative impoverishment of our experience. This process by which things are rendered automatic was deplored by Shklovsky, and provides the historical context for his apparently timeless definition of art as defamiliarization. A few years earlier, Proust, whose point of view was similar, though independently arrived at, had suggested that the task of new artistic experiments was to resist and counteract preconstituted formulae of representation.

Proust did not see such experiments as confined to the domain of painting. Three novels and hundreds of pages after his surprising reference to "the Dostoevskyan side of Madame de Sévigné," Proust makes clear what he means. The narrator explains to Albertine that

> Madame de Sévigné, like Elstir, like Dostoevsky, instead of presenting things in logical order, that is to say, by starting with the cause, shows us first the effect, the illusion which strikes us. This is how Dostoevsky presents his characters. Their actions seem as deceptive to us as those effects of Elstir's in which the sea appears to be up in the sky.[48]

Proust, of course, is another who presents his characters in this way. We think immediately of one of his most extraordinary creations, Baron de Charlus. For a long time the reader is confronted with Charlus's incomprehensible words and actions without being offered any clue (let alone any causal explanation) that might throw light on his demeanor. In a sense, however, the narrator himself lacks any such clue: he, like us, strives to decipher Charlus—who is, like all human beings, a mysterious entity—on the basis of what he knows (and does not know) about him. It has often been pointed out that the character who says "I" in *À la recherche* both is and is not Marcel Proust.[49] Sometimes it is explicitly suggested that these two voices may be identified with one another, as in the double allusion to "the Dostoevskyan side of Madame de Sévigné," made first in the neutral voice of the narrator and then as a comment offered by the "I" in a conversation with Albertine. This kind of identification is deceptive, however. By putting himself as a character into his own novel, Proust suggests that—unlike the omniscient God to whom most nineteenth-century novelists can be compared—he, like us, is in the dark regarding the hidden motives of his own characters. Here is the major difference between nineteenth-century, Tolstoyan defamiliarization and its twentieth-century Proustian analogue. Proust's solution, which endows the narrative voice with a certain ambiguity, may be regarded as a structural development of the strategy used by Dostoevsky in *The Devils*, a story told by a shadowy character incapable of fully grasping its meaning. Indeed, there are strong similarities between the way Stavrogin (the principal character in *The Devils*) is presented to the reader and the way Charlus is presented: we encounter a series of contradictory fragments, which make up a puzzle, a riddle.

2. Why, though—it may be asked—should all this be of interest to historians, to those whose scholarly research brings them to grips with archival evidence, legal contracts, and the like? Why should they waste their time on defamiliarization and other such concepts developed by literary theorists?

One answer to this question may perhaps be suggested by a passage taken from *Le temps retrouvé*, the novel that concludes *A la recherche*. The narrator is talking about his friend Robert de Saint-Loup, recently killed in the Great War. Speaking to his widow, Gilberte, he says:

> I believe he was beginning to appreciate one side of war, I said to her, which is that war is human—we live through it like love or hate, we might tell its story like a novel—and that it follows that if someone goes about saying that strategy is a science, this will in no way help him to understand war, for war is not strategic. The enemy no more knows our plans than we know the ends pursued by the woman we love. Perhaps we ourselves do not know our plans. In their offensive of March 1918, did the Germans intend to take Amiens? We know nothing of their intentions. Perhaps they did not know themselves; perhaps their aim came to be determined by the way things went, by the fact that

they had made ground westward, toward Amiens. If we were to
suppose that war is scientific, we would still have to paint it as
Elstir painted the sea, in reverse, and to begin from illusions,
beliefs which are gradually rectified, as Dostoevsky would
recount a life.[50]

Once again Proust associates Elstir with Dostoevsky, as well as
implicitly—by way of her "Dostoevskyan side"—with Madame de
Sévigné. Here, however, Proust is considering human motivations,
and so adding a new dimension to the usual opposition between
immediate impressions and causality. As his attention shifts from
paintings and novels to the best way of analyzing a great historic
event, Proust reveals the epistemological implications of the observations we have been examining up till now.

We can well imagine how enthusiastically the author of *War and
Peace* would have welcomed Proust's vigorously expressed rejection
of military strategy insofar as the latter embodies the absurd idea
that human existence can be foreseen; that war, love, hate, and art
can be approached on the basis of ready-made prescriptions; that to
know means not to grasp hold of reality but to impose a scheme
upon it. Proust has a "Tolstoyan side," expressed by the word *naturel*,
"natural," of which the narrator's grandmother is especially fond—
a word whose implications are at once moral and aesthetic. But he
has also a "Dostoevskyan side," connected with the way he presents
his characters through a series of corrections and adjustments, and
also with the fascination that crime held for him.[51]

To explore this last point would take me far from my present
path. I prefer to end with a reflection more pertinent to my own
trade. It seems to me that defamiliarization may be a useful antidote to the risk we all run of taking reality (ourselves included) for
granted. The antipositivist implications of this remark are obvious.
In stressing the cognitive implications of defamiliarization, however, I also want to take the firmest possible stand against those
fashionable theories that blur the boundaries between fiction and
history with the aim of making the two indistinguishable. Proust
himself would have rejected this confusion. When he said that war
might be narrated like a novel, he certainly had no intention of
praising the historical novel; on the contrary, he wanted to suggest
that historians, like novelists (or painters), come together in pur-

suit of a cognitive goal. I agree entirely with this point of view. To characterize the historiographical project to which I see myself as contributing, I would use a phrase—slightly altered—that I have just quoted from Proust: "If we were to suppose that history is scientific, we would have to paint it as Elstir painted the sea, in reverse."

2

Myth

DISTANCE AND DECEIT

Continuity of words does not necessarily mean continuity of meanings. What we call "philosophy" is still, despite everything, the "philosophy" of the Greeks, whereas our "economics" and "economy," both the discipline and its object, have little or nothing in common with what the Greeks meant by the term. We often speak of "myth," in general and specifically: "the myths of the new generation," "the myths of the peoples of the Amazon." We have no hesitation in applying the term "myth" to phenomena very distant from each other in both space and time. Is this a manifestation of ethnocentric arrogance?

This question has been more or less explicitly posed in the course of an intensive discussion of Greek myths and the Greek idea of myth (two connected but not identical themes) that began some twenty years ago.[1] Doubts have been raised as to whether it is possible to identify a specific class of narratives that can be called myths. It has been argued that myths did not exist; what existed was mythology, an aggressive discourse carried out in the name of reason and aimed at an ill-defined traditional knowledge.[2] While this conclusion is, to say the least, open to debate, it does have one merit, in that it brings us back to the condemnation of myth expressed by Plato. It is worth examining this once again.

I

1. In the second book of the *Republic*, Plato describes the education that should be provided for the guardians of the state. This comprises "two branches for the cultivation of the mind and of the body," namely, music and gymnastics. But music is accompanied by "stories [*logous*]," which may be "true" or "fictitious." Falsehood is to be extirpated from earliest infancy. The myths (*mythous*) recounted to children "taken as a whole, are fiction, though they contain some truth." It is therefore important to "supervise" those who make "fables and legends" (*epistateteon tois mythopoiois*); some of these may be approved as acceptable, but those that are unsatisfactory must be rejected (376c–377d). Then Plato upbraids Hesiod, Homer, and the other poets in similar terms: they have "composed fictitious tales [*mythous . . . pseudeis*] and told them to mankind." By attributing immoral actions to the gods, the poets have encouraged the anti-religious sarcasm of Xenophanes. Plato rejects the representation of such actions, because they are incompatible with the idea of divinity: no member of the commonwealth should be "suffered to speak of the divine, which is good, being responsible for evil" (379).[3] This concise criticism of false myths cues Plato's condemnation of poets. They cannot be allowed to practice in the ideal state.

Plato does not condemn myths as such; if he did, he could not express the wish that a different kind of myth, purified and properly corrected, might become current. He condemns myths insofar as they are false—even if (as he observes) they have some truth in them. In the *Timaeus*, for instance, the Egyptian priest tells Solon that the story of Phaëthon "is a mythical version of the truth [*touto mythou men skhema ekhon legetai, to d'alethes esti*]" that the movements of the heavenly bodies periodically occasion destruction (22c–22d). In general, however, the distinction between false and true elements within a myth is anything but simple, as we see in a famous passage in the *Phaedrus* (229c–230a).[4]

Phaedrus and Socrates are walking near Athens. "Tell me, Socrates," says Phaedrus, "wasn't it from somewhere just here that it is said [*legetai*] that Boreas seized Oreithuia from the Ilissus?" So it is said, agrees Socrates; it is also said, he mentions a little later, that she was seized from the Areopagus, "for this account [*logos*] is given too." Phaedrus remarks that the pure and clear waters of the stream would be "just right for young girls to play beside." Socrates then points out that there is an altar to Boreas not far away. "I've not really noticed it," replies Phaedrus. Then he asks Socrates: "Do you really believe this myth [*mythologema*] to be true [*alethes*]?"

Phaedrus uses the terms *"logos"* and *"mythologema"* (translated here as "account" and "myth," respectively) as if they were equivalent. Even though it refers to a particular instance, the question he poses bears on the problem broached in the second book of the *Republic*: the truth of myths. Socrates' reply (229c–229e) almost at once raises the discussion to a more general level:

> If I disbelieved it, like the experts, I would not be extraordinary; I might then cleverly say that a blast of Boreas pushed her down the nearby rocks while she was playing with Pharmaceia, and that when she met her death in this way she was said to have been seized by Boreas—or else from the Areopagus; for this account is given too, that it was from there and not from here that she was seized. But, Phaedrus, while I think such explanations attractive in other respects, they belong in my view to an over-clever and laborious person who is not altogether fortunate; just because after that he must set the shape of the Centaurs to rights, and again that of the Chimaera, and a mob of such things—Gorgons and Pegasuses—and strange hordes of other intractable and portentous creatures flock in on him; if someone is sceptical about these, and tries to reduce each to what is likely, with his boorish kind of expertise, he'll need a good deal of leisure.[5]

Socrates is uninterested in interpretations of this kind: "I am not yet capable, in accordance with the Delphic inscription, of 'knowing myself'; it therefore seems absurd to me that while I am still ignorant of this subject I should inquire into things which do not belong to me." In matters like this, he says, he will go along with what is generally believed (*to nomizomeno*): or, as we would say today, with tradition.

Here we have a very clear refusal to interpret myths by reducing them, as the Sophists proposed they should be reduced, to a series of natural and everyday circumstances. When Phaedrus asks him whether the myth of Boreas and Oreithuia is "true," Socrates replies that the "laborious" explanation of the allegory can at the best lead us to a probable conclusion (*kata to eikos*). However, even this degree of probability is hard to attain when we come to interpret the Centaurs, the Chimaera, and the "mob of Gorgons and Pegasuses." By listing these one after another, Socrates emphasizes his own ironic and almost disdainful distance: they are worth as little as each other. Socrates has by now dismissed the narrative (*logos? mythologema?*) that turns upon the abduction of Oreithuia by Boreas, and offers some thoughts about the sphere to which this tale belongs. His words tell us that centaurs, gorgons, and so forth are expected ingredients in stories of this kind. What such figures have in common is their hybrid character: their being simultaneously human and animal-like, or else derived from the combination of various animal species. Almost four centuries later, Dionysus of Halicarnassus identified in these hybrid figures the mythic element (*mythodes*) from which Thucydides (1.22.4) proudly declared that he had freed himself:

> Thucydides . . . claimed that he was to be distinguished from those historians who preceded him . . . because he had added nothing mythical [*to meden . . . mythodes*] to his history, and because he did not use his writings to impose tricks and impostures on the multitude, as all writers before him had done, when they told of certain Lamias in the woods and groves who had come up from the earth, and of amphibious Naiads making their way from Tartarus and swimming through the sea and whose bodies are half-wild yet they enter into relations with men, [or told of] half-divine progeny born of the couplings of mortals and gods, and other stories too, which to us today seem unworthy of credit and full of the greatest folly.[6]

2. To speak of a "mythic element" (*to mythodes*), as do both Thucydides and Dionysus of Halicarnassus after him, implies that

one takes myth to be a homogeneous category (here, a negative one).[7] As we have seen, Plato's approach was different. On one hand, he did not consistently associate the term *"mythos"* with a specific category of discourse; on the other, he sought to distinguish what was true from what was false within the tales handed down by tradition (first of all, those told by the poets). It bears repeating here that Plato's target was not myth itself but myth insofar as it was the bearer of false statements.

The texts of Plato that we have discussed so far, the second book of the *Republic* and the *Phaedrus*, were in all probability composed during more or less the same period (ca. 390–385 B.C.).[8] However, Plato returned to the question of false discourse in the *Sophist*, as part of his closely argued engagement with the philosophy of the Eleatic school.[9] In the radically monist perspective defended by Parmenides and his pupils, negation implied nonexistence: "What is not, is not." In the *Sophist*, the visitor from Elea, who speaks for Plato, rebuts this position, drawing a distinction between absolute negation and determinate negation: between "not being" and "not being something." This argument is further developed toward the end of the dialogue, and it is here that the theme of false discourse is introduced (259e–264b):

ELEATIC: We discovered that *not-being* is one kind of being among the rest, and is distributed over the whole domain of being.

THEAETETUS: We did.

ELEATIC: Then the next question is whether it can combine with *judgment* and *discourse*.

THEAETETUS: Why so?

ELEATIC: If it will not combine with them, it follows by consequence that *all is true*; if it will, there is the possibility of *false* judgment and *false* discourse. In fact, falsity as a character of thought or language is precisely the *thinking or saying of what is not*.

THEAETETUS: Just so.[10]

The Eleatic goes on to introduce another distinction, that between verbs (*remata*) and names or nouns (*onomata*). He illustrates this as follows:

Eleatic: Now a continuous string of nouns by themselves will never constitute discourse, nor yet a series of verbs without accompanying nouns. . . . Take, for instance, *walks, runs, sleeps,* and the rest of the verbs by which actions are denoted; even if they are all enunciated, one after another, they are no nearer constituting a discourse. . . . And so, once more, if one utters the words *lion, deer, horse,* or any of the words which denote the agents performing actions, neither does that succession amount to discourse. In neither case do the vocables denote the action, inaction, or being of anything that is or is not, until verbs have been mingled with nouns.

It is only (the Eleatic concludes) when we take a minimally propositional statement, such as "man learns," which brings together a verb and a noun, that we can speak of true or false discourse: the former refers to what is, the latter to what is not.[11]

3. In his treatise *On Interpretation,* Aristotle reworks the conclusions reached in the *Sophist.* First of all, he softens the distinction between verbs (*remata*) and names (*onomata*). "When uttered just by itself a verb is a name and signifies something . . . but it does not yet signify whether it is or not" (16b.20). Second, he observes that " 'Not man' is not a name. . . . It is neither a phrase nor a negation. Let us call it an indefinite name (*onoma aoriston*)" (16a.30). The same goes for verbs (even though Aristotle gives no examples of "indefinite verbs"):

For a negation must always be true or false; but one who says "not-man"—without adding anything else—has no more said something true or false (indeed, rather less so) than one who says "man." *(20a.31–36)*

The points made here had been introduced in the following passage, from the beginning of the treatise *On Interpretation* (16a.9–18):

Just as some thoughts in the soul are neither true nor false while some are necessarily one or the other, so also with spoken sounds. For falsity and truth have to do with combination and separation. Thus names and verbs by themselves—for instance "man" or "white" when nothing further is added—are like thoughts that are without combination and separation; for so far they are neither true nor false. A sign of this is that even "goat-stag" signifies something [*kai gar ho tragelaphos semainei men ti*] but not, as yet, anything true or false—unless "is" or "is not" is added (either simply or with reference to time) [*he haplos he kata kronon*].[12]

Plato's thesis, formulated in the *Sophist*, according to which a name (for example, "stag," *elaphos*) taken on its own is neither false nor true, is taken up and strengthened by Aristotle by way of the instance of the goat-stag (*tragelaphos*), a nonexistent animal.[13] This last characteristic, nonexistence, no more than implicit here, is repeatedly emphasized elsewhere in Aristotle. In the *Physics* (208a.29–31), it is stated that the goat-stag, like the sphinx, does not exist and is thus to be found nowhere. In the *Second Analytic* (92b.4–8), we read:

> How can one prove the essence? Anyone who knows *what* "man" or any other thing is must also know *that* it is; because no-one knows *what* a non-existent thing is. (He may know the meaning of a phrase, or of a name, if, *e.g.*, I speak of a goat-stag; but it is impossible to know *what* a goat-stag is.)[14]

A few pages earlier (89b.23–35), Aristotle introduces the same argument in a different manner, by way of the question—which he may have taken from the Sophists—"whether a centaur or a god exists." However, Aristotle goes on, "the question of existence refers to simple existence, and not to whether the subject is (say) white or not. When we know that the subject exists, we ask what it is; *e.g.*, 'what, then, is a god?' or 'a man'?"[15]

We have seen that for the Greeks, hybrid creatures were closely associated with the narrative genre that came to be known as "myths." In the passages we've just quoted, the goat-stag, the centaur, and the sphinx have the status of mere logical operators, in that they are (as we would put it today) entities without referential value.[16] In the long run, however, these two strands—logic and reflection upon myth—were to become intertwined.

4. For centuries, in the medieval West, Aristotle's writings on logic were accessible only by way of the translations and com-

mentaries of Boethius. These included his version of the treatise *On Interpretation*, accompanied by a commentary: the latter exists in two texts, one longer than the other. When he comes to the example of the goat-stag, Boethius cannot control his enthusiasm. To demonstrate that a single name is neither true nor false by means of a compound name, and moreover one that names a non-existent being: this example, he exclaims, is "most forceful," because of its "novelty and exquisite subtlety" (*maximam vero vim habet exempli novitas et exquisita subtilitas*).[17] Boethius then goes on to comment on the statement that we cannot determine whether "anything [is] true or false—unless 'is' or 'is not' is added (*either simply or with reference to time*)" (emphasis added). This latter opposition is related by Boethius to that between statements "according to the substance" and statements that add something "that may signify a certain presence" (*praesentiam quandam significet*). He continues:

> For indeed when we say "God is" we do not say that he is now, but rather that he is in substance, so that what we say refers to the immutability of the substance rather than to any particular time. But if we say that it is day, we do not refer to any substance of day but rather to its constitution in time. For this is what we mean when we say "it is," when we mean "it is now." . . . This is one explanation. Another is as follows. "To be something" may be said in two ways: either absolutely (*simpliciter*) or according to time. Absolutely means according to the present time, as when someone says "the goat-stag is." But what we call the present is not a time but the division of times: the end of the past is the beginning of the future. . . . Now there are (as it has been said) two times, the past and the future. Whoever speaks with reference to the present, speaks absolutely; but if he were to speak of the past or the future, his words would be according to time. There is also a third explanation, which is that sometimes we make use of time so that we may speak indefinitely: if anyone were to say, "The goat-stag is, the goat-stag was, and the goat-stag will be," then this would be said indefinitely and absolutely (*indefinite et simpliciter*). But if he were to add "is now," "was yesterday," "will be tomorrow," then to what was said absolutely he would be adding time.[18]

Boethius, then, starts by taking Aristotle's elliptical expression "either simply or with reference to time" and interpreting it relative to the ambiguity by which we may say "is" in a temporal or an atemporal sense.[19] In his second explanation he eliminates this ambiguity, saying that the present ("is") may be identified with the sphere of the atemporal, and the past and the future ("was," "will be") with the sphere of the temporal. Then comes the third explanation: not just the present but also the past and the future may be considered "indefinitely and absolutely (*indefinite et simpliciter*)": "the goat-stag is, was, will be." These three explanations, among which Boethius declines to choose,[20] progressively remove all the temporal determinations by which the verb "to be" is subject to the consideration "according to time." The sphere of the atemporal, absolute, and indefinite—as disclosed in Aristotle's demonstration of the power of the "mere name" (*simplicis nominis*)— meanwhile grows correspondingly broader.[21] The "goat-stag," the exemplar of an empty category, indeed shows itself to be a most potent logical tool. It is like being present at the invention of zero.

Boethius's commentaries on Aristotle have often, and perhaps too summarily, been dismissed as largely or completely unoriginal. It is nowadays generally believed that Boethius had access to a series of glosses in Greek, originating perhaps in the school of Proclus, which accompanied an edition of the *Organon* in his possession.[22] It seems unlikely, however, that glosses of this kind would have included the commentary quoted above. When he declares that there are only "two times, the past and the future," this certainly sounds like a defiant rephrasing of Saint Augustine's famous declaration, in the eleventh book of the *Confessions*, that there are "three times, the present of things past, the present of things present, and the present of future things."[23] Against the present of Augustine, which we might call an existential present, Boethius sets an atemporal and logical present. The same polemical note is sounded, in various keys, elsewhere in his works. God, he writes in his *Quomodo Trinitas unus Deus*, "always is"; but not in the sense that he "always was, always is, and always will be," for we might say as much of the heavens and of other immortal bodies. God "is, because he is in an eternal present," which differs from our own present as the eternal differs from the sempiternal. Although Boethius professes his indebtedness to the *De Trinitate*, nowhere in that work does Augustine draw such a distinction.[24]

5. "God is," "the goat-stag is": the most real of all Beings and the nonexistent being coexist in the atemporal and absolute dimension of the eternal present.[25] This paradoxical rapprochement suggests that it is worth analyzing with some care the reference made by Boethius, a few pages earlier, to the "chimeras and centaurs that the poets *finxerunt*." And we may begin by asking how we should translate this word *"finxerunt"*: "fabricated"? "devised"? "contrived"?[26]

These alternatives arise because the exact meaning of such terms as *"fictiones"* or *"figmenta,"* freely used by both pagan and Christian writers in late antiquity when they seek to define the significance of what we might call myths, seems anything but unambiguous. "This, then, is the fiction of the poets [*fictio poetarum*]," says Augustine in *The City of God* (9.7), in reference to Apuleius's *On the Daemon of Socrates*—"to call gods those who are not gods." However, Macrobius had written, in his commentary on the *Dream of Scipio*, that sometimes "sacred things are made known . . . under the chaste veil of inventions [*sacrarum rerum notio sub pio figmentorum velamine . . . enuntiatur*]": a remark referring in the first instance to Plato's own myths, so unlike the scandalous stories about the gods, but which Macrobius then applies also to Homer, "the fount and origin of all divine wisdom," who "made the truth intelligible to the wise, wreathed in the fictions of poetry [*sub poetici nube figmenti verum sapientibus intellegi dedit*]."[27] We shall see shortly that the opposition between Augustine's lying *fictio* and Macrobius's truth-enwrapping *figmentum* is more apparent than real. Where, however, did Boethius stand?

His enthusiastic response to Aristotle's example of the goat-stag should perhaps be seen as a reflection of the excitement felt by anyone who sees a hitherto uncharted terrain opening up for exploration. Immediately after 515–516, the year in which he probably composed his second commentary on the *De Interpretatione*, Boethius was to begin work on his treatise *On Hypothetical Syllogisms* (516–522).[28] In the Proem, he remarked proudly that this was a topic on which Aristotle had written nothing and Theophrastus only cursorily, and concerning which Eudaemus had done no more than sow some seeds.[29] For Boethius, this was an opportunity to develop the interest in oratory that had led him to write his commentary on Cicero's *Topici*, a work he had dedicated to one Patricius, "quaestor in the Holy Palace," who may also be the dedicatee of the work *On Hypothetical Syllogisms*.[30] Some of the syllogisms that Boethius analyzes, for example, those made up of two hypothetical propositions ("If it is the case that a is b, then it is the case that c is d"), remind one irresistibly of the logical framework of the Roman laws.[31] Let us take an example from Gaius's *Institutiones* (4.37): "If it appears that with the aid and at the suggestion of Dionis, son of Hermetis, a gold *patera* has been stolen, on which grounds he ought to be condemned as a thief were he a Roman citizen [*si civis romanus esset*]," etc. But let it be supposed that the accused (or indeed the victim of the robbery) is a foreigner: in that case, Gaius comments, he is to be endowed, insofar as the law permits (*si modo iustum sit*), with a fictitious Roman citizenship (*civitas romana peregrino fingitur*).[32]

These sorts of legal fictions—*fictiones*—were familiar to the Roman jurists.[33] Boethius, as a senator of Rome, saw Aristotle's goat-stag not as a poetico-religious *fictio* but as a logico-juridical *fictio*: a construction that, within a well-defined sphere, made operative a nonexistent reality.

6. A currently fashionable view sees the history of Western thought as dominated by the contrast between "timeless spirits" and "practical souls"; between authoritarian metaphysicians tracing their descent back to Plato and democratic pragmatists who are the heirs of locally demarcated knowledges such as sophistry, rhetoric, and casuistry.[34] The example of Boethius is enough to show that such an opposition cannot be sustained. The importance of legal and rhetorical *fictiones* was acknowledged in the context of his more or less Platonic ontology—if indeed it was not his Platonism that led to the acknowledgment; and this many centuries before Hans Vaihinger rediscovered the value of such fictions in that seminal text of pragmatism, *Die Philosophie der Als-Ob*.[35]

Boethius's work is important for its intrinsic worth, and still more important for the enormous influence it exercised. In the twelfth century, Aristotle's writings on logic, in Boethius's translation and accompanied by his commentaries, were rediscovered and included in the Scholastic curriculum, thus becoming an integral element in the intellectual formation of generations of students.[36] Abelard was among the moving spirits in this rediscovery. In his glosses on *De Interpretatione*, he remarked approvingly on Boethius's enthusiasm for the example of the goat-stag: Aristotle, he noted, "chose a significative word [*vocem significativam*], though one [referring to] a nonexistent thing, because had he chosen a word lacking signification then the matter of truth and falsehood would have seemed relative to the word's lack of signification rather than to its absoluteness [*simplicitas*]."[37] This passage does not stand alone. Abelard reflects insistently on terms denoting fictitious substances (*fictae substantiae*)—"goat-stag," "chimera," "phoenix"—in order to raise the question of the problematic relationship between language and reality.[38] The realm of signification, no more than a marginal concern in Aristotle, became a central theme in the investigations of the Scholastic philosophers.[39]

Moreover, this kind of reflection on language also had profound repercussions on a less abstract plane. In his *De vulgari eloquentia* (2.4.2), Dante defined poetry as *"fictio rhetorica musicaque poita"*: not as "invention" in general, but rather as a fiction "made with the help of rhetoric and music."[40] Poetry is *fictio*, and this word is linked, etymologically, to the Latin *figulus*, a potter; and in the same vein, Dante in the *Purgatorio* (26.117) hails the poet Arnaut Daniel as *"miglior fabbro del parlar materno"*—the best "smith" of the mother tongue. Language, to Dante, is a physical reality, something to twist and hammer. However, poetry is *fictio* also in another sense, in that like legal *fictio* it constitutes a reality that is true to all intents and purposes, but not true in the literal sense. Saint Augustine had insisted, in a passage that Aquinas quotes and that Dante must certainly have known, on the necessity of distinguishing between *fictio* that is a lie, and *fictio* that is *"aliqua figura veritatis,"* "truth under another aspect": otherwise, "everything that has been said in figurative form [*figurate*] by wise men and saints or even by Our Lord Himself would be regarded as a lie just because, according to the usual understanding, these expressions are incompatible with the truth."[41] What is said by wise men (*sapientibus*) is likened, as figurative speech, to what is said by the saints and in the Bible, and this reflects the conviction that when God spoke to men, he had to accommodate himself to their limited understanding.[42] Duns Scotus Eriugena, again echoing Augustine, compared the moral and material lessons taught by the epic poets "by way of fictitious myths [*fabulas fictas*]" and allegorical similitudes to the "fictitious imaginings [*fictis imaginationibus*]" of Scripture, adapted to our immature understanding. Allegorical readings of Homer licensed allegorical readings of the Bible: Scotus observed that "theology is in a certain sense poetry [*theologia veluti quaedam poetria*]."[43] Petrarch takes up the same idea, in an almost identical phrase, in a well-known letter (*Familiares* 10.4): "Theology, I am inclined to say, is the poetry of God [*parum abest quin dicam theologiam poeticam esse de Deo*]."[44] In his *Trattatello in laude di Dante*, Boccaccio translated, and expanded on, Petrarch's reflections. He rejects the traditional opposition between theology, "which supposes nothing but what is true," and poetry, which "pretends some things to be true, which are most false and erroneous and against the Christian religion." "Theology and poetry," Boccaccio roundly declares,

> may be said almost to be one thing, where they have one theme; and so I say more—that theology is nothing but a poem of God. And what kind of thing is it, if not a poetical fiction [*poetica fizione*], when in the Scriptures Christ is said now to be a lion and now a lamb and now a worm, and then a dragon and then a rock, and so in divers other manners that would take much time to tell should we wish to relate them all?[45]

This way of thinking leads us to Vico's *bestioni*, those relatives of "the first people in the earliest age," who, writes Boccaccio, "since they were so rude and uncouth, were most ardent to know the truth by study."[46] If we consider this notion of a very ancient "poetical knowledge" that found expression in myths, we can see that it presupposed a belief that the truth lay concealed beneath the rind, veil, or *integumentum* of poetry.[47] To this reflection, we may add another, less obvious: namely, that in our intellectual tradition, a consciousness of the mendacious nature of myths, and by extension of poetry, has accompanied, like a shadow, the conviction that they contain a hidden truth. The notion of *fictio*, taken in a positive and constructive sense, has opened a way out of the impasse in which we find ourselves if we try to sustain, on the literal plane, the two incompatible beliefs that poetry is truthful and that it is mendacious.[48] As Isidore of Seville wrote, "the 'false' is what is not true; the 'fictitious' is what is likely ['*Falsum*' *est ergo quod verum non est,* '*fictum*' *quod verisimile est*]."[49] Horace, however, might be invoked as an authority for the doctrine that in the realm of poetry or painting, citizenship could be claimed even by such hybrid and improbable creatures as the siren or the goat-stag.[50]

7. There can be no doubt that as human beings we have the potential to move back and forth between fictitious and real worlds, between one fictitious world and another, and between the domain of rules and the domain of meta-rules.[51] In one particular culture, however—our own—the distinction between these levels has been theorized with sometimes extreme subtlety, under the successive and convergent impulses of Greek philosophy, Roman law, and Christian theology. The elaboration of such concepts as *mythos, fictio, signum* is simply one aspect of the search for ever more efficient ways of manipulating reality. We encounter its results every day, materialized in the objects that we use (among them the computer on which I write these words). The technological inheritance that allowed Europeans to conquer the world included the capacity, developed in the course of centuries, to check and control the relations between the visible and the invisible, between reality and fiction.

One should of course speak not of "Europeans" but of some Europeans, since what we describe was limited to certain spheres. Nonetheless, this technological inheritance makes its presence felt in unexpected places, thanks to the combined action of the school system and the printing press. In the late sixteenth century Domenico Scandella, a miller from Friuli known as Menocchio, was tried by the Inquisition because of his heterodox beliefs. In his defense of religious toleration, he invoked a text (the tale of the three rings) that he had read in an unexpurgated edition of Boccaccio's *Decameron*; and when the Inquisitor asked him: "Do you believe then . . . that we do not know which is the right law?" he replied: "Yes, sir, I do believe that every person believes his faith to be right, and we do not know which is the right one."[52] Is there anything specifically European about this dialogue, at this date? Certainly not, if we have regard to the narrative device used by Boccaccio, in which the tale of the three rings is set within the meta-novel of the Sultan and Melchisedek the Jew.[53] Certainly, if we have regard to the ecclesiastical institutions that control books and individuals. Perhaps, if we have regard to how the miller defends himself by climbing adroitly from the level of "belief" to that of "belief about belief," from the level of discourse to that of meta-discourse. Culturally, Menocchio was closer to the Inquisitor who condemned him to death than to a native of the New World.

What allowed a handful of Spanish soldiers to conquer the empire of the Aztecs was (it has been argued) as much their hegemony in the sphere of communications as their possession of guns and horses.[54] This hegemony, moreover, was the consequence of wider and older historical processes. One is tempted to read the first great modern novel, written by a Spaniard, as an ironical allegory dealing with a decisive aspect of European expansion: the contest between diverse cultures for the power to determine reality. The character who controls the relations between reality and fiction is Sancho Panza, the peasant. The character who proudly concludes the tale by announcing the identity of the creator with his creature ("For me alone Don Quixote was born, and I for him") is Cervantes' fictitious double, the Arab Cide Hamete Benengeli.[55] A peasant and a Moor: in a true Erasmian spirit, here Cervantes performs a magnificent inversion, in which the central place is taken by representatives of the marginal, the rejected, the defeated. Only in fiction, however—a fiction that closes ironically in a condemnation of "all fabulous and absurd stories of knight errantry."[56]

8. So immediate and remarkable was the success enjoyed by *Don Quixote* that we may be fairly sure Velázquez was among its readers. His probable knowledge of the book may be indirectly reflected in two pictures painted during his first visit to Rome, in 1629–1630: *Jacob Receiving the Bloodstained Garments of Joseph*, now in the Escorial, and *The Forge of Vulcan* in the Prado (plates 1 and 2).[57] The two pictures were at first shown together in the wardrobe of the Buen Retiro palace, and even though their original measurements were not identical they probably formed a pair.[58] They both present us with a narrative sequence that unfolds from left to right, and that hinges on a figure drawn from the same model (the third person from the right in the *Jacob*, the fourth from the right in the *Forge*), his head tilted back, looking toward the painting's left.[59] However, despite these formal parallels, the content of the two paintings is disparate. We would expect to find an Old Testament narrative like that of *Jacob Receiving the Bloodstained Garments of Joseph* paired with an episode from the New Testament, not with a mythological scene like *The Forge of Vulcan*. Attempts have been made to explain the anomaly by noting that both paintings refer to a betrayal, unmasked in the very action of the *Vulcan* (where Apollo is announcing to Vulcan that the

latter's wife, Venus, has just been caught *in flagrante* with Mars), awaiting future revelation in the *Jacob* (where his brothers, having sold him into slavery, are announcing that Joseph is dead, holding out his clothes, which they have stained with the blood of a goat).[60] This is somewhat speculative, and we are on firmer ground when we note that the *Vulcan* is indebted to a print by Antonio Tempesta that was among the illustrations to an edition of Ovid (with a moralizing commentary) published at Antwerp in 1606 (plate 3). The verse accompanying the print drew an implicit parallel between Apollo and Christ: "On ne sçauroit tromper la divine Prudence / Elle voit de nos coeurs les plus cachés recoins / Il ne lui faut iamais enqueste ny temoins / Ayant de nos secrets l'entiere cognoissance."[61] Should we then conclude that the Apollo in the *Vulcan* represents the figure of Christ? A further comparison suggests that things are more complex. When Velázquez went to Rome, he was able to see original works by Caravaggio, whose example—direct, or transmitted through echoes in others' work—had been the formative influence on his youth.[62] *The Forge of Vulcan* is an extraordinary pictorial commentary on Caravaggio's *Calling of Saint Matthew* in S. Luigi dei Francesi, which we can glimpse, with a reversed composition, behind the more literal and superficial reference to Tempesta's print.[63] The way the scene is structured; the spare everyday setting, so unusual in a mythological scene; the varying degrees of bewildered surprise, so subtly evoked—all this exactly echoes the *Calling of Saint Matthew* (plate 4). Moreover, Velázquez evidently crossed the nave of the church of S. Luigi and studied the fresco there of *The Death of St Cecilia* by Domenichino, for two of the figures in the second plane of the *Jacob* echo Domenichino's work (plate 5).[64]

It would be ridiculous to suppose that Velázquez, in taking the *Calling of Saint Matthew* as an implicit model, intended to equate the Gospel with a myth. This misses the point, as does the hypothetical (and unproven) identification between Christ and the Apollo of *The Forge of Vulcan*. The reference to Caravaggio, which of its nature can only have been addressed to the few who would pick it up, is a reference to *fictio*: "pictura autem dicta quasi fictura" (painting too may be said to be a kind of fiction), in the words of Isidore of Seville—a writer well known to Velázquez's father-in-law, Francisco Pacheco, who quotes him in his *Arte de la Pintura*.[65] Luca Giordano's remark about *Las meninas*, which he called "the theology of painting," may legitimately be applied also to a metapictorial picture such as *The Forge of Vulcan*. It may be that Velázquez's ideas here owe something to the meta-novel of Cervantes, which he is likely to have read.[66]

It is still sometimes thought that mythology is just a repertory of outworn forms and narrative formulas, the resort of painters and poets in their staler moods. Velázquez's cross-referencing of *The Forge of Vulcan* with *The Calling of Saint Matthew* shows that the encounter between different cultural traditions—which differed above all in the truth-claims that they made—was capable of opening up a profound and unexpected viewpoint on reality. Moreover, Velázquez's act in putting Caravaggio's Christ in quotation marks and using him for the depiction of his own Apollo has a wider symbolic value. The capacity to put into quotation marks both one's own traditions and those of others was a most powerful weapon. Among its effects we may include the extension (thanks to the ethnocentric arrogance mentioned above) of the category "myth" to cultures who had never known such a category. But myth in its turn could throw back a sharp and unexpected light on Christian religion.

II

1. We must turn to Plato once more to examine a theme we have hitherto neglected, namely the political use of myth. In the third book of the *Republic*, Socrates examines the corrupting effects of poetry, drawing his examples mainly from Homer. He then remarks that "gods have no use for falsehood, and it is useful to mankind only as a medicine [*hos en pharmakou eidei*]" (389b). He draws a general affirmation from this restrictive clause: "If anyone, then, is to practise deception [*prosekei pseudesthai*], either on the country's enemies or on its citizens, it must be the Rulers of the commonwealth, acting for its benefit [*ep'ophelia tes poleos*]."[67] Private citizens are explicitly denied any such right to lie: indeed, to lie to the guardians of the city is worse than to lie to a doctor, a gymnastics teacher, or a ship's pilot—that is, those to whom we entrust our bodies and our lives.

These lies told for the public good are myths. Plato recounts one, which may be of Phoenician origin (414b ff.). All men are born of earth, but with an admixture of more or less precious metal (gold, silver, iron, bronze), which designates their place in the hierarchy of the ideal city (guardians, auxiliaries, peasants, and other manual workers).[68] A passage in Aristotle's *Metaphysics* (1074b.1) takes up the same theme of social control through myth, placing it in historical perspective:

> Our forefathers in the most remote ages have handed down to posterity a tradition [concerning the existence of the single primum mobile and the single Heaven], in the form of a myth [*en myhtou skhemati*], that these bodies are gods and that the divine encloses the whole of nature. The rest of the tradition has been added later in mythical form [*mythikos*] with a view to the persuasion of the multitude and to its legal and utilitarian expediency [*pros ten peitho ton pollon kai pros ten eis tous nomous kai to sumpheron kresin*]; they say these gods are in the form of men or like some of the other animals, and they say other things consequent on and similar to these which we have mentioned.[69]

Aristotle sees this use of myth to hold the multitude in check as the transformation of truth into anthropomorphic terms, rather than as truth's negation. He believes that a truly divine "original content" has been maintained, despite everything, with the aid of later additions "in mythical form." Plato's account is more uncompromising, extraordinary myth-maker and extraordinary de-mythologizer though Plato was. Taking the two passages together and reading them with hindsight, we can see that they appear to set out the premises for an interpretation already suggested by the Sophist Critias (who was Plato's uncle), which would enjoy enduring influence: the interpretation of religion as a political imposture.[70]

In Christian Europe between the beginning of the thirteenth century and the beginning of the fourteenth, Moses, Christ, and Mahommed were blasphemously characterized as "the three impostors." The heterogenous group held accountable for this blasphemy included an emperor (Frederick II of Swabia), a theologian (Simon of Tournai), and an obscure friar, the twice-apostate Thomas Scotus.[71] There was nothing new in the claim. In the second century a philosopher called Celsus had declared (as we know from Origen's work against him) that Moses had befooled goatherds and shepherds with his crude tricks, and that Christ had similarly befooled his followers.[72] In later centuries remarks of this kind, which probably became part of oral tradition, were made about Mahommed also, as the founder of the third great monotheistic religion of the Mediterranean. Of course, to denounce religion as a deception or a cheat is not the same as to point out (whether in a condemnatory or in a merely descriptive spirit) that religion plays a socially useful role in securing obedience to the law. Nonetheless, even where the denunciation of religious imposture is not accompanied by any overt political argument, we can see that it does have links with the Aristotelian tradition or, to be precise, with Averroes's interpretation of Aristotle. The apostate friar Thomas Scotus, for instance, charged by a court of the Inquisition with having spoken in the usual terms of the "three impostors," had the insolence to declare that the world was eternal, and that Aristotle was "better than Christ" and "wiser and more subtle than Moses."[73] Was there a connection between these statements? It is probable that there was: but the inquisitor, it seems, had no interest in exploring it.

2. The political implications of these themes become manifest once more in the work of Machiavelli, who treats them with extraordinary boldness, especially in the chapters of *The Discourses* devoted to the religion of the Romans (1.xi–xv). The basis of Roman power, writes Machiavelli, was established by Numa, who "pretended he had lived intimately with a nymph," even more than by his precursor Romulus. Religion is necessary both for the introduction of new laws such as Numa enacted and for the consolidation of old ones:

> And so the leaders of a republic or a kingdom must maintain the foundations of the religion that the people hold: and if they do this, it will be easy for them to keep their republic religious, and consequently good and united. And whatever things favor this they should promote and encourage, even if they judge them to be false; and they should do so all the more the more powerful they are, and the more cognizant of the nature of things.[74]

"Even if they judge them to be false": here we seem to catch an echo of the justification that Plato put forward of lying for the common good. Indeed, Machiavelli may have read the *Republic* in Ficino's translation, though it is less likely that he ever came to grips with Aristotle's *Metaphysics*.[75] There is, however, a closer and more likely parallel, namely the sixth book of Polybius, which was being discussed at the time in philohellenic circles in Florence.[76] Polybius regarded religion as the principal cause of Rome's political power, and attributed the political weakness of his native Greece to the lack there of any real civic religion (6, 56, 6–15). He went on to note:

> It seems to me that the Romans instituted these practices with the nature of the crowd in mind. In a nation peopled exclusively by the wise, it would indeed be needless to have recourse to such means as these, but since the multitude is of its nature fickle and subject to passions of every kind, unchecked in its greed and violent in its anger, there is nothing for it but to hold it in bounds with these sorts of contrivances and mysterious fears. It seems that this was why the ancients introduced to the multitude religious faith and superstitions concerning Hades, and not without reason; and indeed the truly foolish ones would be those who might think we could get rid of such things in our own times.[77]

This judgment bespeaks the viewpoint of a marginal observer, a Greek.[78] Polybius may have read Plato's *Republic*; he certainly did not know Aristotle's *Metaphysics*.[79] However, the fact that we cannot demonstrate any direct textual transmission only highlights the significance of the similarities we have been tracing. On the one hand, we can follow this trace back from those who are "cognizant of the nature of things" (Machiavelli), by way of Polybius's "the wise," to the "philosophers" of Plato and Aristotle; on the other, from Machiavelli's "people," by way of the "multitude" *(pletho)* of Polybius, *hoi polloi* of Aristotle, and Plato's "the rest of the city." Oppositions of this kind, formulated over a period of two thousand years on the basis of widely divergent and even frankly opposed positions, are based on a premise that is sometimes openly and sometimes less openly declared, namely that the majority of mankind, in thrall to passion and ignorance, can be held in bounds only thanks to religion or to the myths introduced by the wise minority "with a view," as Aristotle puts it, "to the persuasion of the multitude and to . . . legal and utilitarian expediency."

It was this idea, as it had been developed in the tradition of the Greeks, that allowed Machiavelli to turn upon the religion of his own time an eye at once keen and dispassionate. Numa, finding "a very savage people," had subjected them to his own laws, pretending that they had been taught him by the nymph Egeria; "the people of Florence do not take themselves to be ignorant or uncouth; yet

they were persuaded by brother Girolamo Savonarola that he con-
versed with God."[80] The analogy between the Christian God and the
nymph Egeria, between Savonarola and Numa, is registered coolly,
as a matter of fact: human nature is always the same, "all men are
born, live, and will die in the same way." Religion is a necessary
imposture: however, Christianity is exposed, when compared to the
religion of the Romans, as a timid and halfhearted affair.[81]

3. The splitting apart of European Christianity consequent upon
the Protestant Reformation eventually also undermined the legitimation that the Church had traditionally given to the existing social
order. It became possible not only to practice regicide but to defend
its legitimacy from a religious and moral standpoint, as the Jesuit
Mariana famously did in print. Dissension between the churches
seemed to shake the foundations of collective civil life. In France,
among the generation born in the wake of the wars of religion, the
so-called learned libertines opted for prudence and caution. One of
the best-known of them, Gabriel Naudé, records in his account of
the journey he made to Italy in 1626–1627 what he was told by Cesare
Cremonini, a professor of philosophy at the University of Padua:

> He has admitted to a few close friends that he believes neither in
> God, nor in the Devil, nor in the immortality of the soul; but I
> take good care (he said) that my valet is a good Catholic, for if he
> believed in nothing I fear that one fine day he would come and
> cut my throat while I lay in bed.[82]

A little earlier, a few miles away (at Venice in 1617), the Inquisition
brought to trial a certain Costantino Saccardino, a converted Jew of
very humble rank who had spent some years playing the jester in the
court of the Medici before devoting himself to the distiller's art. Saccardino was accused, among other things, of having declared:

> Those who believe in it [hell] are dull-wits. . . . Princes want to
> make it believed; then they can have things their way, but . . . now
> the whole dovecote has opened its eyes.[83]

Here is a common recognition, from opposite viewpoints and to
contrary effect, that the pains of the hereafter are a matter of polit-

ical mythology, forming what we would nowadays call the last ideo-logical bulwark of the defense of the existing order. Polybius's warn-ings against doing away with the myth of Hades had never sounded more timely. Misbelievers used their own language—cryptic, ironi-cal, allusive, and intended for the chosen few. This is how the writer whose pseudonym was Orasius Tubero expressed himself in the *Cinq dialogues faits à l'imitation des anciens*, published in Paris in 1632 or 1633:

> To write fables as if they were truths, to hand stories down to posterity as if they were histories, this is to act like an impostor, or a light author worthy of no regard; to set down flights of fancy as divine revelations, and dreams as laws ordained in Heaven, is the way of Minos, Numa, Mahommed, and their like, setting up for great Prophets, and very sons of Jove.[84]

The author (La Mothe Le Vayer) defends himself against potential critics by explaining in his introduction that he has set himself the goal of "researching into the truths or seeming truths of nature" by following his own fancies and caprices; expressing himself, in fact, like "an antique and pagan philosopher, *in puris naturalibus.*" An echo of Plato's *Republic* can indeed be heard in the contrast he makes between "fables" (*fables*) and "truths" (*veritez*), "stories" (*contes*) and "histories" (*histoires*). However, whereas Plato had conceded—through his mouthpiece, Socrates—that the guardians of the City had the right to lie, La Mothe Le Vayer cunningly takes this as grounds for accusing the so-called Prophets of setting down their "flights of fancy" (*caprices*) as "divine revelations." He concludes allu-sively: this "is the way of Minos, of Numa, of Mahommed, *and their likes*, setting up for great Prophets, *and very sons of Jove.*" The percep-tive reader, the "libertine" (that is, one who had liberated himself from superstition),[85] is hereby invited to read between the lines and to recognize the real target aimed at behind the historical parallels and mythological circumlocutions, namely the Christian religion and its founder, who had dared to proclaim himelf the son of God. In a later essay ("De la vertu des payens"), La Mothe Le Vayer drew on the work of pagan polemicists and Christian theologians to illus-trate the similarities between the burning of Sodom and Gomorrah and the myth of Phaeton, between Jacob's fight with the angel and the struggle between Jove and Hercules, and so on. "To be sure," he commented, "great was the ignorance of the pagans, and boundless the malice of the Devil, to have gone about (had they been able to do it) to lessen the import of sacred history by setting up, in place of its divine truth, such agreeable fables [*des fables agréables*]."[86] In this way the truths of religion were implicitly compared to myths, and the relationship suggested by Saint Augustine—pagan *fictio* as *aliqua figura veritatis*—was turned upside down. The critical distance that myth allowed made it possible to set forth, in ironical and polemical tones, the premises for a comparative history of religions.[87]

4. As we have seen, to the libertines religion was a fiction, but a necessary one: without it, Cremonini would have been at the mercy of his valet, and society would have succumbed to the *bellum omnium contra omnes*. At this point we are bound to turn to Hobbes, and not only because the act of the man who "when going to sleep, locks his doors" is cited in the *Leviathan* among the everyday proofs that we are in "that condition which is called war."[88] Religions, whether revealed and thus part of "Divine politics" or "ordered . . . according to invention" and thus part of "human politics," have the end of making the men who believe in them "the more apt to obedience, laws, peace, charity and civil society." Here Hobbes takes his place in the tradition of political reflection upon religion that runs, with varying emphases, from Aristotle to Polybius and Machiavelli. The passage on ancient Rome, in particular, seems to be inspired by Polybius: here Hobbes describes how those in authority openly derided notions of the other world, while at the same time "the more ignorant sort (that is to say, the most part, or generality of the people)" were induced by religious ceremonies "so much the more to stand in fear" of their governors.[89] However, Hobbes takes his distance from this tradition the moment he comes to analyze the question—a very pressing one, when he was writing—of the causes of changes in religious belief. These he attributes first to the discrediting of the wisdom, sincerity, and charity of priests; and secondly to their incapacity to procure "the operation of miracles." Reasons of the first kind appertain particularly to the Church of Rome; those of the second have a wider scope. Hobbes concludes chapter 12 of *Leviathan*, "Of Religion," by declaring: "I may attribute all the changes of religion in the world, to one and the same cause; and that

is, unpleasing priests; and those not only among Catholics, but even in that Church that hath presumed most of Reformation."[90] This sweeping judgment is followed immediately by the thirteenth chapter, with its famous discussion "Of the Natural Condition of Mankind, as concerning their Felicity, and Misery." Here Hobbes sets out his view of mankind's natural equality before the emergence of society and laws, and the war of each against all that resulted from this through the desire for power and the operation of fear. This state, he argues, disposed each individual to lay aside his own personal rights in favor of an unlimited sovereign power. The transition between the chapters is abrupt, but quite understandable both logically and historically. Religion, formerly an instrument of control, has become a factor of social disorder. Hobbes responds by elaborating a radical thesis about the nature of power, drawn "from the principles of Nature only."[91] As the the old myths weaken, Hobbes sets out to legitimize the absolute state by way of a deductive process, seeking to support his argument by explicit reference to the experience of Native American peoples.[92]

An absolute state cannot, by definition, admit the existence of any authority higher than itself. With iron logic, Hobbes writes:

The maintenance of civil society, depending on justice; and justice on the power of life and death, and other less rewards and punishments, residing in them that have the sovereignty of the commonwealth; it is impossible that a commonwealth should stand, where any other than the sovereign, hath a power of giving greater rewards than life; and of inflicting greater punishments, than death. Now seeing *eternal life* is a greater reward, than the *life present*; and *eternal torment* a greater punishment than the *death of Nature*. It is a thing worthy to be well considered, of all men that desire (by obeying authority) to avoid the calamities of confusion, and civil war, what is meant in Holy Scripture, by *life eternal*, and *torment eternal*; and for what offences, and against whom committed, men are to be *eternally tormented*; and for what actions, they are to obtain *eternal life*.[93]

By way of a lengthy exegesis, Hobbes concludes that the Scriptures speak of general salvation, rather than of *"life eternal"* as a reward for particular individuals; of eternal death for reprobates at the Day of Judgment, rather than of *"eternal torments"*; and of eternal fire and of salvation metaphorically, rather than with reference to physical places. Still more important than these answers, however, is Hobbes's question, which clearly expresses the desire to establish the state, the "mortal God" Leviathan, as a religion sui generis.[94]

5. Liberty of conscience was to be extended, in Hobbes's view, only to those who accepted the essential point of Christian doctrine, namely the belief in Jesus as Christ. Hobbes writes:

> Again, the office of Christ's ministers in this world, is to make men believe, and have faith in Christ: But faith hath no relation to, nor dependence at all upon compulsion, or commandment; but only upon certainty, or probability of arguments drawn from reason, or from something men believe already.[95]

In Bayle's view liberty of conscience was a right that all should enjoy. Envisaging an imaginary society of atheists, he argues that human beings can live together even without the constraints imposed by religion; and he invokes the example of China in support of his claim that a country that knows nothing of religious dissension has far more solid foundations than the nations of Europe. In Bayle's view, the stability of civil society was threatened not by unlimited toleration but by Christian political theology in its various opposed forms.[96]

One of Bayle's readers published a book titled *L'esprit de Mr. Benoit de Spinosa* (the Hague, 1719, subsequently republished as *Traité des Trois Imposteurs*). Here it is argued that Christianity, like religion generally, was in fact in itself an instrument of political oppression, and as such should be destroyed.[97] The text cleverly weaves together passages from Spinoza, Hobbes, and various libertine authors (Charron, La Mothe Le Vayer, Naudé). The emendations and additions made by the author endow this collection of disguised quotations with a new significance. Here there is no trace of the caution with which La Mothe Le Vayer had suggested analogies between pagan myths and episodes in the Bible.[98] Hobbes had introduced his myth concerning the foundation of absolute power by hypothesizing the natural equality of men; in *L'esprit de Mr. Benoit de Spinosa*, the hypothesis is invoked to deny that "the prophets and apostles were men of uncommon parts, created especially that they might pronounce God's oracular wisdom."[99] This is one more statement of the old theme that religion is a lie. However, whereas for the libertines the imposture was a necessary one, designed to hold the ignorant multitude in check, the author of *L'esprit de Mr. Benoit de Spinosa* took the view that it was high time that the multitude realized that it was a deceit practiced upon it by "political men" to keep them in "blind obedience":[100]

> If the people were able to understand the depths in which its ignorance sinks it, it would soon enough shake off the yoke placed on its shoulders by those mean-spirited ones who keep it in ignorance because it is in their interest to do so. And such understanding it might reach simply by using its own reason; indeed it is impossible it should not discover the truth if it once allowed reason to operate.

The anonymous author concedes that "the people is much inclined to make itself blind," but he strenuously rejects the "absurd maxim" that holds that truth is not made for the populace, who is incapable of recognizing it.[101]

In the decades that followed, a good part of Europe was flooded with books and pamphlets that reiterated the invitation implicitly extended by the author of *L'esprit de Mr. Benoit de Spinosa*: "the people" had only to "use its own reason," and it would discover the truth. This urgent wish to communicate, impatient of barriers, defiant of censors, typifies the character of the Enlightenment. So also does the conference announced in 1777 by the Royal Prussian Academy of Science and Letters, on the theme "Is it useful to deceive the People?" It was d'Alembert who suggested the topic to Frederick II. That such a question could be openly raised, albeit within the relatively narrow bounds of the republic of learning, is surely significant. "Our age is the age of criticism," and if "the sacredness of religion, and the authority of legislation" are exempted from critical examination, they "become the subjects of just suspicion": so Kant put it not long afterward in the preface to the *Critique of Pure Reason* (1781)—bold words, later suppressed in the second edition (1787), which came out after the death of Frederick II.[102]

Among those who emerged victorious from the debate held in Berlin was a professor of mathematics called Frédéric de Castillon, an émigré from Savoy. Castillon answered d'Alembert's question in the affirmative, though his reply was hedged about with disclaimers and nice distinctions. He noted that d'Alembert was echoing Plato's claim, in the *Republic*, that the guardians of the state had a right to lie for the common good.[103] "It may be for the people's good that it is deceived in matters both of religion and of politics," wrote Castillon, "and that it is either led into new error or confirmed in its existing errors, so long (be it understood) as this is done, as we have already said, for the greater good of the people itself." He went on to warn that "if this principle is to hold good, it is absolutely necessary that the people should not know of it, or it will lose all its efficacy." Truth is "for the eyes of the eagle; to all others, if it is not to blind them, it must appear surrounded by veils that soften its excessive splendour." In Castillon's opinion, the cause of the "disorders, crimes and massacres which have been laid so gratuitously at the door of the Christian religion" was not "the errors spread amongst the people by the preachers of various ages, but rather the indiscretion and imprudence of those who have unmasked them." It was better to proceed slowly, step by step, leading the people from greater to lesser errors, as had happened in the case of heathen religions and even in Judaism. At this point Castillon offered an example of a "new error," which was also a "lesser error," namely patriotism. This (he explained) was a halfway stage between "the true and great fundamental principle" of the brotherhood of men, widely held in antiquity and still dominant "among less civilized peoples," and the subsequent belief in personal interest, according to which individuals were to have regard only to themselves and their families. Patriotism had imposed itself through the combined intervention of "wise and disinterested legislators" and of "heads of state acting out of interest" and motivated exclusively by greed, self-interest, and thirst for domination: a combination of euhemerism and imposture. In this "lesser error," this "lie" intended for the peoples of the modern age, Castillon dimly perceives the lineaments of a religion, the religion that would before long begin to celebrate its sometimes bloody rites across much of Europe.[104] The age of the "preachers of patriotism," whose advent Novalis had foretold, was beginning.[105]

6. "Does Vulcan count for anything, face to face with Roberts and Co, or Jove, in the age of the lightning conductor, or Hermes compared to the Crédit Mobilier? All mythology conquers, controls and shapes the forces of nature in imagination and by way of the imagination; it therefore vanishes once we truly have control over those forces. Can Fame keep its renown, now we have Printing House Square?"[106] Posing these questions in 1857, Marx assumes that they are to be answered in the negative: the symbolic forms of the past, beginning with the outdated mythologies of antiquity, will soon be swept away. We know now that this was not to be, and that Greek and Roman mythology can live on the best of terms with capitalist merchandise, for instance in the sphere of advertising (to which we shall turn shortly). Marx's questions spring, however, from a wider and deeper conviction to which he gave expression in the contrast he drew between "the social [i.e., proletarian] revolution of the nineteenth century" and all earlier revolutions: "In those earlier revolutions, there was more phrase than substance; in the revolution that is to come, there will be more substance than phrase."[107] For now we are in the age of bourgeois society, always synonymous for Marx with "cold reality," reality *sans phrase*, substantially immune from the ideological vapors by which past societies had been afflicted.[108]

The enduring vitality of the old religions on the one hand and the rise and spread of nationalisms and racisms on the other have largely contradicted Marx's prognosis (not that he was alone in holding such views). It has been obvious for some time that the history of the twentieth century cannot be understood without an analysis of the political uses of myth. Marx himself, moreover, made a significant contribution to such a project, as profound in its analysis as it is pertinent in its subject, when he wrote *The Eighteenth Brumaire of Louis Bonaparte*, from which the passage just quoted is taken. Writing in the heat of the moment, immediately after the events that he decribes had taken place (the work originally took the form of a series of articles, subsequently printed as a pamphlet), Marx here sets out to demonstrate how the circumstances arising out of the class struggle had "enabled a grotesque mediocrity to strut around in a hero's garb" and had brought about the return of tragedy as farce.[109] The fiercely demystificatory tone in which Marx writes may be read as an implicit tribute to the effectiveness of the propaganda campaign by which Louis Napoleon sought to cover himself with his uncle's mantle. A further propagandistic analogy, suggested by the term "Caesarism," was rejected as fallacious and superficial in the preface Marx wrote when *The Eighteenth Brumaire* was published in German on the eve of the fall of the Second Empire.[110] In the text of the essay, Marx speaks, rather, of a "cossack republic," a paradoxical resolution to the dichotomy envisaged by Napoleon (who had said, "Within fifty years Europe will be republican or cossack"). Marx rightly foresaw that this "cossack republic" would transform itself into an empire;[111] he can hardly have imagined that it would continue in that form for twenty years. Shortly before the battle of Sedan he wrote to Engels that the Second Empire was about to conclude, as it has commenced, in a parody: "I hit off my *Bonaparte* after all! . . . I believe we two are the only people who grasped the whole mediocrity of Boustrapa [i.e., Louis Napoleon] *from the beginning*, regarded him as a mere showman and never allowed ourselves to be misled by his momentary successes."[112] In point of fact Engels, while his own judgment of the phenomenon was just as scathing as Marx's, had gone so far as to define Bonapartism as "the real religion of the modern bourgeoisie." With the exception of England (he wrote to Marx on the eve of the Austro-Prussian war), where an oligarchy governed on behalf of the bourgeoisie, "a Bonapartist semi-dictatorship is the normal form. The big material interests of the bourgeoisie carry this through, even against the opposition of the bourgeoisie, but allow the dictatorship no share in the real power."[113]

Personal mediocrity but the talent of a "showman," an authoritarianism that makes use of plebiscites: this admixture, contradictory only in appearance, was destined for a great future.[114] Engels was not alone in his farsighted assessment. In 1864, Maurice Joly, an opponent of Bonaparte, published anonymously in Brussels an article featuring a dialogue in hell between Montesquieu and Machiavelli. Montesquieu's feeble arguments, based on his faith in the inevitable progress of liberalism, are swept aside by Machiavelli, whose *post eventum* prophecies foretell how in the middle of the nineteenth century a leader will take hold of the reins of power, suppress the opposition by means of violence and flattery, use military campaigns as a diversionary tactic; his government of society, behind a façade of formal freedoms, will be "a gigantic despotism." "Despotism," concludes Machiavelli/Joly, "is the sole form of government truly adapted to the social condition of modern peoples."[115] Before this, Tocqueville had already drawn from his travels in the United States the chilling prophetic conclusion that "if a despotism should be established among the democratic nations of our day, it would probably have a different character" from the despotisms of the past. "It would be more widespread and milder; it would degrade men rather than torment them. . . . An immense, protective [tutélaire] power . . . provident, and gentle" would stand over "an innumerable multitude of men, alike and equal."[116]

7. "Today, the reign of caste is over, and one can govern only with the masses." It was this conviction that led Napoleon III to his masterstroke, the invention of plebiscites as a way of defusing the potentially explosive charge of universal suffrage.[117] The government of the masses in the twentieth century has taken the most varied forms, and these have not differed only in the crucial matter of the balance between force and consent. The maxim that force may be necessary to seize power but is never sufficient to retain it was current in antiquity (the prince, it was held, must make himself at once a fox and a lion); but winning mass consent has required instruments of propaganda unknown in older societies. These may combine the blatancy of advertising slogans with hidden forms of manipulation, as indeed we see if we consider the paradoxical fortune of the *Dialogue aux Enfers entre Machiavel et Montesquieu.* Joly's work was among the sources drawn upon by an overseas agent of the Tsarist secret police—who may even have been the chief of staff, Rakovsky—when he came, sometime between 1896 and 1898, to compile the work known as *The Protocols of the Elders of Zion.* Translated, and spread across the world in hundreds of thousands of copies, this became the most influential forgery of the last two centuries.[118] Joly had intended to offer a brutally frank description of the techniques used by Napoleon III to seize and maintain power, but in the hands of the author of the *Protocols* (whose aim was probably to discredit the projects of the Russian liberals led by Count Witte) this became an ingredient in the imaginary plans for world domination supposedly laid by a nonexistent organization called the Elders of Zion. The forgery is completely implausible; its content is strikingly at odds with its supposed status as the text for

a Jewish plot. The authorial voice is quite clearly that of an agent of the Okhrana, who repeatedly sings the praises of autocracy ("the gentiles' only healthy form of government") and of the "natural and hereditary" aristocracy. Liberalism and individualism are described as sources of disorder; the idea of progress, except in the sciences, is rejected; and we are invited to look forward to the "universal super-government" of a Jewish emperor, who will restore order and true religion ("since there is only one true doctrine") and who resembles nothing so much as a Tsar turned ruler of the world.[119] To be sure, whoever patched the *Protocols* together insists that the Jews, since theirs was the hidden hand behind the French revolution and the rise of liberalism, are to blame for the downfall of the fine old aristocracy. But the author takes so little pains to give a Jewish tone to his words that in the midst of explaining how the arts of subversion are to be employed, he makes the following amazing admission:

> We know of only one society that can compete with our own in the use of these arts, namely the Jesuits. However, we have successfully discredited the Jesuits in the eyes of the foolish mob, because they operate openly as a society, whereas we for our part remain in the wings and keep our existence secret. The world will care little enough, when it comes down to it, whether it is governed by the head of the Catholic church or by an autocrat of the blood of Zion. However, for us, the "chosen people," this cannot be a matter of indifference.[120]

These words are as revealing as a set of fingerprints. Bakunin, twenty years earlier, had invoked the "system of the Jesuits" as a model for his revolutionary organization, but had then gone on to reproach his former friend and comrade-in-arms Nechaev with having adopted that very model. Bakunin had in mind the hierarchical structure of the Society of Jesus, and the absolute obedience expected of its members, which goes so far as to negate their individual will. He recoiled, however, when he came upon the passage in the *Catechism of a Revolutionary* (1869) that took this principle to its logical extreme, bringing into the revolutionary cell modes of behavior that had in the past been regarded as admissible only for the good of the city or the state:

The fundamental plan of every duty or action undertaken by the section must be known only to the section; as for the individuals charged with carrying an action out, they should not know the nature of what they are entrusted with, but only the details of what is to be done. To stimulate their energies, it is necessary to give them a false explanation of the nature of the action.[121]

Whoever put together the revolutionary *Protocols* must have been very well acquainted with the Nechaev case and with the *Catechism of a Revolutionary*, which had even been the subject of an official publication. This unknown agent of the Tsarist secret police saw revolutionaries, Jews, and Jesuits as interchangeable figures, all sharing the common belief that the people are stupid, that politics is the art of "governing the masses and the individual by means of cleverly chosen phrases," and that despotism is the only rational form of government for the future. What is more, he, too, shared these beliefs. "It will be said," he writes, echoing Joly, "that the kind of absolute power I am suggesting goes against the grain of the present progress of society, but I shall prove that the exact opposite is true."[122] The *Protocols* embodies the dreams of a thuggish policeman, clumsily projecting his own nostalgia and his own ambitions onto an enemy whom he seeks to portray as repugnant and diabolical. This ambivalence, which on occasion amounts almost to an ambiguous pro-Semitism, allowed the Nazis to see the omnipotence that the *Protocols* attributes to the Jews both as a looming threat and as an objective to emulate.[123]

8. Why, though, has myth acquired such importance in the modern world? In *The Birth of Tragedy* (1872), Nietzsche gives the following pitiless and lucid explanation:

Our whole modern world is caught in the net of Alexandrian culture. . . . One thing should be remembered: Alexandrian culture requires a slave class for its continued existence, but in its optimism it denies the necessity for such a class; therefore it courts disaster once the effect of its nice slogans concerning the dignity of man and the dignity of labour has worn thin. Nothing can be more terrible than a barbaric slave class that has learned to view its existence as an injustice and prepares to avenge not only its own wrongs but those of all past generations. Under such conditions, who would dare appeal confidently to our weary and etiolated religions, which have long since become "Brahmin" religions? Myth, the prerequisite of all religions, has been paralyzed everywhere, and theology has been invaded by that optimistic spirit which I have just stigmatized as the baneful virus of our society.[124]

These words, written just after the Paris commune, were to have a lasting impact (Sorel's theory of myth, intended to serve the proletarian cause, amounts to a reworking of them with the political signs reversed).[125] Nietzsche was stating the conclusion he drew from the historical vicissitudes we have been tracing here. Myth in classical Greece had contributed to the maintenance of social control, on one hand justifying social hierarchy and on the other brandishing the threat of punishment in the life to come. This dual role had been inherited by Christianity. After the Reformation, however, things had gone to the bad. Religion no longer sufficed to hold in check the proletariat (the slave class of modernity); new myths were needed. Nietzsche dreamed of a rebirth of German mythology, thinking of Wagner (to whom *The Birth of Tragedy* is dedicated).[126] However, the rebirth of myth had already been under way for some time—and not just in Germany. The masses who for years slaughtered each other on the battlefields of Europe were mobilized not by religion, but by patriotism. On 31 March 1917, in the midst of the great conflict, the London *Economist* breathed a sigh of relief at England's narrow escape:

Just as in July, 1914, in the political sphere, the country was drifting into civil war over the Irish controversy, so in the industrial sphere we were approaching general strikes upon a scale which could have been scarcely distinguished from civil war. The transport workers of all kinds had amalgamated their forces for a trial of strength, and the engineering trades expected the autumn of 1914 to see the break up of the Agreement of 1897, which had been renewed in 1907. We were upon the edge of serious industrial disturbance when *the war saved us* by teaching employers and men the obligation of a common patriotism.

A year earlier the leading Scottish industrialist J. A. Richmond had given an address to the Glasgow University Engineering Society, of which he was the president. In the course of this he observed that "such inroads had been made into the powers of management in factories that, *had the war not happened*, the autumn of 1914 would have witnessed the most serious industrial disorder."[127]

The war marked an irreversible change in the organization of society in every sphere, and this included the organization of consent. The return of peace saw no demobilization of the propaganda techniques that had been used to conduct the battle on the home front and to carry it among the troops both allied and enemy. Blood was joined to the soil, and mythic communities of origin began to be invoked in racist tones.

"I foresee the possibility of neutralizing the press by means of the press itself," Joly's Machiavelli had told Montesquieu. "Since journalism is such a great force, my government will take to journalism. It will be journalism incarnate."[128] This prophecy was to come true in the twentieth century. Among the materials for Walter Benjamin's grand work on Paris, which was destined to remain unfinished, we find the following passage:

> A perceptive observer once said that fascist Italy was run like a great newspaper, and run—what is more—by a great journalist: one idea per day, competitions, sensational stories, a clever and pervasive drawing of the reader's attention to certain facets of social life which have expanded beyond measure, a systematic distortion of the reader's understanding in pursuit of certain practical goals. Truth to tell, fascist regimes are regimes based on publicity.[129]

Gustave Le Bon had suggested as early as 1896 that commercial advertising was a good model for political propaganda. Mussolini, who greatly admired Le Bon, put his ideas into practice.[130] Hitler, too, spoke of propaganda in similar terms:

> Its task, just like that of commercial advertising . . . , is to capture the attention of the masses. . . . The masses are always to be activated primarily through the emotions, and only to a very sec-

ondary degree through the so-called intellect. . . . Whoever wishes to win over the great mass of the people must know the key which unlocks their heart. Its name is not objectivity, or in other words weakness; but rather will and energy.[131]

Yet the triumph of the will can collapse into weakness, for while it is true that *mundus vult decipi* ("the world wishes to be deceived"), it is true also that the deceiver is part of the world. The Nuremberg rally, transformed into a completely controlled spectacle, reveals the manipulatory will equally of Leni Riefenstahl, who filmed the rally as *Triumph of the Will*, and of the Nazi party that staged it. Reality, however, is not a film; in the end objectivity asserted its rights.[132]

The Nazi regime lasted twelve years, and the Soviet regime lasted seventy-four. The former was brought down by military defeat; the latter dissolved and wasted away of itself, under the pressure of the so-called Cold War and its concomitant technological challenges. The Soviet regime went through a process of delegitimization that the Nazis never experienced. The process was slow: so powerful was the myth of Stalin that in some cases even its victims had persuaded themselves of its truth. In the long decades following Stalin's death, the language of propaganda was worn down to the point of exhaustion. Compulsory optimism, exaltation at the prospect of the radiant future toward which Soviet society was bound: nobody, including the bureaucracy, believed in these ritually uttered formulae. Anyone prepared (as Gorbachev was) to put the potentialities of the system to the test had to begin their political campaign by denouncing the lies of official propaganda. The Soviet regime was an empty shell long before its inglorious demise. It wielded tremendous powers of coercion, and was totally discredited. Nobody, from the Red Army down, lifted a finger to defend it.

The capitalist system that has emerged victorious from the Cold War is characterized by a reduction of working time, and by the consequent tendency for free time to be brought under the control of the laws of production. This has provided an objective basis for the transformation of politics into spectacle.[133] The confusions between political propaganda and commercial advertising, between politics and the culture industry, are thus inherent in the nature of things—whether or not we reach the point where the two domains find themselves embodied in a single individual. Technology has changed, but the production of myths is more than ever on the agenda.

III

The "mythic foundation," wrote Nietzsche, is the most "potent unwritten law" of the commonwealth itself.[134] As we have seen, since Plato's time this idea has been invoked in support of a common good identified sometimes with a social order yet to be founded and sometimes with the actually existing order. However, behind this use of myth as a form of lying, something deeper is concealed. In order to legitimate itself, power necessarily has recourse to an exemplary story or history, a principle, a founding myth.[135] This becomes plain in times of civil war, when legitimacy, no longer regarded as a fact of nature, becomes for everyone a matter of choice (tacitly, at any rate). This limit case illustrates a more general phenomenon: if the foundations of power are not subjected to the scrutiny of reason, then their invocation becomes a matter of outward show, formulaic utterance, and routine. But the founding myth is inevitably returned to.

The political use of lying takes us back to the other topic we began with, false discourse. At the intersection of these two, we find myth—a phenomenon with deep roots in oral culture. Plato was able to analyze it thanks to the critical distance made available to him by writing, a phenomenon that he ambiguously condemned.[136] It was the written word, the word purified of the intonations and gestures that in the language of orality may transform a noun or a verb into an affirmation or a negation, that allowed Plato (and Aristotle following in his footsteps) to recognize that a noun or verb standing on its own is "neither true nor false."

In the *Timaeus* (22a–23b), we read that an Egyptian priest, having listened to Solon telling (*mythologein*) about the flood, about Deucalion and Pyrrha and their descendants (*kai tous ex auton genealogein*), remarked ironically that these stories of "generations" told by the Greeks were stories fit for "children" (*paidon . . . mython*).[137] We still find this identification between mythology and genealogy as late as Boccaccio, who gave to his collection of classical myths the title *Genealogia deorum gentilium*. Aristotle seems to adopt a contrary view when he says that the author of a tragedy should add the names of the dramatis personae only once the plot of the work has been composed (*Poetics*, 1455b).[138] This is contradicted, however, by another passage in the *Poetics* (1453a), where he remarks that tragedies now always revolve around the same names and the same families. Athenaeus, quoting the comedian Antiphanes, writes:

> We need only say the name "Oedipus" and we know all the rest—
> his father Laius, his mother Jocasta, the sons and daughters, what
> will happen to him, what he has done. The same goes for
> Alcmaeon: we need only name him, and any child will tell us that
> in a fit of madness he killed his mother.[139]

Names, in truth, were micro-tales.[140] They were the epitomes of myth, offering a powerful mechanism of identification for members of the group who shared in their meaning and excluding all outsiders—a function similarly fulfilled by nonmythical genealogies.

The name standing alone, "neither true nor false," which Aristotle likened to the verb standing alone, is the nucleus of myth.[141] Marcel's friend Bloch, in Proust's *À la recherche du temps perdu*, displayed his aesthetic snobbery by singling out "La fille de Minos et de Pasiphaé" as the one decent line in Racine, because it had the merit of "meaning absolutely nothing": but no line in *Phèdre* has so dense a mythic content.[142] Myth is, by definition, a story already told, a story that we already know.

3

Representation

THE WORD, THE IDEA, THE THING

"Representation" is a much-used term in the human sciences, and has been for a long time. No doubt this is because of its ambiguity. On one hand the "representation" stands in for the reality that is represented, and so evokes absence; on the other, it makes that reality visible, and thus suggests presence. Moreover, this opposition can easily be reversed: the representation is present in the former case, even if only as a surrogate; in the latter case it ends up recalling, in contrast to itself, the absent reality that it is intended to represent.[1] I do not plan to amuse myself with such tedious mirror games; my point here is simply to draw attention to the reason why the term "representation" has often been attractive, in recent times, to critics of positivism, postmodern skeptics, and devotees of the metaphysics of absence.[2]

As Roger Chartier has remarked, we already find this oscillation between representation as substitute and as mimetic evocation in the article on *représentation* in Furetière's *Dictionnaire universel* of 1690. This refers to the waxen, wooden, or leather effigies that were placed on the royal catafalque during the funerals of French and English sovereigns, as well as to the funerary bed, empty and covered with a pall, which in earlier times "represented" the dead sovereign. The first instance bespeaks a mimetic intention not found in the second, but in both cases the term "representation" was used. Let us make this our starting point.

2. Our earliest evidence concerning the use of an empty catafalque in a royal funeral dates back to 1291. In that year, as we learn from a document preserved in the archives at Barcelona, the Saracen inhabitants of the Aragonese city of Daroca assaulted the Jews who were surrounding a bier that "stood there to represent [*in representationem*]" the recently dead king, Alfonso III.[3] Only considerably later do we find effigies used in the funerals of sovereigns: the practice goes back to 1327 in England (the death of Edward II) and to 1422 in France (the death of Charles VI).[4] These figurines were fragile objects, intended only for brief use, and almost all of the very few that have survived have been heavily restored.[5]

Ernst Kantorowicz argued that the figurines exhibited at the funerals of English and French sovereigns gave palpable expression to the legal doctrine of the king's double body. The effigy was the eternal body of the king inasmuch as he was associated with a public institution (*dignitas*); the corpse was his ephemeral body inasmuch as he was an individual.[6] Kantorowicz makes his case convincingly, even though we must note that in France at least the practice of exhibiting effigies of the deceased—the term for which was, precisely, *"representacion"*—was not limited to royal funerals.[7] How, though, did it come about that both corpse and effigy were exhibited together? Ralph Giesey takes the view that effigies were used as "substitutes for the body" for practical reasons: embalming techniques were so little developed that if the exhibiting of a half-putrefied body was to be avoided, it was necessary to have recourse to a wooden, leather, or wax figurine.[8] This, however, is unconvincing as an explanation. It would have been possible to display within the catafalque the coffin covered with a pall, an alternative based on a non-mimetic evocation and sanctioned by tradition.[9] Instead of doing this, it was decided in London in 1327 to pay a craftsman to make *quandam ymaginem de ligno ad similitudinem dicti domini Regis*, an image that would resemble the dead king, Edward II. Why was this done? Why did it take a century for this innovation to be adopted in France, and why did the practice then continue for so long in both kingdoms?[10]

I have just spoken of "innovation," but this term may not be legitimate. Julius von Schlosser noted that there were strong similarities between the wax images used in the funerals of Roman emperors during the second and third centuries and the waxen, wooden, and leather images exhibited in similar circumstances a thousand years later.[11] Should we assume that the two practices are linked, or was the latter a spontaneous rediscovery? Schlosser inclined toward the first hypothesis, though there is very little evidence for such continuity.[12] Other historians, including Giesey, have preferred the second view. Giesey does not deny that there are resemblances (to which we shall shortly return) between the funerals of French and English kings and those of Roman emperors. However, he regards the exercise of comparing rites that took place in cultures remote from one another, tempting as it is to "the human instinct to draw analogy," as facile from a historical point of view. "In terms of cultural anthropology," he declares, "these likenesses are provocative; but the historical link is weak."[13]

Here I proceed on the basis of exactly the opposite hypothesis. I shall seek to show that transcultural similarities can help us to grasp what is specific about the phenomena I am considering here. The task is laborious, and requires a constant shuttling from one space and time to another. The effigies of the kings of France and England will serve as our reference point.

3. Giesey himself tells us that his starting point, doubtless suggested to him by his mentor, Kantorowicz, was Elias Bickerman's article of 1929 on the apotheoses of the Roman emperors.[14] Bickerman's brilliant essay, which gave rise to the liveliest debate, analyzes the rites of *consecratio*. This involved a double cremation, first of the emperor's body and then a few days later of his waxen image. Thanks to this *funus imaginarium*, this "funeral of the image," the emperor, having already shuffled off the mortal coil, could be received among the gods. As well as noting the precise analogies between these rites and late medieval ceremonies in France and

England, Bickerman referred briefly (in a note) to the funeral rites studied by Frazer. He seems not to have been aware of Robert Hertz's article, "A Contribution to the Study of the Collective Representation of Death," that had appeared in *L'Année sociologique* in 1907.[15] Be that as it may, Bickerman ends his first paragraph with a statement that Hertz would have seconded: "Death does not constitute the end of the body's life on earth: it is not the biological fact, but the social deed—the funeral ceremonies—that separate those who depart from those who remain behind."[16] The analysis in Hertz's splendid essay considers the ritual of double burial, discussed by Bickerman in the Roman context, within a very broad perspective. He shows that death, any death, is a traumatic happening for the community, a true crisis that needs to be overcome by way of rituals that transform the biological event into a social process, controlling the passage by which the putrefying body—that most unstable and threatening of objects—becomes a skeleton. Such rituals include temporary burial, or in other cultures mummification and cremation (sometimes combined): in Hertz's view, these are particular solutions to a very general problem.[17] The funerals celebrated over the bodies of emperors in Antonine Rome and of sovereigns in fifteenth- and sixteenth-century England and France performed a function analogous to that of the provisional burials that Hertz analyzes. In either case they were followed by the funerals of the images, which is to say by a ritual that was not just definitive but eternalizing. The emperor was consecrated as a god; the king, since it was declared that the monarchical function was everlasting, would never die. Waxen imperial images and royal effigies, through which the rulers' deaths as a social process came to a conclusion, were equivalents on another level to mummies or skeletons. This is the same conclusion as was recently reached by Florence Dupont through a different research itinerary.[18]

By placing them within this wide transcultural horizon, we are better able to evaluate what is specific about the solutions arrived at both by the Romans of the Antonine period and by the English and French of the fifteenth and sixteenth centuries. In these latter cases we know that the effigy showed the king as if alive; and in Rome too the image became caught up in what has been called a "fiction of the *post mortem* livelihood" of the ruler.[19] A well-known description in Dio Cassius's *Roman Histories* (quoted by Giesey) describes the waxen statue of the emperor Pertinax, who died in 193, "laid out in triumphal garb," and tells how a young slave was stationed before it "keeping the flies away from it with peacock feathers, as though it were really a person sleeping."[20] Herodian gives us an even more detailed account of the ceremonies that followed the death of Septimius Severus, whose waxen image, reclining on a large ivory bed with a gilded counterpane, was visited for seven successive days by doctors who pronounced that the sick man was getting worse and worse.[21] These descriptions are very reminiscent of what happened in France following the death of Francis I in 1547, when banquets were held for eleven days, first in the presence of the king's corpse and then of his effigy: people ate and drank beside him, and "basins of water . . . [were] presented at the chair of the Seigneur, as if he had been living and seated in it."[22] Giesey remarks that Herodian's description was already available in France by approximately 1480, and that the earliest known evidence of funeral banquets being practiced there dates to the end of the fifteenth century, but (as we have noted) he does not regard the analogies as attributable to any conscious imitation of Roman antiquity.[23]

Giesey's arguments are not always entirely convincing. A difference in detail, for instance the fact that the practice of banqueting beside the corpse was inaugurated at the obsequies of Francis I, does not suffice to prove that French usages were entirely independent of Roman ones.[24] Nonetheless there is no doubt that autonomous recreation is possible in this sphere, even between societies further removed in space than Septimius Severus's Rome and Francis I's France were in time. Francisco Pizarro, the conqueror of Peru, tells us (and his evidence on this point is confirmed by other accounts) that on the most solemn occasions the Incas would exhibit the carefully preserved mummies of their kings, feasting with them and drinking toasts to them.[25] This is a truly astonishing analogy, but we may be able to offer at least a hypothetical explanation for it. In Peru, the royal palace of Cuzco was the property of the dead sovereigns, together with its animals and slaves. The management of these goods was in the hands of a group that included all the male heirs with the exception of the king: the latter inherited nothing material from his predecessor.[26] In theory, then, the dead sovereigns retained power, and the Incas kept up a reciprocal relationship, expressed by way of ritual banquets, with their mummies. In France, too, a legal fiction attributed power to the dead sovereign, even though this was only for the limited period (which Giesey calls a "ceremonial inter-regnum") immediately preceding the coronation of the new king.[27] In other words, similar constraints produced convergent results, in quite heterogeneous circumstances.

All this helps us to reformulate the problem that has often been stated in connection with French royal funerals of the sixteenth century. To set "imitation of Rome" against "independent invention" is to engage with only one aspect of this problem. As Marc Bloch and Claude Lévi-Strauss, discussing altogether different questions, have strongly insisted, contact—if indeed there is contact, something of which in the present case we cannot be sure—does not explain the persistence of a given practice.[28]

4. Why, then, in Rome and elsewhere, were images made of dead emperors and kings? Florence Dupont has argued that the search for an answer should begin with the practice of Roman aristocratic families who would have wax masks (*imagines*) made of their ancestors. The *imago* was regarded as equivalent to the bones, since both were considered to be a part of the whole constituted by the body.[29] It is worth noting that in his analysis of the notion of the person (*persona*), M. Mauss had earlier emphasized the close relation that existed in the Rome of antiquity between the *imago* and the *cognomen*, which is the most personal element in the three-name system.[30] However, this use of ancestral masks was not confined to aristocatic families.[31] Bickerman cites a law dating from the period 133–136, in which a certain college or association of Lanuvius reserves the right to celebrate a *funus imaginarium*, "funeral of the image," should an ill-disposed proprietor refuse to hand over the body of a slave belonging to the college.[32]

In such a case as this the funerary *imago* was a substitute for the absent body. This fact is in accordance with the conclusions reached in the discussion of a topic—the meaning of the Greek word *kolossos* —which despite its narrow focus has broadened out until it bears on the status of the image as such. This discussion began with Pierre Chantraine's article of 1931, in which, discussing the etymology of the word "*kolossos*," he argued that its origins had to be sought outside the Indo-European sphere. When he was correcting the proofs of his article, he added that the sacred laws of Cyrene (which had

recently been published) showed that the term *kolossos* did not originally have the meaning of "large statue" with which we have
become familiar thanks to the Colossus of Rhodes, but signified simply "statue." Two years later, research was given a new direction
thanks to an article by Emile Benveniste. It was laid down in the
sacred laws of Cyrene (dating from the second half of the fourth
century) that anyone who welcomed into their house supplicants
who were foreigners or strangers should, for three successive days,
invoke the name of the person who protected their guests. Should
this person be dead or unknown, whoever pronounced the invocation must make *kolossoi*, dolls or lay-figures of wood or clay, of both
male and female sex, and must later "plant them in an uncut wood."
This explanation had seemed strange, even downright illogical, to
some scholars. However, argued Benveniste, "to concede that a living person who is unknown is as if he really did not exist might perhaps be said to obey a deeper logic." And he therefore concluded:
"Here, then, is the authentic meaning of the word: [*kolossoi* were]
funerary statues, ritual substitutes, doubles who took the place of
absent ones and perpetuated their earthly existence."[33]

We will add: they were representations. In terms of both form and
function, there are striking similarities between these Greek *kolossoi*
and the funeral effigies of French and English sovereigns that were
made in wax, leather, or wood. The sacred laws of Cyrene included
explicit provision for a ritual banquet to be held with the funerary stat-
uettes—like those that were held in the sixteenth century, in Paris or
in Cuzco. In Sparta, so Herodotus (6.58) informs us, when a king died
in battle a simulacrum (*eidolon*) was made and then exhibited on a
well-decorated bed, a practice compared by J.-P. Vernant to those provided for in the sacred laws of Cyrene.[34] At this point references are
usually made to magic, but it is best to avoid these, since they explain
nothing.[35] Rather, let us take these observations concerning the links
between funerary images and images in general as the basis for a
rereading, from a new perspective, of two essays: Ernst Gombrich's
Meditations on a Hobby Horse and Krzysztof Pomian's equally important work on collecting and collections. Gombrich, too, made representation his starting point. His reflections on the hobby horse as substitute for a horse led him to emphasize the role played by substitution
in the furnishing of tombs: "The clay horse or servant, buried in the
tomb of the mighty, takes the place of the living." This remark, exem-

plified by reference to ancient Egypt, provided Gombrich with the foundation for a more general hypothesis: "substitution may precede portrayal, and creation communication." Only in certain particular societies—Greece, China, Renaissance Europe—did "a change in function" lead to "the emergence of the idea of the image as a 'representation' in our modern sense of the word." These brilliantly sketched ideas were developed by Gombrich when he came to write his seminal work *Art and Illusion*, ten years later.[36] Pomian, for his part, seeking to understand what there is in common between the disparate objects found in collections, makes funeral offerings his starting point: in them—as in relics, curios, images—he detects "intermediaries" between "this world and the next, the secular and the sacred . . . symbols of the distant, the hidden, the absent . . . intermediaries between those who can see them and an invisible world." Once withdrawn from the sphere of useful objects and isolated in the separate space of the tomb or the collection, these objects become "semiophores": bearers of signs.[37]

Substitution, Gombrich assumed, came before imitation. In both *kolossoi* and funerary *representationes*, the element of substitution clearly predominates over that of imitation. Before commenting further on this, I wish to emphasize that not only have all these investigations been focused on quite different themes, they have all been independently conducted. This makes the convergences that we have noted all the more significant. How, though, are they to be interpreted? Should they be accounted for in terms of the universal characteristics of the sign and the image? Or are they related to a specific cultural milieu—and if so, which milieu?

The alternative I sketch here is a central concern of J.-P. Vernant's essay on the *kolossos* and the double, in which Vernant takes up and develops the work of Benveniste. He emphasizes that *"kolossos"* was one of a group of terms—*"psuche," "dream-image," "shade," "supernatural apparition"*—which, taken together, entitle us to speak of "a true psychological category . . . the category of the double" which "presupposes a different conceptual framework from our own." Toward the end of the essay, however, Vernant's tone suddenly changes:

Here, perhaps, we are touching upon a problem that goes far beyond the case of the colossos, and concerns one of the essential characteristics of a religious sign. The religious sign is not simply a piece of mental equipment. Its purpose is not limited to evoking in men's minds the sacred power to which it refers. Its intention is always also to establish a true means of communication with this power and to really introduce its presence into the human world. But while it thus aims, so to speak, to establish a bridge with the divine, it must at the same time emphasize the gap, the immeasurable difference between this sacred power and anything that attempts to manifest it, perforce inadequately, to the eyes of men. In this sense, the colossos is a good example of the tension which is to be found at the very heart of the religious sign, and which gives it its peculiar character. In effect the colossos's function is to establish a real contact with the beyond and to bring about its presence in this earthly world. Yet, in so doing, it at the same time emphasizes all the elements of the inaccessible, the mysterious, and the fundamentally foreign that the world beyond death holds for the living.[38]

On one hand, there is the "conceptual framework" of the Greeks, which was different from ours; on the other, there are the tensions inherent in the religious sign, which we may detect in Greek times as in our own. This oscillation between a historical and a universalistic pespective, which has inspired Vernant's extremely fertile research, is more than understandable inasmuch as our own culture has a quite special relationship, compounded of both distance and derivation, with the culture of the Greeks.[39] In the matter of the image, however, as in other matters, a deep fracture separates us from the Greeks, which deserves closer examination.

5. Let us return to the *consecratio* of the Roman emperors. This rite, as Florence Dupont has emphasized, involves a paradox. In Rome, in order to consecrate a dead person,

it was necessary to pull him out of the tomb in order to place him in the sacred space in which his temple would be located. This is unthinkable, both from the point of view of the dead person (who would thus be deprived of his burial place) and in respect of the sacred space, which would be horribly contaminated by the presence of a cadaver. . . . Tombs were excluded from the city . . .

it was prohibited to erect a tomb upon public land, within whose confines temples were dedicated.

We have seen how the obstacle was overcome:

Two bodies allowed the dead person to be present in the two distinct spaces of the tomb and the temple, in the two incompatible times of the funeral cult and the cult of public worship. After his death, the emperor remained present among men in two different ways.[40]

This state of things was undermined by the victory of Christianity. Cemeteries, cities of the dead, established themselves within the cities of the living. Jean Guyon has recognized that this millennial abolition of the religious ban on burial *intra muros* marks a true historical turning point.[41] Now among the dead, there were some—the martyrs—who had a special status in the eyes of the faithful. Peter Brown has argued forcefully that the relics of martyrs, and of saints in general, are the signs of their presence. There is every justification for granting these relics the metonymic status that has sometimes been attributed to the *imago* of the Roman emperors. Martin's soul, declared the inscription on his tomb at Tours, is with God (*"cuius anima in manu Dei est"*); and yet Martin *"hic totus est praesens manifestus omni gratia virtutum* [he is entirely here, as miracles of all sorts bear witness]."[42]

The function attributed in the Christian world to the relics of the saints must have led to deep changes in our attitude toward images. This hypothesis is no more than a corollary to the one we have already formulated, which proposed a close link between the image and the world beyond. The relics themselves, however, belong to a realm of which our knowledge is inadequate.[43] Above all, there is the phenomenon that Christian polemicists called idolatry. It is time we took this seriously, and time we acknowledged two things: that we know very little about it and that what we do know is difficult to interpret.[44] Thanks to the work of scholars such as Fritz Saxl, Erwin Panofsky, and Jean Seznec, associated at first with the Warburg library and subsequently with the Warburg Institute, we have long had an understanding of the artistic survivals and metamorphoses of the gods of the ancients.[45] What we still largely lack is an exploration of the range of responses (absorption, metamorphosis, rejection) that resulted from the encounter on the religious plane between such images, including those in popular use, and the aniconic if not explicitly anti-iconic tendencies rooted in Judeo-Christian tradition.

A sufficient indication of the complexity of this encounter is provided by the case of Saint Foy of Conques (Saint Faith). According to the legend, she was martyred at the age of twelve, early in the fourth century. Her image, preserved among the treasures of the church at Conques (plate 7), has long been regarded as a centrally important example of Carolingian sculpture and goldsmith's work. The image plays a significant role in the *Liber miraculorum sancte Fidis*.

The first two books of this hagiographical text were compiled between 1013 and 1020 by Bernard d'Angers, a cleric studying at the school of Chartres. Bernard, a fervent devotee of Saint Foy, had set off with a friend called Bernier, a student, to visit Conques, where the saint's relics had been kept for a century and a half, since their theft from the basilica at Agen built especially to house them.[46] As he journeyed through Toulouse and the Auvergne in the course of his pilgrimage, Bernard was struck by the number of statues he came across, made of gold, silver, and other metals, and housing relics of various saints. Cultivated persons such as himself and his companion could only regard these as works of superstition, carrying a whiff of paganism if not of outright devil worship. On one altar he saw a statue of Saint Gerard, encrusted with gold and jewels, and seeming to gaze with glittering eyes at the peasants who knelt in prayer before it. Turning to his friend, and speaking in Latin (*latino sermone*), Bernard said in mocking tones: "Well, my brother, and what do you think of this idol? Do you suppose that Jove or Mars would have thought such a statue unworthy of them?" The crucifix, he remarked, was the only admissible statue. It was permitted also to depict the saints on a wall—*imagines umbrose coloratis parietibus depicte*. But to venerate statues of the saints struck him as an abuse rooted in inveterate ignorance: if he were to declare what he thought of this statue of Saint Gerard hereabouts, the people would treat him as a criminal.

Three days later, Bernard and Bernier arrived in Conques. The saint's image, known as "the majesty of Saint Faith" (*Majestas sancte Fidis*), was kept in a narrow room, crammed with people on their knees. Bernard found himself incapable of following their example.

"Saint Foy," he exclaimed, "a fragment of whose body is preserved in this statue, come to my aid in the hour when I am judged." As he spoke, he glanced smilingly at his friend. His words showed his disparagement of this saintly statue-reliquary: it seemed to him comparable to a likeness of Venus or Diana, an idol to which sacrifices were offered.

However, things had changed by the time Bernard set down his account. There, he explains that he has come to see the error of his ways, thanks to the miracles performed by Saint Foy, which he describes. He tells the story of one Hulderic, who spoke derisively about the statue of Saint Foy. Next night, the saint appeared to him, holding a stick: "And how is it that you have dared to insult my statue, you rogue?" Bernard concludes that the statue can do no harm to the Christian faith and need cause no apprehensions lest we fall back into the errors of the ancients. It had been made in honor of God, and to preserve the memory of the saint.[47]

Peter Brown has remarked that the saint's vengeful anger is, so to speak, the correlative of the community's sense of justice: "She was the heavy voice of the group."[48] This is undeniable. At the same time we must note that the miracles of Saint Foy, handed down from an oral culture, were bound up within a written text that includes passages like those we have just quoted, which hinge upon a series of asymmetrical oppositions: learned persons/peasants, Latin/the vernacular, painting/sculpture, Christ/the saints, religion/superstition (not to mention masculine/feminine—tacit, but all-pervasive). These can be traced back to a double opposition, both cultural and social: on the one hand, between written culture (in Latin) and oral culture (in the vernacular); on the other, between written culture and images.[49] In relation to images, we become aware of a new hierarchy, which harks back to Hebrew tradition: in terms of their tendency to incite idolatry, statues are far more dangerous than pictures.[50] It is true that when he comes to the end of the chapter, Bernard acknowledges his mistake: there is nothing superstitious in the peasants' devotion to the statues of Saint Gerard and Saint Foy, and their religious attitudes should be tolerated (*permittantur*). Nonetheless, his point of view remains indulgently hierarchical: he looks at all this with the eyes of a learned man from the very different culture of northern France.[51]

6. The statue of Saint Gerard, which prompted Bernard to draw half-ironic, half-shocked comparisons with the idols of Jove and Mars, has not survived. However, in the process of restoring the statue of Saint Foy (which Bernard also compared to pagan idols, those of Venus and Diana), it has been discovered that the body was joined, toward the end of the tenth century, to a much older head, which dates back to the fourth or early fifth century. This head, made of gold and crowned with laurels, was that of a Roman emperor who had been made a god. Bernard's initial reaction was not altogether wide of the mark.[52]

There has been much debate about the chronology of the statue at Conques and of its remodeling. Jean Taralon, who restored it, has argued for an early date, toward the end of the ninth century. Among the works made in the pre-Romanesque rebirth of sculpture in the round, the statue of Saint Foy may well be "the earliest western example that has come down to us."[53] Bernard of Angers tells us that statue-reliquaries of male and female saints were widespread in southern France. Representations of the Madonna and Child in Majesty may be considered a variation of this genre.[54] Their use as reliquaries is by no means incidental; it was probably this that provided an excuse for the return of sculpture in the round.[55] The fragment of Saint Foy's body, which Bernard refers to somewhat cynically in his prayer, allowed the peasants of Conques to possess the case that enclosed the relic—the gold doll with the wide-open eyes and jewel-encrusted cloak that represented the martyred child.

In the miraculous tales that Bernard of Angers relates, the image of Saint Foy is regarded in a characteristically ambivalent manner. On the one hand, it aroused hostility and sarcasm among its detractors; on the other, it appeared in the visions of the faithful.[56] The monks carried it in procession so that, in accordance with established practice, it might take possession of a piece of land left to the monastery of which they had been unlawfully deprived.[57] The people of Conques made no distinction between the image of Saint Foy and the saint herself. Bernard's suggestion that the image was an aid to memory—an argument that he put forward to ward off the suspicion of idolatry—would have been acceptable to only a tiny minority of believers.

The perplexity that Bernard of Angers felt when he looked at the image of Saint Foy disappeared when he turned to consider the crucified Christ. The Church, Bernard remarked, spread crucifixes, in sculpture or bas-relief, as a way of keeping alive the memory of the Passion.[58] Nonetheless, even Christ's image might be looked upon idolatrously. Throughout Europe, from Venice to Iceland and Norway, images of Christ crucified and Christ in glory are to be found, together with Latin verses along the lines of this example (from the twelfth century or earlier):

Hoc Deus est, quod imago docet, sed non Deus ipse
Hanc recolas, sed mente colas, quod cernis in illa.

This is God, as the image teaches, but the image itself is not God. Think upon this, but in spirit worship what you see in it.[59]

The whole of the European Middle Ages shows this ambiguous attitude: fear of images, depreciation of images. But the term *"imago"* (like the term *"figura"*) has many meanings.[60] One more example from the *Liber miraculorum Sancte Fidis* will suffice to suggest a range of themes that we can only touch on here. Bernard has been discussing the case of a knight who is punished for his pride. Addressing himself, he exclaims:

And so you should count yourself fortunate, o learned one, in that you have seen Pride not in image [*imaginaliter*], as you read in Prudentius' *Psychomachia*, but in its authentic and corporeal presence [*presentialiter corporaliterque proprie*].[61]

There can be no doubt that the sacramental connotations of this passage are involuntary—and all the more revealing for being so. The word *"imago"* had long been associated with the Gospel: *Umbra in lege, imago in Evangelio, veritas in caelestibus*, as Saint Ambrose had written—the shadow in the law, the image in the gospel, the truth in heavenly things.[62] In the passage just quoted, however, *"imago"* connotes the fictitious, perhaps the abstract; at all events, a faded and impoverished reality. *"Presentia,"* by contrast, a term long associated with the relics of the saints will be more and more often connected to the Eucharist.[63]

The opposition between the Eucharist and the relics of the saints is expounded in Guibert de Nogent's treatise on relics, *De pignoribus sanctorum*, completed in 1125.[64] Guibert not only dismissed such false relics as the supposed milk tooth of the infant Jesus that the monks of San Medardo had put on show; he insisted that the Eucharist was the sole memorial left by Christ. This led him to deprecate both the use of relics as substitutes (*repraesentata pignora*) and, as a corollary, the figure of synecdoche, since the latter was a trope beloved of the ignorant.[65] Here we see the emerging outlines of the way of thinking that was to lead in 1215 to the proclamation of the dogma of transubstantiation.

As other scholars have emphasized, this was a decisively important event in the history of how images have been perceived.[66] However, its implications are not entirely clear. I shall attempt to state some of them, on the basis of my discussion thus far. It is immediately obvious that there is a profound discontinuity between the ideas we can glimpse behind the Greek *kolossos* and the notion of the real presence. To be sure, in both cases we are dealing with religious signs. However no one could apply to the Eucharist what Vernant says of the *kolossos*, namely that its function is to "establish a real contact with the beyond and to bring about its presence in this earthly world." The way in which the doctrine of transubstantiation is formulated makes it impossible to speak simply of "contact"; *presence* in the strongest sense of the term is involved. The presence of Christ in the Host is in effect a super-presence. All other evocations or manifestations of the sacred—such as relics and images—are dim and feeble by comparison, at least in theory. (In practice, this was not how it turned out.)

Let me conclude by putting forward some hypotheses, more or less rash, which may stimulate further thought on the subject of this essay. After 1215, the fear of idolatry begins to lessen. Ways are found of domesticating images, including those that have come down from pagan antiquity. Among the fruits of this historical change is the return to illusionism in sculpture and painting: only the disenchantment of the image made possible the work of Arnolfo di Cambio, Nicola Pisano, Giotto. "The idea of the image as a 'representation' in our modern sense of the word," to which Gombrich refers, was born at this moment.

The process had bloody consequences. The miracles of the Eucharist were linked, we know, to the persecution of the Jews.[67] It has been thought that the accusations of ritual sacrifice brought against the Jews from the mid-twelfth century onward may have constituted a projection onto an externalized other of a deep anguish bound up with the idea of the real presence connected to the Eucharist.[68] Traditional themes of anti-Jewish polemic, such as the charge of idolatry centered on the worship of the Golden Calf, or of excessive literal-mindedness in interpreting the word of God, were given new meanings. The dogma of transubstantiation, inasmuch as it denied sense data in the name of a profound and invisible reality, may be interpreted—at any rate, by an outside observer—as an extraordinary victory of abstraction.

In this same period, abstraction was also triumphing in the spheres of theology and of political liturgy. In Kantorowicz's great book on the king's two bodies, references to the Eucharist are strangely marginal.[69] In fact, the dogma of transubstantiation probably had a decisive influence in the relevant historical process. I shall refer to just one example, drawn from the description of the ceremonies that took place at Saint-Denis to mark the obsequies of the Constable Bernard du Guesclin, in 1389. The monk who wrote the chronicle of Saint-Denis describes a scene that he saw with his own eyes. The bishop of Autun, who was celebrating the mass, at the moment of the offertory left the altar, together with the king, and went over to where four knights stood at the entrance of the choir, displaying the arms of the dead man "as if with the aim of showing, so to speak, his bodily presence" (*ut quasi ejus corporalem presenciam demonstrarent*).[70] The Eucharistic implications of this extraordinary heraldic and knightly communion, normally reserved for barons and princes, are readily explained in the light of the hypothesis I have just advanced. It is the real, concrete, corporeal presence of Christ in the sacrament that makes possible the crystallization, between the late twelfth and early thirteenth centuries, of that extraordinary object from which I started and which became a concrete symbol of the abstraction of the state: the effigy of the king, known as *representation*.

4

Ecce

ON THE SCRIPTURAL ROOTS OF

CHRISTIAN DEVOTIONAL IMAGERY

In the following pages, I shall seek to connect two spheres of research—New Testament studies and studies of Christian iconography—between which there has been no communication. Given the limits of my competence, I have made much use of the work of other scholars. I remain responsible for the conclusions, as well as for the errors I must inevitably have made.

I

Let us begin with Matthew 1:21–23. An angel appears to the sleeping Joseph and tells him that his wife, Mary, has conceived a son, but not by him:

"She will bear a son; and you shall give him the name Jesus (Saviour), for he will save his people from their sins." All this happened in order to fulfil what the Lord declared through the prophet: "BEHOLD, THE VIRGIN will conceive and bear a son, and he shall be called Emmanuel," a name which means "God is with us."[1]

"What the Lord declared through the prophet": Matthew here refers to Isaiah 7:14; and Luke, too, indirectly evokes the same passage ("BEHOLD you shall conceive and bear a son"—Luke 13:1). To be more precise, Matthew's reference is to the Greek of the Septuagint, where Isaiah's word *almah*, "girl," is rendered *parthenos*, "virgin."[2] As we know, two millennia have borne witness to the consequences that flowed from this translation, or distortion, which in the passage from Hebrew into Greek transformed a prediction that although made in a discourse with possible messianic implications was in itself entirely normal ("Behold: the girl will conceive and bear a son"), into a preternatural prophecy: "Behold, the virgin will conceive and bear a son." I shall not be concerned with these consequences here. I must simply note that the divergences between the evangelists on the question of Jesus' birthplace may be traced back to the reference to Isaiah 7:14, which is explicit in Matthew and implicit in Luke. Matthew and Luke tell us that Jesus was born at Bethlehem, because Isaiah 7:14 in turn involves a reference to "the city of David, called Bethelehem" (Luke 2:4; John 7:41), the birthplace of "Jesse of Bethlehem" (1 Samuel 16:1), father of David, from whose "stock"—so Isaiah (11:1) had prophesied—a "shoot" would grow. Mark and John know nothing of Bethlehem, just as they know nothing of Joseph's descent from David, which is emphasized by both Matthew and Luke. Mark (1:9) says simply that "Jesus came from Nazareth in Galilee" to have himself baptized in the Jordan. We know from John that some people refused to acknowledge that the Messiah might be a Galilean, as Jesus was, because according to Scripture the Messiah was supposed to be "from David's village of Bethelehem" (John 7:42). It is John, too, who reports that Philip referred to Jesus as the "son of Joseph, from Nazareth" (1:45 ff.), in reply to which Nathaniel asks scornfully: "Can anything good come from Nazareth?"

Since the end of the nineteenth century, various scholars have conjectured that allusions in the Gospels to biblical passages may depend on and imply chains of reference and quotation, or *testimonia*, organized thematically or in terms of key words. This hypothesis has been strongly resisted. Some scholars have formulated it anew by arguing that we may need to postulate *testimonia*, connected to preaching, which came into existence immediately after the compo-

sition of the Gospels.[3] Others again have argued that *testimonia* date back only to the era of the church fathers, which saw the composition of the best-known example, Cyprian's *Ad Quirinum: Testimoniorum libri tres*.[4] The possibility that these chains of reference may have been intended to play a part in anti-Jewish polemic has also been much debated. Some time ago, the hypothesis that *testimonia* existed when the Gospels were written was confirmed in the eyes of some scholars by the discovery in the fourth cave at Qumrân of a fragment that included quotations from Deuteronomy, Numbers, Joshua, and Amos. J. A. Fitzmayer remarked that we might infer that such chains of citation constituted a "pre-Christian literary procedure, which may well have been imitated in the early stage of the formation of the New Testament. It resembles so strongly the composite citations of the New Testament writers that it is difficult not to admit that *testimonia* influenced certain parts of the New Testament."[5] This is an important statement, especially given its author's standing; but it is perhaps a little evasive, as appears if we examine the quotations taken from the prophets, particularly Isaiah, and inserted into the Gospels to prove to the Jews that Jesus was the Messiah.[6] In regard to this group of quotations—in many ways significant from a methodological point of view—to speak of "imitation" and "influence" is euphemistic.

This is in fact shown by the example we began with. The reader will have noticed that I took it for granted that Matthew 1:22 and Luke 1:26 ff.—that is, the passages referring to Jesus' being conceived by a virgin—are the result of a messianic reading of Isaiah 7:14, which is in turn influenced by the (probably deliberate) distortion in the Septuagint's Greek. I am well aware that the relationship between the two series of texts can be read differently, indeed inversely: Jesus' conception in the virgin's womb can be seen as the realization of Isaiah's prophecy (Isaiah 7:14), and more generally the events of Jesus' life and death can be seen as the fulfillment of biblical prophecy. However, such a point of view, though quite legitimate in religious terms, cannot guide scientific research.[7] The link between the reference (open or tacit) to Isaiah 7:14 and the naming of Bethlehem as Jesus' birthplace seems to imply the existence of a *testimonium* that also included 1 Samuel 16:1 and Isaiah 11:1 ff. If the inference is correct, then one or more strings of citation, organized

thematically, would not simply have influenced the narrative; they would have generated it. Krister Stendahl arrives by a different route at the same conclusion: in the nativity story, "the whole context seems to be constructed with the quotations as its nucleus—and as its germ from the point of view of growth."[8]

Is it helpful to go on using the term *"testimonia"* to designate these citation strings? Stendahl, on the basis of an analysis of Old Testament citations in the Gospel according to Saint Matthew, answers this question firmly in the negative: most of the features that Rendel Harris sought to explain by postulating the existence of a book of *testimonia* can be accounted for in terms of methods of reading the Bible (*midrash, pesher*) linked to liturgical or instructional elements in Hebrew tradition.[9] The consequences to be drawn from this conclusion are such as to modify considerably the accepted image of the Gospels and of Jesus' life. Stendahl, who is quite aware of this, prefers, however, not to make these consequences explicit.[10] I shall attempt to do so, bringing together the results of his researches and those attained by other scholars.

II

Let us turn to Luke 2:26–32. The young Jesus (*to paidion*) is taken to the temple. Simeon, an upright and devout man, has been assured that before dying, he will set eyes on the Messiah. He goes to the temple, takes the child in his arms, and gives thanks to God, saying:

> "This day, Master, thou givest thy servant his discharge in peace; now thy promise is fulfilled.
> For I have seen with my own eyes
> the deliverance which thou hast made ready in full view of all the nations;
> a light that will be a revelation to the heathen,
> and glory to thy people Israel."

Simeon's hymn is based on a mosaic of passages taken from the verses in Isaiah (52:13, 49:6, 42:1) concerning the "suffering servant" or "servant of the Lord" (*'ebed Yahweh*). The child Jesus, referred to in the Gospels by the term *"paidion,"* is tacitly assimilated to the "servant of God" mentioned by Isaiah (nowadays identified as Second Isaiah), who is nearly always referred to in the Septuagint by the term *"pais"* (servant), but also "boy." Such an assimilation was perhaps encouraged by the messianic tone that the Greek translators introduced into Isaiah 53:2 by rendering the Hebrew term *"joneq"* (suckling), as *"paidion"* (boy)—this latter word being one that might recall the prophecy of Isaiah 9:6 ("For a boy has been born for us") just as the term *"rhiza"* (root), which immediately follows in Isaiah 53:2, might recall the other prophecy of Isaiah 11:1 ("a shoot shall grow from the stock of Jesse, / and a branch shall spring from his roots").[11] Such a hypothetical string of citations (Isaiah 53:2, 9:6, 11:1) would allow a boy truly or supposedly descended from David to be compared with the "servant of God," understood in a messianic sense, and would also allow him to be compared to the "sheep [led] to the slaughter" (Isaiah 53:7) who would "vindicate many, himself bearing the penalty of their guilt" (Isaiah 53:12). Just as in the case of Isaiah 7:14, we may trace the origins of this citation string to a distorted translation, inspired by a messianic reading, and probably accountable to a rigorous hermeneutics based on the comparison of similar passages.[12] It is hard to escape the impression that the premises of the Gospel narrative were established in the Hellenistic Judaism of Alexandria, where the translations that make up the Septuagint were carried out, beginning with the Torah and later including the historical and prophetic books (Isaiah being translated between 170 and 150 B.C.).[13]

In Matthew 12:15–21, the comparison between Jesus and the "servant of the Lord" is explicit, and is based on Isaiah 42:1–4, in this case cited in a version different from the Septuagint:

But the pharisees, on leaving the synagogue, laid a plot to do away with him.

Jesus was aware of it and withdrew. Many followed, and he cured all who were ill; and then gave strict injunctions that they were not to make him known. This was to fulfil Isaiah's prophecy:

"BEHOLD MY SERVANT, whom I have chosen,
my beloved, on whom my favour rests;

I will put my Spirit upon him,
and he will proclaim judgement among the nations.
He will not strive, he will not shout,
nor will his voice be heard in the streets.
He will not snap off the broken reed,
nor snuff out the smouldering wick,
until he leads justice on to victory.
In him the nations shall place their hope."[14]

Here, too, Matthew sees the event he is recounting as the fulfillment of a prophecy.[15] Since what happens here is within the range of natural possibilities (rather than preternatural, as in the case of Mary's virgin conception), it would be over-hasty to conclude unequivocally that the prophecy generated a corresponding narrative event: the reference to Isaiah 42:1–4 may have been for embellishment. However, such a hypothesis certainly cannot apply in the case of the description of Jesus' Passion. Jesus is insulted, spat upon, and beaten (Mark 10:34; Matthew 26:67, 27:26), in just the same way as the "servant of the Lord":

I offered my back to the lash,
and let my beard be plucked from my chin,
I did not hide my face from spitting and insult.   (Isaiah 50:6)

There are numerous parallels of this kind. Sometimes the link with Second Isaiah is more indirect, but deeper, as when Jesus appears before the governor:

Jesus came out, wearing the crown of thorns and the purple cloak.
"BEHOLD THE MAN!" said Pilate.   (John 19:5)

The sublime idea of the messianic king subjected to scorn and humiliation draws, as Christian tradition was quick to recognize (Acts 8:6 ff., 3:13), on the description of the "suffering servant" in Isaiah 53:2–8:

He had no beauty, no majesty to draw our eyes,
    no grace to make us delight in him . . .
He was despised, he shrank from the sight of men,

tormented and humbled by suffering;
we despised him, we held him of no account,
a thing from which men turn away their eyes . . .
He was afflicted, he submitted to be struck down
and did not open his mouth;
he was led like a sheep to the slaughter,
like a ewe that is dumb before the shearer.
Without protection, without justice, he was taken away.[16]

Jesus, too, "did not open his mouth." His silence in the course of his trial (Matthew 26:63; John 19:9) mutely echoes the demeanor of the "servant of the Lord" in Isaiah 53:7:

He was led like a sheep to the slaughter,
like a ewe that is dumb before the shearer.[17]

It is absolutely certain that the image of Jesus—an image that has changed the course of world history—is deeply colored by this identification with Second Isaiah's "servant of the Lord." It is equally certain that the authors of the Gospels made and subscribed to that identification. But did Jesus do so too? Joachim Jeremias, following a trail pointed out by Harnack, has maintained that the epithet *"pais theou"* that is applied to Jesus originally meant "servant of God" rather than "son of God"; that the preaching of Jesus as the "servant of God" was intended from the first to characterize him as the servant of the Lord prophetically spoken of in Isaiah 42 and 53; and that this socially humiliating identification, linked to a very long-standing tradition, met with strong resistance in the earliest Christian churches and eventually disappeared. He concludes, on the basis of some very suggestive evidence, that Jesus himself claimed to be the "servant of the Lord" prophesied by Second Isaiah.[18]

This thesis, which seeks to isolate certain elements of the Gospel text and declare them immune from any intervention by those who compiled it, so as to reinstate for us Jesus' own thoughts about himself, inevitably runs into serious difficulties. One such difficulty, which Jeremias does not explicitly consider, is that the compilers of the Gospel may have begun from a series of citations that turned upon the "servant of the Lord" of Second Isaiah, probably as these were transmitted by way of the Septuagint version, and may then have incorporated them into a narrative altogether independent—especially in its description of the Passion—of the person and deeds

of Jesus. One example suffices to show the extensive implications of this hypothesis. It has been emphasized that the Aramaic word "*talja'*," "servant," also means "boy" and "lamb." According to Jeremias, the epithet "Lamb of God," which John the Baptist applies to Jesus (John 1:36) and which prepares the way for Jesus to be recognized as the Messiah, derives from a distortion that took place when the linguistically ambiguous Aramaic expression meaning "servant of God" was translated into Greek.[19] But of course this translation does not stand alone. The Evangelist is implicitly echoing the epithet in the phrase "Behold the Lamb of God" when he concludes his description of the crucifixion (John 19:31–36):

> Because it was the eve of Passover, the Jews were anxious that the bodies should not remain on the Cross for the coming Sabbath, since that Sabbath was a day of great solemnity; so they requested Pilate to have the legs broken and the bodies taken down. The soldiers accordingly came to the first of his fellow-victims and to the second, and broke their legs; but when they came to Jesus, they found that he was already dead, so they did not break his legs . . .
>
> This happened in fulfilment of the text of Scripture: "No bone of his shall be broken."

Taken literally, the passage is incomprehensible: there is no reason to think that those condemned to be crucified had their legs broken to bring their sufferings to a speedier end.[20] The explanation is to be sought elsewhere, in the biblical passage whose fulfillment is here declared, namely Exodus 12:46. Among the divine prescriptions concerning the Passover meal, we there find the following: "Each lamb must be eaten inside the one house, and you must not take any of the flesh outside the house. You must not break a single bone of it."

As Joseph Henninger has brilliantly demonstrated, the prohibition against breaking the legs of sacrificial animals was linked, both within Semitic culture and across a much wider Eurasian geographical and cultural region, to beliefs concerning resurrection.[21] Moreover, another citation would have facilitated the application to Jesus of the sentence in Exodus 12:46, namely verse 20 of Psalm 34: "He guards every bone of his body, and not one of them is broken."[22] The analogy between the "servant of the Lord" and the lamb in Isaiah 53:7, reinforced by the comparison between the sacrificial lamb of Exodus 12:46 and the good man whose troubles are described in Psalm 34:20, gave rise to the detail of Jesus' unbroken legs.

John the Evangelist in the following passage goes on to tell how the spear pierced Jesus' side. Then he refers to himself: "This is vouched for by an eyewitness, whose evidence is to be trusted. He knows that he speaks the truth, so that you too may believe."

It has often been noted that this insistence on eyewitness evidence has no parallel elsewhere in the Gospels. What the double reference to the fulfillment of Scripture indicates ("No bone of his shall be broken"; "They shall look on him whom they pierced," which refers to Zechariah 12:10) is that John did not see an event—the soldiers not breaking Jesus' legs, and then piercing his side with a spear—that in all probability never happened; rather, he saw a *theologoumenon*, a messianic idea that is presented as an event.[23] A string of citations had generated a narrative situation that Saint Paul was later to sum up in the formula equating Jesus with a sacrificial lamb: "Our Passover has begun; the sacrifice is offered—Christ himself" (1 Corinthians 5:7). It was probably the Evangelist's messianic perspective that led John to place the crucifixion on Passover, rather than on the following day (as the synoptic Gospels do).[24] Factual truth, as we understand it, was not the first concern of whoever compiled the Gospels. But then, "what is truth?" (John 18:38).

III

The word "true" has many meanings. We can distinguish "truth" according to faith from "truth" according to history. Historical truth has different, distinct levels. The historical existence of Jesus is a truth that cannot reasonably be called into doubt. However, it is difficult to say who Jesus really was, because the accounts we possess of his life and especially of his death are entangled in and obscured by the desire to prove that he was indeed the Messiah foretold by the prophets. Within this perspective we can make out a figure that was probably much less distorted: the doer of miracles and master of wisdom, or in other words the Jesus of the *logia*.[25]

In a recent book, John D. Crossan has tried to conjecture how the account of Jesus' Passion came to be constructed. He argues that all that the disciples closest to the Passion knew about the event was that Jesus had been crucified. The intense interest with which the Passion was then studied developed, Crossan emphasizes, in a learned and sophisticated milieu. Here, verses and images were discovered that were applicable to the Passion as a whole—though obviously not to specific details, since of these no memory had been preserved. Eventually, Crossan argues, it was possible to construct a coherent narrative based on these scriptural connections and on the fulfillment of particular detailed prophecies.[26] Of one thing, however, Crossan is certain (though it does not amount to much): Jesus was indeed crucified under Pontius Pilate.[27]

However, the crucifixion too has its scriptural connections and suggestions of prophecy fulfilled. Since the earliest centuries of the Christian era, verse 16b of Psalm 22—"and they have hacked off my hands and feet"—has been understood as a prophecy of Christ's crucifixion. Gregory Vall has lately reconstructed the history of this interpretation, which was based on yet another mistranslation in the Septuagint. The verse probably originally ran "They bound my hands and feet."[28] We may hypothesize the existence of a pre-Christian citation string, which brought together the "servant of the Lord" of Second Isaiah and the just man persecuted in Psalm 22 ("But I am a worm, not a man, abused by all men, scorned by the people") and saw both as messianic figures.[29] The sharing out of Jesus' clothes between the soldiers who have played at dice for them (Mark 15:24; Luke 23:24; John 19:23–24) takes a verse from Psalm 22— "they share out my garments among them and cast lots for my clothes"—and transforms it into a narrative sequence. The first verse of Psalm 22—"My God, my God, why hast thou forsaken me?"—became Jesus' final invocation on the cross (Matthew 27:46; Mark 15:34).

Krister Stendahl has put it thus:

The relation between historical facts and O. T. quotation is often regarded as an influence of the O. T. on the facts recorded, particularly in the accounts of the Passion. This is surely true in such a case as Ps. 22 which in its entirety has become a liturgical text on the Passion. An increasing number of details creep into the story and it is hard to distinguish between the facts which related the Psalm to the Passion and the details in the story evoked by the Psalm.[30]

Details of this kind may have generated further developments of the narrative, as when the soldiers, misunderstanding Jesus' citation of Psalm 22 on the cross ("Elì, Elì, lemà sabactàni"), are led to make the gibe "He is calling Elijah" (Matthew 27:46–49; Mark 15:34–36). Even the misrecognition of the Messiah takes its place in the logic of prophetic fulfillment, in the spirit of Second Isaiah.[31]

IV

The messianic element, based on citations of the prophets (above all, Isaiah), may thus be taken as the prime impulse behind the narrative development in the canonical Gospels, which in this regard differ greatly from collections of Jesus' sayings such as the Gospel of Saint Thomas.[32] From this kernel of prophecy, we have seen the following series gradually emerge: "behold the virgin," "behold my servant," "behold the lamb of God," "behold the man." In the Vulgate, the series runs: *Ecce virgo, ecce puer meus, ecce agnus dei, ecce homo.* Around 1535, Hans Holbein the Younger took the first element (and, more discreetly, the third) and used them to express vividly the link that joins the Old and the New Testaments (plate 8).

"Ecce" translates the Hebrew word *"hinné."* In the version of the Septuagint, *"hinné"* is rendered *"idou"* or *"ide"*—adverbial expressions, colloquial in character, cognate with the verb "to see," and used much like "look!" in modern English to catch the ear of a listener.[33] The terms *"idou"* and *"ide"* occur very irregularly as between the different Gospels, being used respectively 62 and 4 times in Matthew, 59 and no times in Luke, 12 and 7 times in Mark, and 6 and 16 in John.[34] *"Idou"* is abundant in Revelation (30 occurrences); this has been interpreted as an imitation of the style of the prophets, in which nominal phrases are often used.[35] The very frequent employment of *"idou"* in Isaiah (88 usages), Jeremiah (132), and Ezekiel (100) certainly confirms that the translators of the Septuagint associated the term above all with prophetic dreams and visions.[36] "This," Saint Jerome was to write, "was why the prophets were called seers [*videntes*]—because they saw the one whom others could not see": that is, Jesus.[37]

As I shall attempt to show, the references to the prophets that were contained in the Gospels opened up a quite unexpected range of iconic possibilities. It was a long time, however, before these were realized. To begin with, Christian art took an altogether different direction.

One of our earliest pieces of written evidence concerning what were taken to be images connected to the Gospels comes from the beginning of the fourth century. In a very well-known passage in his *Ecclesiastical History* (6:18), Eusebius recounts seeing a bronze bas-relief in the city of Paneas (Caesarea Philippi). This depicted "a lady kneeling and with hands outstretched, in the manner of a suppli-cant"; opposite it was another bas-relief of the same material that showed "a man on foot, wrapped splendidly in a mantle, and hold-ing his hand out to the lady."[38] A local tradition held that the two sculptures represented Jesus in the act of curing the woman who suf-fered from bleeding (Matthew 9:20–22; Mark 5:26–34; Luke 8:43–48). The woman herself was supposed to have had them made; and the same tradition held that she was a native of Paneas, the bas-reliefs being placed opposite her house. The passage shows that Eusebius accepted the *interpretatio christiana* of this group of figures, which presumably represented Aesculapius, as we may infer from his ref-erence to a curative herb that grew on the monument. It is clear, however, that Eusebius was uneasy at the possibility of Christian images—so much so that he regarded not only this group thought to represent Jesus and the woman cured of bleeding, but other painted images of Peter, Paul, and Jesus, as the products of a hea-then impulse.[39] At all events, when Constantia, the sister of the Emperor Constantine, asked Eusebius to send her an image of the Redeemer, he refused quite sharply, citing (if the text we have is authentic) both the Mosaic prohibition against images and the per-fection of Christ, which no image could communicate.[40]

The image-making impulse that we can detect in these texts of the early fourth century overwhelmed the feeble resistance of the clergy, which was linked to Hebrew tradition. The woman cured of bleeding became a common subject for the bas-reliefs that adorned Christian sarcophagi representing Jesus the worker of miracles, a figure who, unlike the Jesus of the Passion, was immediately com-prehensible to the pagan mind. Jesus became an Aesculapius—with mightier powers than his pagan analogue.[41] The popularity of the miracle of the woman cured of bleeding is significant also because here we see Jesus' miracle-working power, his *dunamis*, acting without his volition or awareness, like an irrepressible electrical charge that connects him instantaneously with the woman.[42] This is a quite exceptional moment, for in the Gospels Jesus always plays an active role, even in times of suffering or in the desperate rebellion on the cross that is expressed in the words of Psalm 22. In the case of the woman cured of bleeding (a woman who would have been regarded as in a state of impurity) Jesus does not act; he is, rather, put into action—as if the narrative wished to tone down the breach of the Law involved in the physical contact between the two.[43] One crucial detail, recorded in the synoptic Gospels, emphasizes that Jesus had not even registered the woman's presence: she "came up from behind" (*opisthen*) "and touched the edge of his cloak" (Matthew 9:20; Mark 5:7; Luke 8:44).[44] It is significant that other representations of this same scene, by contrast, focus on the immediately following moment, when Jesus suddenly becomes aware of the woman's presence (plates 10 and 11).

These images, concentrated on this point in time, this decisive instant, evince the extraordinary novelty of Christian iconography: an anonymous sick woman had never been endowed with such importance in the art of Greece or Rome.[45] Miracles, as T. F. Mathews has observed, constitute the kernel and the foundation of early Christian iconography.[46] In the fifth and sixth centuries, however, this tradition was supplanted and replaced by something completely different, as devotional images developed that had little or no narrative content. Is Kurt Weitzmann right to suggest, as he does in his introduction to the symposium accompanying a well-known exhibition that he curated, "The Age of Spirituality," that we can see here a return of the Greco-Roman tradition of devotional imagery?[47] Ernst Kitzinger, in the same volume, proposes an alternative explanation: the appearance or reappearance of devotional images may have been a response to the need for a more direct and intimate connection with the heavenly realm. Kitzinger suggests that it was no longer enough for images to be apprehended as factual or historical documents, or as elements in a self-sufficient system: rather, the image had to be available for use here and now.[48] This and other factors may indeed have contributed to the popularity of devotional images. All the same, it is difficult to see any need for such direct and intimate connection with the celestial realm behind the imposing mosaic (ca. 425–450) that covers the apse of the church of Hosios

David at Salonika (plate 12). The mosaic depicts the vision of Ezekiel (1:4–5), here interpreted according to the Christian tradition, which saw it as a revelation of Christ.[49] In Ezekiel's text, we again find the formula used to introduce prophetic passages that are cited in the Gospels:

> I looked and BEHOLD a storm wind was coming from the north, a vast cloud with flashes of fire and brilliant light about it; and within was a radiance like brass, glowing in the heart of the flames. In the fire was the semblance of four living creatures in human form.

"I looked and BEHOLD": *kai eidon kai idou.* The vision of the Son of Man (Daniel 7:13), which inspired Matthew 24:30 and hence the iconography of Christ in majesty (*Maiestas Domini*), opens in similar vein.[50] This formula takes us a long way from the sarcophagi that recount Jesus' miracles with dramatic immediacy; a long way, indeed, from any narrative dimension. We are in the dimension, rather, of what we might call the ostensive mode: the term *"idou"* is a device to project us into another realm, the realm of prophetic vision. This is emphasized by the scroll Jesus holds, on which are written some words based on Isaiah 25:9–11: "BEHOLD THE LORD [*idou ho theos hemon*] for whom we have waited; let us rejoice and exult in his deliverance. For the hand of the Lord will rest on this mountain."[51]

"Idou," as we have noted, is often associated with nominal sentences. The Septuagint translation of the passage from Ezekiel just quoted, while not strictly speaking a nominal sentence, is characterized by a long series of substantives and adjectives dependent on a single verb (*"erkheto"*). In Christian devotional imagery, the ostensive, non-narrative mode provided a visual equivalent to these prophetic nominal sentences.

This is what is demonstrated by the nominal sentences with messianic implications that I have singled out in the Gospels. These phrases inspired some of the most widely diffused devotional images, from the Annunciation (often accompanied by the phrase *"Ecce ancilla domini,"* "Behold the Handmaid of the Lord") to John the Baptist (generally depicted holding a scroll that reads *"Ecce agnus dei,"* "Behold the Lamb of God").[52] The image-type of the Madonna and Child (plate 13), which has no specific scriptural basis, probably derives from the expression *"idou o pais"*; the semantic ambiguity made it possible to displace the socially scandalous "servant" by "son" or "boy," as happens in the Vulgate where the phrase in Isaiah 42:1 (*"Ecce servus meus"*) becomes, when Matthew cites it (12:28), *"Ecce puer meus."*[53] Moreover, Isaiah's "servant of the Lord" is also the source (as we have said) for *"Idou ho anthropos," "Ecce homo"*—the iconographic type that became famous in the West by way of the celebrated icon kept in the Roman church of Santa Croce in Gerusalemme (plate 14).[54]

"The analogy between the experience of the image and mystical experience," Hans Belting has written, "is confirmed by the fact that visions have included images of the Man of Sorrows and the Throne of Grace, both examples of modern devotional imagery."[55] The evidence I have assembled here allows us to place this remark in a much broader context, which makes it clear that "the analogy between the experience of the image and mystical experience" was rooted in a textual tradition going back to Jewish prophetic literature. This tradition, reanimated by the authors of the Gospels, played a decisive role not only in the "experience" of images but in their production.

This point is sufficiently illustrated by just one example. John the Evangelist refers to the crucified Christ in terms that are a variation on the customary ostensive formulae (John 19:26–27) and that are faithfully reproduced in detail in the most widespread iconographic type (plate 15):

> Jesus saw his mother, with the disciple whom he loved standing beside her. He said to her, "Mother, BEHOLD YOUR SON [*ide ho huios sou*]!"; and to the disciple, "BEHOLD YOUR MOTHER [*ide he meter sou*]!"[56]

By an extraordinary paradox, a recurring feature of Jewish prophetic texts created the premises for something new and altogether different: the emergence of Christian devotional imagery.

PLATE I.
Diego Rodriguez de Silva y Velázquez, *Jacob Receiving the Bloodstained Garments of Joseph* (Madrid, Escorial)

PLATE 2.
Diego Rodriguez de Silva y Velázquez, *The Forge of Vulcan*
(Madrid, Prado)

PLATE 3.
Antonio Tempesta,
The Forge of Vulcan
(from Ovid,
Metamorphoseon . . .,
published in
Antwerp, 1606)

Coniugis furtum Sol Vulcano detegit.

Above
PLATE 4. Caravaggio, *Calling of Saint Matthew* (Rome, San Luigi dei Francesi)

Left
PLATE 5. Domenichino, *Death of Saint Cecilia* (Rome, San Luigi dei Francesi)

PLATE 6.
Royal figurine (London,
Westminster Abbey)

PLATE 7.
Saint Foy, Conques

PLATE 8.

Hans Holbein the Younger, *Allegory of the Old and New Testament*
(Edinburgh, National Gallery of Scotland)

PLATE 9.
Latin sarcophagus (no. 191) (Vatican Museums)

PLATE 10.
Sarcophagus with trees (Arles, Musée Réattu)

PLATE II.
Fragment of sarcophagus, depicting Jesus and the woman
cured of bleeding (Rome, Catacomb of San Callisto)

PLATE 12.

The Vision of Ezekiel (Salonika, church of Hosios David)

PLATE 13.

Madonna and Child (Rome, Santa Maria Antiqua, sixth–seventh century)

PLATE 14.
Ecce Homo (Israel von Meckenem, late fifteenth century)

PLATE 15.
Crucifixion (Ohrid, early fourteenth century)

PLATE 16.
Pall depicting Anubis (Moscow, Pushkin Museum)

PLATE 17.
Capital depicting a sphinx (church of Saint Foy, Conques, cloisters)

PLATE 18.
Capital depicting a siren (church of Saint Foy, Conques, cloisters)

Ceci n'est pas une pipe.

PLATE 19.
René Magritte, *La trahison des images* (Los Angeles, County Museum of Art, copyright SIAE 1998)

PLATE 20.

The Temple of Solomon, from Johann Bernhard Fischer von Erlach,
Entwurf einer historischen Architectur . . . , 1721

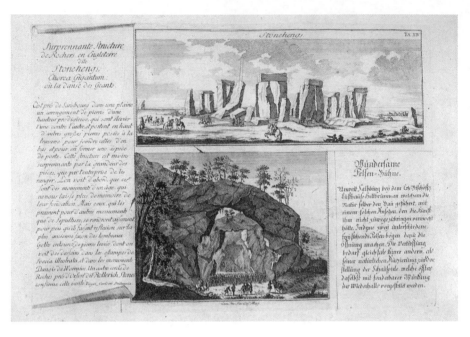

PLATE 21.

Stonehenge, from Fischer von Erlach, *Entwurf* . . .

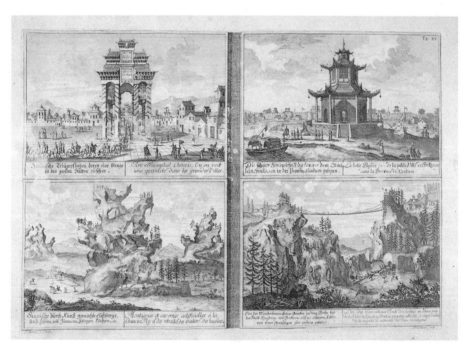

PLATE 22.

Chinese Bridges, from Fischer von Erlach, *Entwurf* . . .

M. Denman   Printed by C.Hullmandel

Sculpture from Persepolis.

Pl. 25.

W. Walton.   Printed by C.Hullmandel.

One of the Figures on the Pediment at Egina.

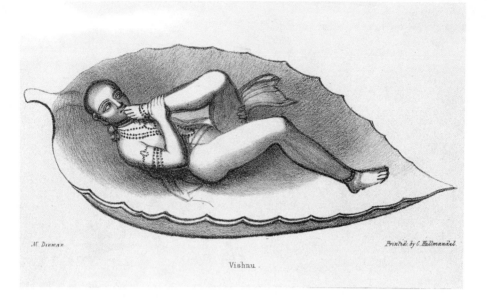

M. Denman   Printed by C. Hullmandel.

Vishnu.

B. Walton,   Printed by C. Hullmandel

Transfiguration.

Above
PLATE 25. Vishnu, from Flaxman, *Lectures on Sculpture*

Left
PLATE 26. Transfiguration of Jesus, from Flaxman, *Lectures on Sculpture*

Idols and Likenesses

A PASSAGE IN ORIGEN AND ITS VICISSITUDES

1. During the first centuries of Christianity, a largely hostile attitude toward images was gradually replaced, for reasons that we are still unable fully to understand, by a largely favorable attitude. The text that I am about to examine—Origen's *Homilies on Exodus* 8.3—throws an unexpected light on this crucially important change and on its long-term consequences.[1]

Origen's *Homilies on Exodus*, like much of his vast literary work, has survived only in the Latin translation made by Rufinus of Aquileia early in the fifth century.[2] Rufinus, working from a text pieced together by shorthand writers around the years 235–245, omitted a few passages, inserted some repetitions, and supplied material to fill gaps.[3] However, two fragments of the text with which we are concerned do survive also in the original Greek. The first was published by the seventeenth-century scholar François Combefis on the basis of the so-called *Catena Romana*

("Roman Chain") (*Vat. Barb. gr.* 569).[4] The second, which is longer, and which Baehrens included in his edition of Origen's *Homilies on Exodus*, is found in a manuscript (*Monac. graec.* 358) of the *Catena* assembled by Procopius of Gaza (which remains as yet unpublished).[5] Although they differ slightly in length and content, these two fragments do give us a less indirect (though still hazy) picture of Origen's thoughts. We are nonetheless obliged to work with Rufinus's translation, above all because this was the means by which Origen's name was kept alive in the West despite the fact that certain of his ideas had been condemned.

2. "You shall not make an idol for yourself nor the likeness of anything in the heavens above, or on the earth below, or in the waters under the earth" (Exodus 20:4): so runs the second commandment, which in the Latin West eventually became so closely associated with the first that they were virtually fused into one. In commenting on these words, Origen insists that "idols" and "gods" (on the one hand) and "idols" and "likenesses" (on the other) are not synonyms. He is especially concerned with the second distinction, and refers to the passage in the first letter to the Corinthians in which Saint Paul affirms that it is no sin to eat the flesh of animals offered in sacrifice, because "an idol is nothing in the world" (1 Corinthians 8:4: "*hoti ouden eidolon en kosmo*"; Latin Vulgate, "*quia nihil est idolum in mundo*"). However, Origen remarks, the Apostle "has said that idols are nothing" ("*de idolis dixit quia non sunt*"), but he has not said that likenesses are also nothing. He continues:

If, for instance, someone reproduces—in whatever material, be it gold, silver, wood, stone—the features of a quadruped or a serpent or a bird and decides to adore this, then he makes not a likeness [*similitudinem*] but an idol. And should he reproduce it in a picture for the same reason, again we should say that he has made a likeness.

An idol (*idolum*), on the other hand, is "that which is not":

But what is that which is not? Something whose features are not seen by the eyes but fashioned by the mind itself. Let us suppose, for example, that someone forms the head of a dog or a ram with human limbs, or fashions a man with two heads, or joins together a human bust and the lower parts of a horse or a fish. Whoever makes these things or things like them makes not images but idols.

In this latter case, "no form is drawn from existing things; it corresponds to what the idle and curious mind has discovered within itself." At all events, Origen concludes, the divine prohibition applies to both idols and likenesses.[6]

3. In his comments on the commandment that God gave Moses, Origen refers on the one hand to centaurs and sirens (idols that join together "a human bust and the lower parts of a horse or a fish") and on the other to the Egyptian god Anubis, who had "the head of a dog . . . with human limbs" (plate 16).[7] It is harder to identify what he has in mind in referring to the "likenesses" of animals: possibly (for instance) the Egyptian god Mendes, depicted at first in the form of a ram, and later in the form of a goat.[8] Origen's homilies on Exodus were given shortly before he was obliged to leave Alexandria in 231. In them we hear echoes of the huge diversity of voices and languages that resounded in the streets of the great city that was the true center of Hellenistic civilization.

Origen's conclusion, which simply repeated the Mosaic prohibition against images, held nothing new; but the argument that precedes it, based on the clear distinction drawn between idols and likenesses, seems unusual. We need only compare it with the beginning of Tertullian's treatise *De Idololatria*, written a couple of decades earlier, around 203–206: "*Eidos* is the Greek term for *form*; similarly its diminutive *eidolon* gives us our word *formula*. Therefore both *form* and *formula* always really mean *idol* (*idolum*)."[9] We see that Tertullian's point of view is quite different from Origen's. How, then, had Origen come to develop the distinction that he draws?

4. Origen's argument turns on two words, "idol" ("*idolum*") and "likeness" ("*similitudo*"). If we consider the latter, we encounter a difference between Rufinus and Origen, or more precisely between the versions of the Bible they refer to. In the *Vetus Latina* text, the term "*similitudo*" is used in both Exodus 20:4 and Genesis 1:27: "You shall not make an idol for yourself nor the likeness of anything" ("*non facies tibi ipsi idolum neque omnem similitudinem eorum*"); and

"So God created man in his own image and likeness" ("*ad imaginem
et similitudinem Dei*").[10] The Septuagint version, by contrast, has
"*homoiosis*" in the first instance and "*homoioma*" in the second—a difference that did not prevent those Greeks who favored icons from
invoking Genesis 1:27 as an argument against their adversaries.[11]

G. Ladner has argued that the choice of a term like "*homoiosis*"
(rather than "*homoioma*" or "*homoiotes*"), a term that in Platonic and
neo-Platonic texts implied a deliberate intention to liken humanity
to God, marks a decisive moment in the history of ideas.[12] Both
"*eidolon*" and "*homoioma*," the key terms in Origen's commentary on
Exodus 20, carry Platonic resonances that take us beyond the scope
of their use in the letters of Saint Paul.[13] Plato had used these words
to describe how the celestial Ideas came to be embodied, perforce
inadequately, in earthly likenesses.[14] May we then catch a Platonic
echo in Origen's distinction between images and likenesses? To
answer this question we must examine the arguments that Plato
develops in the *Sophist*.

The visitor from Elea distinguishes, within the general category
of "mimicry," between two arts, which he calls the arts respectively
of "copying" (*eikastiken*) and of "illusion" (*phantastiken*) (*Sophist*,
235e–236c, 260d–e, 264c, 266d–e). He explains that the art of copying
or portraiture is found particularly where "the copy is made to
reproduce the proportions of the original in length, breadth, and
depth, and its various parts moreover receive their proper tints."
However, "those who have to model or paint colossal figures" must
work differently. "Were they to reproduce their beauties in their true
proportions, the upper parts of the figures, you know, would appear
too small, and the lower too large" (235e–236a).[15] The effort made to
achieve a more convincing illusion has in it an element of trickery:
in this sense, the sophist is one who "professes an art of illusion"
(*phantastiken technen*). This is not simply an analogy. The hypothesis
that the sophist is a "maker of images" (*eidolopoion*) takes us into the
heart of the dialogue, the confutation of Parmenides' thesis that
"not-being is not." The image (*eidolon*) is not true but "it has being
of a kind" (*all'esti ge men pos*) (240b).[16] Consequently, negation qua
difference is not to be confused (as Parmenides confuses it, in his
radically monistic argument) with negation qua non-entity.[17]

Plato's argument, which does not refer to existence as such, pays
no heed to nonexistent beings: for instance, poetic fictions like sirens

or centaurs.[18] Origen's argument, by contrast, turns on precisely this question of the depiction of fictitious beings, which are produced by the mind through a "comprehensive representation" (*kata perilep-* *tiken phantasian*).[19] This expression combines the Platonic notion of "comprehensive reason" (*perileptikos logos*) that fuses "evidence and truth" (Sextus Empiricus, *Against the Logicians*, 1:143) with the Stoics' concept of "apprehensive representation" (*kataleptike phantasia*), upon which hinges the crucial problematic of the Stoics' logic and their theory of perception, namely the "criterion of truth."[20]

Sextus Empiricus writes that an "apprehensive [*kataleptike*] representation" is one that "comes from an existing object [*apo hupark-* *hontos*], and which is impressed upon and taken up by the subject in conformity with that same existing object [*kai kat'auto to hupark-* *hon*], and is such as cannot be derived from an object that does not exist [*apo me huparkhontos*]. . . . Many representations strike us that come from things that are non-existent [*me huparkhontos*], as happens in the case of madness, and these cannot be apprehensive [*kataleptikai*]." Origen, when he speaks of idols that are produced in the mind by "comprehensive representation" [*kata perileptiken phan-* *tasian*], uses the same words: these are "images of things that are non-existent [*ta de eidola anuparkhon estin*]."[21]

The expression *"to huparkthon"* (that which exists), another fundamental term in the vocabulary of the Stoics, implied (so A. Graeser argues) the idea that between language and reality there exists a complex relation, rather than the simple isomorphic correspondence assumed by Plato and Aristotle.[22] Some while earlier, A.-J. Festugière had remarked that in the *Posterior Analytics* 89b.23–25 Aristotle (who never uses the abstract term *huparksis*) had attempted to isolate an existential core within the Greek verb "to be" (*einai*). Aristotle draws on a scholastic argument, which presumably went back to the Sophists:

There are four kinds of questions that we ask, and they correspond to the kinds of things that we know. They are: the question of fact, the question of reason or cause, the question of existence, and the question of essence. When we ask whether this or that is so, introducing a plurality of terms (e.g., whether the sun suffers eclipse or not), we are asking the question of fact. . . . It is when we know the fact that we ask the reason; *e.g.* if we know that the sun suffers eclipse and that the earth moves, we ask the reasons for these facts. That is how we ask these questions; but there are others which take a different form: e.g. whether a centaur or a god exists. The question of existence refers to simple existence, and not to whether the subject is (say) white or not. When we know that the subject exists, we ask what it is: *e.g.*, "what, then, is a god" or "a man?"[23]

A few pages further on (*Posterior Analytics* 92b.4–8), Aristotle emphasizes this point, writing:

> Anyone who knows *what* "man" or any other thing is must also know *that* it is; because no-one knows *what* a non-existent thing is [*to gar me on oudeis oiden ho ti estin*]. (He may know the meaning of a phrase, or of a name if, *e.g.*, I speak of a goat-stag [*trage-laphos*]; but it is impossible to know *what* a goat-stag is.)[24]

It was Festugière's hypothesis that in drawing such a clear-cut distinction between the use of "is" as a copula and its use in an existential sense, Aristotle was inspired by the Sophists' skeptical attitude toward religious tradition. We must note, however, that when he follows his remarks on how we proceed "when we know that the subject exists" by posing the question "What, then, is a god, or a man?.," he distances himself from any polemical inference that might be drawn from the juxtaposition of gods and centaurs. Still, when he sets forth the difficulties raised by fictitious beings such as centaurs or goat-stags, or in other words by terms that possess meaning but lack referential content, Aristotle does open up the line of thought that leads to the Stoics and to the way they concentrated on nonexistent beings as a means of calling in question the isomorphic relation between words and things. Sextus Empiricus writes as follows:

> Indeed every thought [*noesis*] is produced either by way of a sensation or not without a sensation, or by way of an event in experience or not without an event in experience. So we shall find that not even those events that are called false [*pseudeis phantasias*]— for example, those that occur in dreams or in the state of madness—are clearly to be separated from those of which we are conscious by way of sensation in accordance with an event in

experience. And, in truth, whoever might in madness imagine beings just like the Furies, *Maidens all bloody and snakelike* [Euripides, *Oresteia* 256], has in mind a form made up of things that have already appeared to him; and in the same way whoever, being asleep, sees in his dreams a winged man, does not dream this without having formerly seen a winged thing and a man. And, speaking more generally, it is not possible to encounter in thought a thing we do not already possess as something already known to us by way of an event in experience.

This happens, continues Sextus Empiricus, by analogy, either because we enlarge the dimensions of things (as in the case of a Cyclops) or because we diminish them (as in the case of a pygmy), or again

by composition, when from a man and a horse we think of a hippocentaur, such as has never stood before us (Sextus Empiricus, *Against the Logicians* 2.56–60).[25]

Let us return to Origen's argument: the centaur, given that it has a composite nature, is an image and thus does not exist. Origen here brings together the fact that the centaur does not exist (as Aristotle insists) and the fact of its composite nature (emphasized by the Stoics). This network of ideas reveals Origen's relationship with what has been called middle-Platonism, in which Stoic themes and elements taken from Aristotle were grafted onto the dominant stock of Platonic ideas.[26] Echoes of Stoic terminology can be found, indeed, in Origen's paraphrase of the first letter to the Corinthians (1 Corinthians 8:4): *"nihil est idolum [hoti ouden (esti) eidolon] in mundo"* parallels the Stoics' *"ou gar huparksis to eidolon."*[27] I am not in a position to embark on a discussion of the first letter to the Corinthians, and in any case this would not be relevant to my present theme. However, my impression is that Origen's translation was by no means inexact. It might be argued that the statement that "an idol is nothing" (*idolum est nihil*), which is implicitly repeated in a later rhetorical question (1 Corinthians 10:19: *"ti oun phemi . . . hoti eidolon ti estin"*; "What do I imply by this? that an idol is something?"), takes up and reworks the schema developed in scholastic argument, which, as Aristotle declares in the *Posterior Analytics*

(89b.23–25), called in doubt the existence alike of centaurs, of gods, or of both together.[28]

5. Anyone who spoke of images (above all, religious images) in third-century Alexandria inevitably used ambiguous terms, even when speaking the same language, for instance, Greek. We are to demonstrate this ambiguity by comparing Plato's words with those of Paul: "the image surely is, in some sense" (*eidolon esti ge men pos*), says Plato; and an idol "is nothing in the world" (*hoti ouden eidolon en kosmo*), says Paul (1 Corinthians 8:4). There is an obvious opposition between "*pos*" (of a kind) and "*ouden*" (nothing), but this is less significant than the hidden divergence between the two uses and meanings of "*eidolon*" and "*esti*," which we may translate respectively as "image" and "idol" and as "is" and "exists."[29]

Origen was deeply indebted to the Platonic tradition, as we may clearly see from his propensity for metaphors that turn on images and similes. He did not hesitate to compare God the Father to "a statue so large as to hold the entire earth . . . whose immensity is such that no-one may properly examine it," and the Son to

> another statue perfectly alike in the aspect of its members and the lineaments of its face, in form and matter, but which does not have this measureless immensity, so that those who could not observe and examine that immense one may look upon this and may faithfully believe they have seen the other one, since it reproduces with absolute likeness [*similitudine*] all its features, the aspect of its members and of its face, its form and its matter.[30]

We do not know whether in the original Greek the likeness (*similitudo*) between the two statues was expressed by the word "*homoioma*" or "*homoiosis*." In Origen's view, the likeness between God the Father and the Son, like that between God and mankind, was to be understood in a purely spiritual sense.[31] Nonetheless, it is significant that he chooses a sculptural metaphor. Passages like the one just cited prompt the thought that the distinction between the image (*eidolon*) and the likeness (*homoioma*) formulated by Origen in his comment on Exodus 1:4 was inspired by a typically Alexandrian compromise between Greek philosophy and Judaic tradition.[32] It might seem that the latter gained the upper hand, since the conclusion of Origen's homily is decidedly anti-iconic in spirit, being equally condemnatory of images and of likenesses. In the long run, however, this conclusion was undermined by the very distinction on which it was based.[33]

Sometime late in the seventh century or early in the eighth, Stephen of Bostra wrote a treatise titled *Against the Jews*. From the few fragments that survive, we can see that he sought to reformulate the Mosaic commandment by counterposing *eikones*—likenesses, icons—to *eidola kai agalmata*.[34] Man, being created in the image of God, might be adored; the serpent, created in the devil's image, might not. In the course of his polemical arguments against Jewish iconoclasts, Stephen mentions the images of cherubim to be found in the Tabernacle.[35] Now in the *Catena* compiled by Procopius of Gaza the passage taken from Origen's *Homily on Exodus* is immediately followed by a question posed by an unnamed adversary: "If images are to be condemned, why then has God desired that there should be images of cherubim in his tabernacle?" I am unable to judge whether this question, and the reply that is given, are drawn from some other homily of Origen's.[36] What seems probable is that Stephen of Bostra took as the starting point for his own reflections the texts on Exodus 20:4 collected in the *Catena* of Procopius of Gaza. We do not know the context in which Stephen's polemical defense of images against the Jews was put forward. It may have been that he was seeking an opportunity to express his opposition to a current of hostility toward images linked to the aniconic tradition of the Nabateans, which still survived in the region of Bostra.[37] At all events, as has been pointed out, the distinction between idols and likenesses that was formulated by Origen reappears in iconophile writings by Theodoretus of Cyrus and Theodore of Studion.[38]

6. Origen's ideas, condemned in part as heretical, had a wide circulation in the West in the form of passages included in the *Glossa Ordinaria*, the great compilation of biblical commentaries made by Anselm of Laon. This is the context within which it has been noted that Bernard of Clairvaux's writings contain echoes of Origen.[39] What has not been noted is the close relationship between Origen's commentary on Exodus 20:4 (which is among the passages included in the *Glossa Ordinaria*)[40] and Bernard's famous condemnation of the sculptures that adorned the cloisters of Romanesque churches

(*Apologia in Guillermum Abbatem*, 1125)—a condemnation not without its nuances and ambiguities (see plates 17 and 18):[41]

In the cloister, under the eyes of the brethren who read there, what profit is there in those ridiculous monsters, in that marvellous and deformed beauty, in that beautiful deformity [*ridicula monstruositas, mira quaedam deformis formositas ac formosa deformitas*]? To what purpose are those unclean apes, those fierce lions, those monstrous centaurs [*monstruosi centauri*], those half-men, those striped tigers, those fighting knights, those hunters winding their horns? Many bodies are there seen under one head, or again, many heads to a single body. Here is a four-footed beast with a serpent's tail; there, a fish with a beast's head [*cernitur hinc in quadrupede cauda serpentis, illinc in pisce caput quadrupedis*]. Here again the forepart of a horse trails half a goat behind it, or a horned beast bears the hind-quarters of a horse. In short, so many and so marvellous are the varieties of shapes on every hand, that we are more tempted to read in the marble than in our books, and to spend the whole day wondering at these things rather than meditating on the law of God. For God's sake, if men are not ashamed of these follies, why at least do they not shrink from the expense?[42]

From late antiquity on, centaurs and sirens spread right across the Latin West, by way of both texts and likenesses.[43] One important text was the opening lines of Horace's *Ars Poetica*, well known to Bernard of Clairvaux and to some of his contemporaries.[44] However, Origen was a special case. The catalog of the library of the Abbey of Clairvaux in the twelfth century lists eleven manuscripts of his work, which include Rufinus's translations of his *Homilies* on the Old Testament.[45] We can imagine that Bernard's spirit of monastic piety would have been deeply touched by these phrases in Origen's attack on images: "the likeness is not drawn from things that exist; it corresponds to what the idle and curious mind has discovered within itself" (*non enim aliqua ex rebus exstantibus assumitur species, sed quod ipsa sibi otiosa mens et curiosa repererit*). After all, Bernard had written at length against the sin of curiosity, and had deplored—perhaps with an echo of Origen—the dangerous practice of spending "the whole day wondering at these things rather than meditating on the law of God" (*totumque diem occupare singula ista mirando, quam in lege Dei meditando*).⁴⁶

Bernard's words bespeak an attraction repressed with some difficulty, which suggests a profound ambivalence toward the proliferation of images. His great adversary Peter Abelard expressed this ambivalence differently, by listing in his book *Sic et Non* a series of texts for and against "the corporeal representation of God." The first of these was the passage from Origen distinguishing between idols and likenesses.⁴⁷ It is probable that this distinction, which had become current thanks to the inclusion of the passage in the *Glossa Ordinaria*, helped to draw out the ambiguous status of the image—itself an element in the more general ambiguity that Christians felt toward Jewish tradition.⁴⁸

7. We find another echo of the passage from Origen (though its author is not named) in Thomas Aquinas's commentary on 1 Corinthians 8:4. To exemplify a likeness of a nonexistent being, Aquinas mentions not centaurs as such, but the head of a horse joined to a human body. It is clear that the problem for him was a matter not of idolatry but of what we now call "the referential quality of the image." In his *Adnotationes in Novum Testamentum*, Erasmus cites the distinction formulated by Aquinas between *"idolum"* and *"similitudo"* or *"simulacrum"* (idol and likeness)—unaware, it seems, that this derived from his beloved Origen (in the translation of Rufinus). The distinction, declared Erasmus, was not unworthy of the *Catholicon*.⁴⁹ This was a frankly ironic remark: the *Catholicon*, a Latin vocabulary compiled by Giovanni Balbi of Genova, had been singled out by Lorenzo Valla as an instance of linguistic barbarism.⁵⁰ One of Valla's closest friends and collaborators, Giovanni Tortelli, indeed correctly defined idolatry in his *De Orthographia* as *"simulachrorum cultura,"* the cult of images.⁵¹ Erasmus was right: in classical Latin no meaning could attach to the distinction that Aquinas had taken from Origen (or, more precisely, from Rufinus). However, a deeper analysis shows that the implications of Origen's distinction, along with the questions raised by Aquinas in his commentary on 1 Corinthians 8:4, are more complicated than they seem.

One of the objections that Aquinas lists (in order to confute them) states: "An artist can only represent what he has seen." How, then is it possible to have images of nonexistent beings? To this,

Aquinas replies that when we speak of an idol's lack of resemblance, we refer to the whole, and not to its parts, which are depictions of natural objects.[52] This reply recalls the Stoics' remarks on the "comprehensive" powers of *phantasia*—a comparison that may seem absurd but is not. Aquinas wrote his commentary on the first letter to the Corinthians (up to the tenth chapter) during his second stay in Paris, from January 1269 to June 1272.[53] Before his departure from Italy, he had been working on a very different project, a commentary on Aristotle's *Peri hermeneias*, which was largely based on two commentaries of the early fifth century, by Ammonius (this had just been translated from the Greek by the Dominican, William of Moerbeke) and by Boethius (this was in turn largely based on Porphyrius's earlier commentary).[54] In the passage I have just quoted from Aquinas's commentary on 1 Corinthians 8:4, we can catch an echo both of Aristotle's *Peri hermeneias* and of the commentaries made on it in antiquity.

Right at the start of the *Peri hermeneias* (16a.9 ff.), we once again come across the *tragelaphos*, the goat-stag:

> Just as some thoughts in the soul are neither true nor false while some are necessarily one or the other, so also with spoken sounds. For falsity and truth have to do with combination and separation. Thus names and verbs by themselves—for instance "man" or "white" when nothing further is added—are like the thoughts that are without combination and separation; for so far they are neither true nor false. A sign of this is that even "goat-stag" signifies something but not, as yet, anything true or false [*kai gar ho tragelaphos seimainei men ti, oupo de alethes e pseudos*]—unless "is" or "is not" is added (either simply or with reference to time).

A word like *"tragelaphos,"* in which meaning and referentiality are so clearly disjoined, highlights a more general phenomenon, namely the conventionality of language. Substantives, Aristotle continues, have a meaning fixed by convention: the parts of which they are made up have no meaning, except in the case of compound nouns:

> I say [names are significant] "by convention" because no name is a name naturally but only when it has become a symbol. Even

inarticulate noises (of beasts, for instance) do indeed reveal something, yet none of them is a name.[55]

Ammonius, in his commentary on the *Peri hermeneias*, gives a longer list of possibilities. This develops the reflections of the Stoics on the question of meaning: (a) a sound may both be a word and have a meaning—for instance, "man"; (b) a sound may have a meaning but not be a word—for instance, the barking of a dog; (c) a sound may be a word but have no meaning—for instance, *"blituri"* (this was the traditional designation for the sound of the harp); (d) a sound may neither be a word nor have any meaning—for instance, a whistling or buzzing, or a sound made by some wild animal, by chance and not with the aim of signifying or representing anything.[56]

This passage considers *mimesis*, or *repraesentatio* (this is the term used by William of Moerbeke); however, neither in antiquity nor in the Middle Ages do we find comparably far-reaching discussions of visual representation. The fact that we keep encountering comments about centaurs and other nonexistent beings demonstrates, indirectly, that the theme of meaningless signs and images remained largely unexplored. The partial exceptions—such as the commonplace of the chance-made likeness—only confirm the general rule.[57] One is tempted to discern a kind of visual *blituri* in the act of the Greek painter Protogenes, who supposedly threw a sponge at his own incomplete work in an excess of despair: here a meaningless sign is caught in the moment at which it is transformed into a perfect representation of the slaver of a dog. However, it was only because of this extraordinary outcome that the anecdote—true or false—was ever set down. Those intrinsically meaningless signs that (as Ernst Gombrich has taught us) communicate the experience of illusion to those who behold them through the deployment of specific visual conventions became the subject of theoretical reflection only when the artistic tradition centered on mimesis began to be called in question.

8. Antiquity and the Middle Ages had asymmetrical attitudes toward words on one hand and images on the other, and this fact can be traced to a historical divergence. Since images were interpreted in mimetic terms, their relation with the natural world was taken for

granted. Aristotle, arguing against Plato, had put forward the idea that human language was to be interpreted as a convention, and this encouraged a profound exploration of all those phenomena that stand before, alongside and beyond language. Such an explanation is inadequate, however, because it takes no account of a deeper and (so far as I can see) intrinsic difference between the word and the image. A word like "goat-stag" may be said to predicate "nonexistence"; but we cannot say this of the corresponding image.[58] Images—whether they represent objects that exist, nonexistent objects, or non-objects—are always affirmative.[59] If we want to say *"Ceci n'est pas une pipe,"* we have to use words (plate 19). Images are what they are.

The reference to Exodus 3:14: "I am who I am," is intentional. We are used to believing that both idolatry and the condemnation of idolatry belong to a past that we have left behind. But probably Origen was not altogether wrong to detect a deep contiguity between idols and likenesses.

6

Style

> Monotheism of reason and of the heart, polytheism of the imagination and of art, that is what we need.[1]

1. In 1605 two Venetian priests, accused of minor offenses, were imprisoned, and this unleashed a bitter diplomatic war between the Venetian Republic and the Holy See. Pope Paul V, basing his position on the principle of indirect power (*potestas indirecta*) formulated by Bellarmino, took the view that he had the right to intervene in the internal affairs of the Venetian state by requesting that the two priests be released. A lively debate ensued. The immediate stakes concerned the juridical and political independence of the Republic of Venice; in a longer perspective, the respective limits of church and state were at issue. Paolo Sarpi, the official theologian of the Republic, vigorously upheld the Venetian point of view. Sarpi, a Servite friar who was to gain a European reputation as the pseudonymous author of the *History of the Council of Trent*, was excommunicated in 1607; a few months later, he was attacked in the precincts of the monastery to which he

belonged by five men who attempted to kill him by stabbing him with daggers. Sarpi, gravely wounded, whispered to the doctor who was tending him that, as everyone knew, his wounds had been caused *"stylo Romanae curiae"*—that is, "by the knife of the Roman Curia," but also "by the legal procedures [literally, by the stylus or pen] of the Roman Curia."[2]

Sarpi's splendid conceit can hardly be bettered as an introduction to a discussion of the political implications of style. Style, as we shall see, is often used as a means of delimiting, demarcating, and cutting out: as a weapon. At the same time, style has also played an important (and too little recognized) role in the acceptance of cultural diversity. I shall consider this ambiguity as it presents itself in the field of the visual arts; toward the end of my argument, certain implications concerning the history and philosophy of science will also become apparent.

2. I shall begin by discussing some passages taken from Cicero's *De oratore* (55 B.C.). Crassus, the representative of the author's point of view, begins his account of rhetoric by recalling Plato's dictum that all intellectual activities are bound together by a certain internal coherence. However, what comes next (3.26–36) is anything but Platonic in flavor. Crassus/Cicero starts by stating the obvious: that in nature certain things exist, such as the pleasures of hearing or of smell, which are different in kind but equally agreeable.[3] The scope of this observation is extended first to the arts, both visual and verbal, and then to oratory. In the field of a single art, like sculpture, says Crassus, we find excellent artists such as Myron, Policletus, and Lysippus, whom everyone appreciates even though they are very different from one another. It is the same in painting (Crassus names Zeuxis, Aglaophontis, and Apelles) or in poetry. Poets such as Ennius, Pacuvius, and Accius differ from one another, as do the Greek poets Aeschylus, Sophocles, and Euripides: "And yet they gain almost the same kind of praise, different though they are in their various manners of writing" (*"in dissimili scribendi genere"*). Their excellence defies comparison; perfection, as Cicero demonstrates, proceeding to define concisely the characteristics of various orators, may be pursued by each artist in his own particular manner.[4] In the final analysis, if we could bring the orators of all times and places together under review, would we not conclude that there are as

many kinds or manners (*genera dicendi*) as there are orators?[5] Thus the notion of kind or manner (*genus*) eventually becomes something like our notion of individual style.

Cicero's insistence on the importance of different kinds of oratory, which he takes so far as to identify these different kinds with individual orators, was inspired by the rhetorical notion of "appropriateness," of what is "fitting" (in Greek, *to prepon*).[6] Cicero explictly chose not to consider any all-encompassing oratorical manner, adapted to every cause, every audience, every orator, and every circumstance. He advised his readers only that they should choose an oratorical style—high, middling, or low—appropriate to the particular case they were engaged in (3.210–212). We are a long way from Plato and his quest for a universal idea of the beautiful.

This argument could be taken outside the sphere of the visual and verbal arts, with unexpected consequences. We can appreciate this if we consider a letter sent by Saint Augustine to the imperial commissioner Flavius Marcellinus.[7] The Roman senator Volusianus had asked a provocative question: how was it possible that God had looked favorably upon the new sacrifices of Christianity and had condemned the old sacrifices (in other words, the ceremonies of the Jews)? Could he ever change his mind? In his reply, Augustine emphasized the difference between the "beautiful" (*pulchrum*) and the "fitting" (*aptum*), a theme he had explored in his lost youthful treatise *De pulchro et apto*. The seasons of the year and the phases of human life show us, wrote Augustine, that both nature and human activities change in accordance with the necessities of the times, following a certain rhythm, but this does not affect the rhythm of their change. We can recognize the same principle in religious matters. In the earliest times, Augustine remarks, the sacrifice established by God was fitting (*aptum*); but it is so no longer. The change that is fitting for the present day has been willed by God, who knows infinitely better than any human being what is adapted to each time (*quid cuique tempori accommodate adhibeatur*). Augustine, seeking to express the idea that the Old Testament was both true and superseded, could not speak in terms of a "jealous" vision of truth (Exodus 3:14; Deuteronomy 4:24). He needed something different, and this he found in the *De oratore*, in the idea that the ways leading to artistic excellence are various and not to be compared with one another. However, the essentially atemporal model we find in Cicero is given a new formulation by

Augustine, who adapts it to a temporal perspective. Thus the rhetorical notion of the appropriate, the fitting, allowed Augustine to sustain simultaneously the ideas of divine immutability and of historical change—a truly crucial step. Diversity of style, although conceived in ahistorical terms, contributed to the development of an idea of historical perspective that remains substantially current today.[8]

3. Cicero's argument surfaces again in a passage of Baldesar Castiglione's *Courtier*, published in 1528 but written some ten years earlier. This is one of the earliest known uses of the term "style" in connection with the visual arts. The discussion on *"sprezzatura,"* which was to become so celebrated, leads into the theme of literary imitation, which was much discussed at that time. Count Ludovico di Canossa, who represents Castiglione's own views in the dialogue, rejects the imitation of classical models in the name of "custom," remarking that "the summit of every excellence can almost always be reached by diverse routes." This implicit allusion to *De oratore*— often mentioned by the speakers—is followed by references to music and to contemporary painting. In this context, the terms "manner" (*"maniera"*) and "style" (*"stile"*) are used as synonyms, which endow with a specific significance the general capacity to "make":

And again various things are equally pleasing to our eyes, so that it is with difficulty that we can judge which delights them most. Consider how in painting Leonardo Vincio, Mantegna, Raphael, Michelangelo, Giorgio da Castelfranco are all most excellent: and yet nonetheless each in his manner of making is different from the others; so that it seems that none of them is in any way lacking in his manner, for we recognize that each is altogether perfect in his own style.[9]

The presence among this group of Mantegna, a painter of the preceding generation, is astonishing: still more astonishing is the absence of Titian. Titian, to be sure, was still too young to be mentioned in 1507, the year in which Castiglione sets his fictitious dialogue at the court of Urbino; but clearly his name could still not be included in 1528, when *The Courtier* was published.[10] Leonardo, Raphael, Michelangelo, and Giorgione remain at the center of the canon established by Vasari, who saw them as the initiators of the so-called modern manner. To order them hierarchically would seem to many of us today an obvious waste of time, just as it did to Castiglione. However, this "obviousness" is misleading. The passage from Cicero was by no means a mere familiar *topos* or commonplace; rather, it was a formula that opened up a new cognitive model—a *Logosformel*, we might say, paraphrasing Aby Warburg.[11] It formed an integral part of Vasari's perspective, which on this point is still our own today.

4. In what remains a fundamental essay, Erwin Panofsky describes Vasari's historical perspective as the hybrid result of two antithetical principles. The first is pragmatic, considering all phenomena as parts of a causal process; the second is dogmatic, considering all phenomena as more or less adequate incarnations of a "perfect rule of art."[12] However, the antithesis is easily overcome in the teleological perspective that Vasari adopted, inasmuch as he is able to evaluate every artist and each work on the basis of their contribution to the progress of art. At the end of his own work, Vasari wrote as follows (using terms that, as Panofsky noted, echo the Scholastic distinction between *simpliciter* and *secundum quid*):

I mean to have praised not simply [*semplicemente*], but rather, as we say, in accordance with [*secondo che*] and with respect to place, time, and other such circumstances.[13]

The notion of *secundum quid*, far from contradicting the notion of perfection, was in a sense the latter's corollary. Vasari continues:

It is true that Giotto, to take his example, was greatly praised in his time; I do not know what would have been said of him or of other old painters, if they had been of the same time as [Michelangelo] Buonarroto: except that the men of this century, which stands at the summit of perfection, would not be as able as they are had not such others been beforehand, and had they not come before us.[14]

Vasari, Panofsky argues, essentially understood history as theology.[15] Vasari, who called Michelangelo "divine," would not have demurred. However, this was an artistic theology, which saw in

Michelangelo the outcome of a process that had begun with Cimabue and Giotto; it was not a matter of any extrahistorical norm. When Vasari declares that he has always judged artists "in accordance with and with respect to place, time, and other such circumstances," we are bound to think of the insistence on what is appropriate and fitting that we find in Cicero's advice to orators and that Augustine made the foundation of his theology of history.[16]

However, Vasari's linear construction of history was indeed threatened by an antithesis, though not the one suggested by Panofsky. The first edition of Vasari's *Lives*, published in 1550, had no life of Titian, who was then at the peak of his European renown (he had just painted two portraits of the emperor Charles V). By this time Vasari was already familiar with some of Titian's works, and he had met the painter at Rome a few years earlier. At the end of his life of Giorgione, and after praising his works elaborately, Vasari explains why no biography of Titian is included: "But because [Titian] is alive, and his works are to be seen, there is no need to give an account of them here."[17] Michelangelo, whose biography concludes the 1550 edition of the *Lives*, was to be the only living artist included in the work. Vasari probably thought the inclusion of Titian would have encroached on the absolute preeminence he wished to accord to Michelangelo; and he may have had reasons to believe that Michelangelo would not especially have welcomed the presence of a life of Titian. For whatever reason, the second edition of Vasari's *Lives*, published in 1568, after Michelangelo's death, did include a biography of Titian, where praise alternated with criticism. In a celebrated passage, Vasari, speaking of himself in the third person, reports a conversation with Michelangelo at Rome in 1546. The two had visited Titian, who had shown them his *Danae*:

> After they had left him, and were discussing Titian's manner of working [*il fare di Tiziano*], Buonarroto gave him considerable praise, saying how pleasing he found his coloring and his manner [*maniera*]; but it was a pity, he said, that in Venice artisans did not learn to draw well from the beginning, and that Venetian painters did not have a better method of study . . . because whoever has not done enough drawing, and has not made sufficient study of choice things both ancient and modern, cannot do well by himself, nor can he improve those things that are taken from life.[18]

These words were probably occasioned by the derivation of Titian's *Danae* from Michelangelo's *Night*.[19] Michelangelo's criticism was aimed not at Titian's "manner," his individual style, which he praised as "very beautiful and lively"; rather, he had in mind the intrinsic weakness of the tradition inaugurated by Titian's master, Giorgione, who (according to Vasari) "acquired a reputation . . . to compete with those who were working in Tuscany, and who were the authors of the modern manner."[20] The second edition of the *Lives* was still a celebration of the triumph of Florentine drawing, from Cimabue to Michelangelo. Vasari was, however, such an open-minded critic, with so little in his makeup of the conventional or (*pace* Panofsky) the dogmatic, that he succeeded in writing a memorable tribute to the mythological paintings of Titian's old age, profoundly alien though these are to Florentine tradition: "executed with bold strokes, broadly done, smudged, so that from nearby they cannot be made out whereas from a distance they appear perfect."[21] Here the tension between style as an individual phenomenon and style in a broader sense is pushed to an extreme.[22]

5. In 1557, the Venetian writer Ludovico Dolce had replied to the first edition of Vasari's *Lives* in his *Dialogo della Pittura*. Here we again discern the argument put forward by Cicero and spread by Castiglione: "it is not to be believed . . . that there is one single form of perfect painting." Dolce concludes by praising the "divine and peerless" Titian, who mingles the "greatness and fierceness" (*terribilità*) we find in Michelangelo with the "pleasant and lovely" quality of Raphael, and with the colors of nature.[23] Two opposed models were emerging, founded respectively on drawing and on color.[24]

The debate went on from the late seventeenth century until the early nineteenth, opposing first Poussin to Rubens, later Ingres to Delacroix.[25] There was some degree of connection between this antithesis and that which set "ancients" against "moderns"; the proponents of color were identified with those who favored the moderns. (When it was first suggested, in the early nineteenth century, that the statues and buildings of the Greeks had originally been colored, many admirers of ancient art were left deeply shocked.) In the introduction to his *Parallèle de l'architecture antique avec la moderne* (1650), Roland Fréart, sieur de Chambray, provided a disdainful summary of the objections put forward by the champions of the "moderns":

That the spirit is free, and that we have as much right as did the ancients to invent and to follow our own genius, without making ourselves as it were their slaves, since art is something infinite that grows in perfection from day to day, while it adapts itself to the humor of centuries and nations whose judgments differ and which all define the Beautiful in their own way; and many more such arguments, vague and frivolous enough, but apt all the same to sway half-learned people who have not yet been enlightened by the practice of the arts, and simple workmen whose only trade is what they have at their fingertips.

Art that "adapts itself," *l'art . . . s'accommodant* to the "humor of centuries and nations whose judgments differ": the notion of adaptation, of accommodation, of what is fitting, having already passed from rhetoric into theology and from theology into history, here continues to display its richness. Such variety and diversity were a long way indeed from the chosen and changeless classical model that the "great moderns, Michelangelo and Raphael" had rescued— so Fréart de Chambray maintained—from the ruins of antiquity.[26] To the champions of the ancients, a liberal attitude toward classical models smacked of the Gothic; in other words it bordered on the worst of treasons against architecture. The sixteenth-century architect Philibert Delorme had proposed a reconstruction of the Corinthian style, but Fréart de Chambray made short work of this: Delorme was "a fine fellow, a student and amateur of ancient architecture; but for all that, his modern genius led him to see the most beautiful things in Rome through Gothic eyes."[27]

6. We are already on the verge of the birth of an anti-classical architecture, which occurred indeed in Rome but which gave sustenance to a revolt against the Roman and the traditional, opening the way to a less narrow architectural canon. An early and impressive statement of this attitude is found in Johann Bernhard Fischer von Erlach's book of 1721, *Entwurf einer historischen Architectur in Abbildung unterschiedener berühmten Gebäude des Altertums und fremder Völker* (Project for a historical architecture, illustrated by a variety of famous edifices built in antiquity and by foreign peoples). Fischer von Erlach, a key figure in Austrian baroque architecture, had spent many years in Rome (1670–1686) and had been much influenced

while there by the work of Francesco Borromini.[28] Among the sumptuous illustrations in his book we find representations of the Temple of Solomon, according to the reconstruction suggested by the Spanish Jesuit Villalpanda (plate 20); of the megaliths at Stonehenge (plate 21); of a series of mosques, from Pest to Constantinople; of the residence of the king of Siam and of the imperial court at Peking (Beijing); and of a series of Chinese bridges (plate 22)—as well as of a number of buildings designed by the author himself. In his introduction, Fischer von Erlach justifies this admixture of heterogeneous edifices by invoking a more general notion of diversity, which he connects with the idea of taste (*goût*):

> Draughtsmen and designers will see here that the tastes of nations [*les goûts des nations*] differ in architecture no less than they do in matters of clothing or of dressing meat; and by comparing one with another, will be enabled to make a judicious choice among them. In the end they will come to see that in truth custom can authorize certain bizarre elements in the art of building, as for instance the decorative apertures of the Gothic style, or ribbed vaulting, or church towers and steeples, or ornaments and roofs in the Indian style—and in all this the diversity of opinions is as little subject to argument as is the diversity of taste.[29]

No Gothic edifices were included in Fischer von Erlach's book. However, Borromini's opponents regularly used the epithet "Gothic" as an insult: the classicist Bellori referred to him as "a most ignorant Gothic architect."[30] The reference to the "bizarre" also brings Borromini to mind, since this was a term that he applied to his own works.[31] One begins to wonder whether some of Borromini's most extravagant ideas, such as the lantern of Sant'Ivo alla Sapienza (which may have been indirectly inspired by Oriental models), may not have played a part in Fischer von Erlach's attempt to develop a broader architectural canon that would have room for instances of non-European work.[32] Fischer von Erlach's openness to the diversity of national tastes (though he continues to uphold a few universal architectural principles, such as the rules of symmetry and stability) recalls the attitude of the Jesuit missionaries of the time toward the non-European cultures they encountered, which was based explicitly on the principle of adaptation or accommodation (*accommodatio*).[33] In this regard it should be noted that the *Entwurf* was largely (though not explicitly) based upon the works of the very learned Jesuit Athanasius Kircher, whom Fischer von Erlach had met in Rome.[34]

This attitude in time made possible a phenomenon without precedent, namely the simultaneous employment of different styles. At first this was restricted to architectonic experiments within the space of the garden, intermediate between nature and culture and between town and country.[35] The juxtaposition of Gothic ruins with Chinese pagodas in English gardens was often regarded as a transgression of the rules of taste and provoked polemical responses, as we see in this contribution of 1755 to *The World*:

> The applause which is so fondly given to Chinese decorations or to the barbarous productions of a Gothic genius . . . seems once more to threaten the ruin of that simplicity which distinguishes the Greek and Roman arts as eternally superior to those of every other nation.[36]

7. "Noble simplicity and calm grandeur": so Johann Joachim Winckelmann famously defined the character of Greek sculpture in his *Gedanken über die Nachahmung der griechischen Werke in der Malerey und Bildhauerkunst* (Thoughts on the imitation of Greek works of painting and sculpture), likewise published in 1755.[37] These same qualities, Winckelmann remarked, are to be found in Greek writing of the period, for example in the works of Socrates' pupils, as well as in the productions of those, such as Raphael, who imitated classical models.[38] "There is," Winckelmann once wrote, "only one Beauty as there is only one Good."[39]

The Platonic overtones of these words are evident. However, in his most influential work, *Geschichte der Kunst des Altertums* (History of the art of antiquity) (1764), Winckelmann does not place such exclusive stress on the revelations of sempiternal Beauty. Rejecting the biographical framework adopted by Vasari (and by Pliny before him), he declares that the task of art history is to examine the origin, development, change, and decay of art itself, and at the same time to consider how style varies in accordance with differences among peoples, times, and artists.[40] He analyzed not only Egyptian, Etruscan, and Greek styles but, within the Greek, four separate phases of style.

For the first time, style was identified as the specific object of art history, while at the same time it was connected with history in general.

In order to analyze stylistic changes, Winckelmann investigated the various factors that conditioned them. As well as noting (in fairly traditional terms) the influence of climate, he emphasized the importance of political liberty for the arts, and thus the value of style itself as historical evidence.[41] There is, moreover, a third aspect of Winckelmann's work, much less obvious and indeed often ignored by his commentators, which throws an unexpected light on his overall approach. In his summary of the principal characteristics of the Etruscan style, Winckelmann remarks that these were also to some extent the characteristics of the Etruscans as a people. A tendency to dwell excessively on details is found in the literary style of the Etruscans, which is strained and artificial and thus very different from the pure clarity of Roman style. This style of the Etruscan artists is still discernible in the work of their successors, including the greatest of them, Michelangelo; and these same characteristics account for the faults of such artists as Daniele da Volterra or Pietro da Cortona. Raphael and his followers, by contrast, were spiritually closer to the Greeks.[42]

Winckelmann had praised Raphael as an imitator of the Greeks in the aphorism we have already noted from his *Gedanken*, which hinges on a comparison between Greek language and Greek sculpture. In the passage from the *Geschichte*, however, the disparaging comparison between Etruscan writing and the works of Tuscan painters implies not conscious imitation but an alleged ethnic continuity linking the Etruscans and the Tuscans. This form of argument developed in a rather unexpected direction the reflection of two authors, Caylus and Buffon, whose work had had a profound (if unacknowledged) influence on Winckelmann.[43]

In his *Recueil d'antiquités egyptiennes, etrusques, grecques et romaines*, which came out from 1752 onward, Caylus had rejected a merely antiquarian perspective. He had argued instead for a method whose aim would be

> to study accurately the spirit and the handiwork of the artist, to grasp its intentions and to follow its execution, in a word to regard these monuments as the evidence and the expression of the taste that held sway in a given century and in a given country

... Once we have determined the taste of a country, we have but to follow it in its progress or alterations; thus we shall be able to know, at least in part, the taste of every century.[44]

Here Caylus expresses the view that the history of art must be connected to history in the broad sense, a view later emphasized in the much more influential work of Winckelmann.[45] Winckelmann, who as a rule tended to patronize Caylus as a pedant, acknowledged his debt to the French scholar in a letter that he wrote to the antiquary Bianconi:

He is the first who can be credited with the glory of having set out to enter into the substance of the style of the Art of the Peoples of antiquity. To attempt this in Paris, however, was to undertake a task that would be most difficult to accomplish.[46]

At all events, the presumption of an ethnic link between the Etruscans and the Tuscans involved much more than a notion of national tastes. Here, the indirect influence of Buffon should be noted. On two separate occasions, in 1750 and in 1754, Winckelmann noted down long extracts from Buffon's *Histoire naturelle*.[47] It was from the Frenchman that he learned to communicate his own observations, based on the most accurate scrutiny, in a vivid style that aspired to a kind of classical impersonality.[48] Styles constituted for Winckelmann the same kind of object as animals constituted for Buffon in the latter's great comparative project; Winckelmann too focused his attention both on the species (the style) and on the individual (the single work of art or artist). It may have been this analogy that led Winckelmann to maintain that style could not only be created or imitated, it could also be transmitted biologically—a step that was to have unforeseen consequences.

8. The nineteenth century was a period of political upheaval (the aftermath of the French Revolution, the Napoleonic wars), of European expansion overseas (in India, the islands of the Pacific, Egypt, and elsewhere), and of profound intellectual and social changes. Historical events radically transformed the way visual culture was understood by educated people in Europe, who now found themselves in direct or indirect contact with artefacts that bore witness to

civilizations quite remote in time or space.[49] Winckelmann's image of Greek art constituted, for many people, a point of orientation from which they could survey this mass of heterogeneous material.

This is strikingly demonstrated in John Flaxman's *Lectures on Sculpture*, given at the Royal Academy from 1810 onward and published after Flaxman's death in 1829.[50] Flaxman worked as a sculptor, but he was and is best known for his illustrations to Homer, Hesiod, Aeschylus, and Dante, based on sober, concise line drawings that are clearly inspired by the artistic principles that Winckelmann proclaimed.[51] However, as Goethe pointed out, Flaxman's line drawing echoes not just the vase paintings of the Etruscans (that is of the Greeks), but also the work of the Italian primitives.[52] In the *Lectures on Sculpture*, this double reference takes its place within the theoretical and historical perspective that Flaxman develops. Style, for him, was an original principle of art, and he describes it, in his florid prose, as a

well-known quality which originates in the birth of the art itself—increases in its growth—strengthens in its vigour—attains the full measure of beauty in the perfection of its parent cause—and, in its decay, withers and expires. Such a quality will define the stages of its progress, and will mark the degrees of its debasement. . . . Such a quality immediately determines to our eyes and understanding the barbarous attempt of the ignorant savage—the humble labour of the mere workman—the miracle of art conducted by science, ennobled by philosophy, and perfected by the zealous and extensive study of nature.

This distinguishing quality is understood by the term Style, in the arts of design.

It is very probable that Flaxman was the first person to broaden the notion of "style" so that it comprehended what was produced by "mere workmen" and even by savages.[53] Let us follow his argument:

This term, at first, was applied to poetry, and the style of Homer and Pindar must have been familiar long before Phidias or Zeuxis were known; but, in process of time, as the poet wrote with his style or pen, and the designer sketched with his style or pencil, the name of the instrument was familiarly used to express the

genius and productions of the writer and the artist; and this sym-
bolical mode of speaking has continued from the earliest times

through the classical ages, the revival of arts and letters, down to
the present moment, equally intelligible, and is now strengthened by the uninterrupted use and authority of the ancients and
the moderns.

From the instrument—the style, the stylus—to its products, in
the broadest sense. Flaxman continues as follows:

> And here we may remark, that as by the term style we designate
> the several stages of progression, improvement, or decline of the
> art, so by the same term, and at the same time, we more indi-
> rectly refer to the progress of the human mind, and states of soci-
> ety; for such as the habits of the mind are, such will be the works,
> and such objects as the understanding and the affections dwell
> most upon, will be most readily executed by the hands.

Style, as a concept connecting the mental and the manual,
thereby refers to well-defined phases of social and cultural history.
As he develops this idea, Flaxman expresses himself in terms that are
worth noting:

> Thus the savage depends on clubs, spears, and axes for safety and
> defence against his enemies, and on his oars or paddles for the
> guidance of his canoe through the waters: these, therefore,
> engage a suitable portion of his attention, and, with incredible
> labour, he makes them the most convenient possible for his pur-
> pose; and, as a certain consequence, because usefulness is a
> property of beauty, he frequently produces such an elegance of
> form as to astonish the more civilized and cultivated of his
> species. He will even superadd to the elegance of form an addi-
> tional decoration in relief on the surface of the instrument, a
> wave-line, a zig-zag, or the tie of a band, imitating such simple
> objects as his wants and occupations render familiar to his obser-
> vation—such as the first twilight of science in his mind enables
> him to comprehend. Thus far his endeavours are crowned with
> a certain portion of success; but if he extend his attempt to the
> human form, or to the attributes of divinity, his rude concep-

tions and untaught mind produce only images of lifeless deformity, or of horror and disgust.[54]

The admiration that Flaxman here expresses for the art of savages (circumscribed though it is by well-defined limits) is decidedly
surprising. In praising its "elegance of form," he connects such art
with a quality we have already met with: "convenience," the property of being adapted or accommodated (*aptum, to prepon*). However, Flaxman understands "convenience" in utilitarian terms: "use-
fulness is a property of beauty"—an observation that need not surprise us when we recall that he had worked for Wedgwood, making
drawings for vases and cameos.[55] The new relationship between art
and industry was encouraging a more open-minded approach to the
variety of artefacts produced in the course of history, and indeed to
that history itself; this is exemplified by the illustrations accompanying the *Lectures on Sculpture*, which are based in part on drawings by
Flaxman and in part on books by others. Flaxman's fluid, wavy line
proved able to convey and translate an extraordinarily wide and
diverse range of visual languages—relief-work at Wells Cathedral
and Persepolis (plate 23), statues from archaic Greece (plate 24) and
from India (plate 25), buildings at Mycenae, miniatures taken from
medieval manuscripts (plate 26), and so forth. By contrast, Flaxman
produces a very bland, weak, and watery version of Michelangelo's
"fierceness" (*terribilità*), especially if we compare his attempts with
the work of his great contemporary Fuseli.

One of his listeners wrote that Flaxman's lectures pleased the
public because of their "John-Bullism."[56] Flaxman did not conceal
his admiration for English medieval sculpture, but the political
implications of the *Lectures* go well beyond this appreciative judgment. The accompanying illustrations may be regarded as an
attempt to comprehend diverse cultures, to penetrate them, to
translate them, and to appropriate them: a visual equivalent to
British imperialism.

9. At more or less the same time, the greatest living philosopher
was also addressing an audience—of students, at Heidelberg and
Berlin—on the exotic art of the Asian countries. In his posthumously published lectures on aesthetics, Hegel noted that if Chinese
or Indian works of art turned away from the representation of real-

ity, this was not the result of technical weaknesses but a matter of deliberate distortion: in this respect, notes Hegel, we may have an imperfect art that is technically and in other ways perfectly accomplished within its own determined sphere, though it appears lacking when compared with the very concept of art and of the ideal.[57]

Behind this statement, we glimpse a fundamental theme of Romanticism: the freedom of the artist. Hegel, however, drew back from its more radical implications, which are forcefully expressed by Heinrich Heine in his essay on French painters ("Französische Maler"):

It is always a big mistake when the critic brings up the question "What should the artist do?" Much more correct would be the question "What is that the artist wants to do?" or even "What does the artist have to do?" The question "What should the artist do?" comes by the way of those philosophers of art who, though they possessed no sense of poetry, have singled out traits of various works of art and then, on the basis of what there was, determined a norm for what everything ought to be, and who delimited the genres, and invented definitions and rules. . . . Every original artist, and certainly every artistic genius, brings with him his own aesthetic terms and must be judged according to them.[58]

Heine wrote these words at the start of his long exile in Paris, in a congenial milieu. We can pick up a distant echo of them in an article published many years later (1854) in the *Revue des Deux Mondes*, by Delacroix, the painter who had embodied for decades the rejection of traditional values. In an impassioned defense of artistic variety, Delacroix argues that the Beautiful may be attained by diverse ways: by Raphael and Rembrandt, by Shakespeare and Corneille. To take antiquity as a model is absurd, he says, since antiquity does not offer or constitute a single homogeneous canon.[59] It may have been reading this article that inspired Baudelaire to write "Les phares," an extraordinary exercise in *ekphrasis* that starts with some of the painters admiringly referred to by Delacroix (Rubens, Leonardo, Rembrandt, Michelangelo) and ends with Delacroix himself, the only living artist in the series. The "beacon burning on a thousand citadels" ("*phare allumé sur mille citadelles*"), which in the poem's conclusion is a metaphor for the Beautiful, is made plural in the title, as if to underline the idea expressed by the extreme diversity of each strophe. In May 1855 Baudelaire returned to the same theme in an article, published in the journal *Le Pays*, about the Paris Universal Exposition in which Delacroix finally attained fame, being represented by thirty-five pictures. "The Beautiful," wrote Baudelaire, "is always bizarre":

> Now how can this quality of the bizarre—necessary, irreducible, infinitely varied; dependent on setting, climate, custom, race, religion, and the temperament of the artist—how can this quality ever be governed or set to rights by utopian rules drawn up in a little temple of science somewhere on the planet, without art itself falling into mortal peril?[60]

Baudelaire therefore rejects any idea of aesthetic norms:

> Faced with these unaccustomed phenomena, what would any of these *jurymen professors* of aesthetics say or write?—so they are called by Henri Heine, that charming spirit who would be a genius if only he would turn more often towards the divine.[61]

If Heine's principal target was probably Friedrich Schlegel, Baudelaire's was the rhetoric of French democracy:

> There is one more very fashionable error from which I desire to preserve myself as I do from Hell.—I refer to the idea of progress. This obscure lantern, invented by the philosophising chatter of the day . . . Whoever wants to gain a clear view of history must above all extinguish this perfidious lantern.[62]

This passage, not present in the article as it appeared in *Le Pays*, was added by Baudelaire after the publication of "Les phares." The "phare allumé sur mille citadelles" first evoked, by contrast, the "obscure lantern" ("*fanal obscur*") of the idea of progress—followed, in a sudden *coup-de-théatre*, by the lines written by "a poet" (Baudelaire himself) and an interpretation of them: "Delacroix, lake of blood, haunted by evil angels" ("*Delacroix, lac de sang hanté des mauvais anges*").[63] Heine had written that all great artists have their own individual aesthetic; Baudelaire takes this line of reasoning to its limit:

Flourishing is always spontaneous, individual. Was Signorelli really the progenitor of Michelangelo? Did Perugino contain Raphael? The artist depends only on himself. He promises to the ages nothing but the works he has made. He is responsible to nobody but himself. He dies without children.[64]

His insistence on the multiple elements that influence artistic works in their variety had taken Baudelaire to the point where he rejected the very possibility of any historical approach to art. As we shall see, this tension would continue to make itself felt.

10. The trail we have been following seems to lead, thus far, to a victory of diversity over uniformity of style. Nineteenth-century architecture, in the movement known as *Historismus* (historicism), authorized the coexistence of diverse styles. In Germany, the leading advocate of this approach was Gottfried Semper (1803–1879). Semper produced a comparative analysis of style in his ambitious work *Der Stil in den technischen und tektonischen Künsten oder praktische Aesthetik* (Style in the technical and tectonic arts, or practical aesthetics), the first two volumes of which appeared in 1860 and 1863. (The third was never completed.) Semper's project originated, he said, in his experiences as a student in Paris, between 1826 and 1830, when it was his custom to spend hours in the Jardin des Plantes looking at the collection of fossils made by Cuvier. He mentioned these youthful memories on two separate occasions: first in a letter to a Brunswick publisher, Eduard Vieweg (dated 26 September 1843),[65] and then in a talk given in 1853 in London, where he had gone as a political exile, being obliged to leave Germany in 1848 because of his involvement in Dresden with revolutionaries.[66] On both occasions Semper draws an analogy between Cuvier's comparative approach and his own. However, the shift from the German of the letter into the English of the lecture (the first in a series given by Semper in the Department of Practical Arts) resulted in significant changes. On one hand, Semper got rid of all terms inspired by the morphology of Goethe: "einfachte Urform" (the original and simplest form), "ursprüngliche Ideen" (original ideas), "Urformen" (original forms), "das Ursprünglichte und Einfache" (that which is original and simple). On the other, he transformed a neutral reference to "den Werken meiner Kunst" (the products of my art) into a precise refer-

ence to "industrial art," prompted perhaps by the International
Exhibition of 1851 in which he had collaborated, or perhaps by the
particular audience he was addressing:

> We see the same skeleton repeating itself continually but with
> innumerable varieties, modified by gradual developments of the
> individuals and by the conditions of existence they had to fulfill.
> . . . If we observe this immense variety and richness of nature,
> notwithstanding its simplicity, may we not by Analogy assume,
> that it will be nearly the same with the creations of our hands,
> with the works of industrial art?[67]

Semper probably had a fairly vague idea of Cuvier's work, and he
was certainly not qualified to derive an adequate biological model
from it.[68] However, there is no denying that Cuvier exerted a considerable influence on the metaphors he thought in. Goethe, paradoxically, was equally influential, even though Goethe, in the debate
between Saint-Hilaire and Cuvier at the Académie Française in 1830,
had taken sides with the former. Semper's notion of a "method analogous to that which Baron Cuvier followed applied to art and especially to architecture, [which] would form the base of a doctrine of
Style" implies a considerable degree of continuity with his early
Romantic formation.

A similar path, from Goethe's morphology to Cuvier's comparative osteology (eventually reinterpreted in accordance with Darwin's
evolutionary theory), was followed by another art historian and well-
known connoisseur with a German background, Semper's slightly
younger but equally eccentric contemporary: Iwan Lermolieff, alias
Giovanni Morelli.[69] Both critics analyzed style in a morphological
perspective, but Morelli concentrated on individual artists while
Semper considered larger cultural entities. This difference in scale
prompted a difference in method. Morelli always held to the idea that
stylistic features must be investigated from within, whereas for Semper style was the product of an interaction between internal and
external factors, requiring separate analysis. His doctrine of style
undertook first of all to examine "the exigencies of the work itself
based on some natural, necessary laws, which are the same at all
times and under every circumstance"—a somewhat obscure way of
putting things, alluding to the constraints exercised by materials and

tools (the latter being subject, as Semper himself acknowledged, to historical change). In the second place, it set out to examine

local and personal influences, such as the climate and physical constitution of a country, the religious and political institutions of a nation, the person or corporation by whom a work is ordered, the place for which it is destined, and the Occasion on which it was produced. Finally also the individual personality of the Artist.[70]

One element is missing from this list: race. At more or less the same time, the renaissance of the Gothic was described by George Gilbert Scott, one of the principal collaborators in the restoration of Westminster Abbey, as

the resumption of our national architecture, the only genuine exponent of the civilization of the modern as distinguished from the ancient world, of the Northern as distinguished from the Southern races.

Scott went on to write:

We do not wish to adapt ourselves to medieval customs, but to adapt a style of art which accidentally was medieval, but is *essentially national*, to the wants and requirements of our own day.

And he hence concluded that "the indigenous style of our race must be our *point de départ*."[71] His was by no means an isolated voice. In the course of the nineteenth century, the admixture of historical, anthropological, and biological discourses had facilitated a parallel convergence between the ideas of national character, style, and race. In the discussion of architectural styles, race was eventually to occupy a predominant position. Semper's silence on this theme is remarkable.[72] He strongly believed in the "national genius" and also in his own ability to grasp this by way of humble archaeological remains, which he compared, following Cuvier, to fossils. Egyptian sacred boats and Greek *situlae*, with their close links to the Doric style, provide us, Semper argues, with a means of access to the architecture through which the two peoples expressed their essences

(*Wesen*) in monumental form.[73] Nowhere in this ambitious project, however, does Semper seek to invoke race as a conceptual shortcut.

11. Semper spent the last part of his life in Vienna, where his major architectural works, the Hofburg Theatre and the Museumplatz, were radically to transform the city's appearance and image.[74] His book on style had a wide impact among archaeologists and art historians. Toward the end of the century, it was vigorously challenged when Alois Riegl, in his *Stilfragen* (Questions of style, 1893), rejected the materialistic determinism of Semper—though in a number of places, for mainly tactical reasons, Riegl distinguished between the position of Semper's followers and Semper's own more subtle point of view. Where Semper had seen artistic development as essentially determined by tools and instruments, Riegl argued that decoration and form exercised an autonomous countervailing power, to which—emphasizing its historical features and aspects—he subsequently gave the name *Kunstwollen*, artistic will.[75] In his great book *Spätrömische Kunstindustrie* (late Roman artistic industry, 1901), Riegl argued that the artistic productions of what had traditionally been regarded as a decadent era, beginning with the bas-reliefs on the Arch of Constantine, which Vasari had scornfully dismissed as clumsy, could be understood as coherent expressions of a specific and homogeneous *Kunstwollen*, inspired by principles no less legitimate than, though quite different from, those of classical art.

It has often been pointed out that there is an obvious connection between Riegl's researches and artistic events in the Vienna of his time. When we read that "geometrical style" was not a primitive phenomenon attributable to an incapacity for representation (as Semper had hypothesized), but was rather—so Riegl argued—the deliberate product of a refined artistic will, we think of Gustav Klimt's almost contemporaneous pictures, with their geometrical decorations.[76] However, Riegl's theoretical approach had a different and longer ancestry, as we can see from its fundamentally Hegelian inspiration.[77] The passage on Chinese and Indian art that we cited earlier from Hegel's lectures on aesthetics might have been the point of departure for Riegl's reflections on European art. Moreover, Riegl accepted Hegel's teleological perspective, which allowed him to defend late Roman art both in terms of its own specific criteria and as a necessary transition within the overall course of historical development.[78]

Riegl's *Kunstwollen*, inasmuch as it is deployed as a weapon against materialistic determinism, seems to echo the Romantic notion of artistic freedom that prompted Heine's question: "Was will der Künstler?" "What is it that the artist wants to do?" However, Riegl does not dwell on the individual artist as a subversive genius; instead, he analyzes collective entities—the *Kunstwollen* of late Rome or of the Netherlands.[79] Stylistic analysis based on an ethnic perspective (however "ethnic" may have been understood) was itself part of the intellectual inheritance of Romanticism. This, as we have seen, is a context where the word "race" often recurs. Baudelaire himself includes race in his heterogeneous list of factors that condition art, along with custom, climate, religion, and the individual character of the artist. However, given the growth of an openly anti-Semitic atmosphere in late-nineteenth-century Vienna, the remarks Riegl made in his university lectures concerning the rigidity of the Jewish worldview, which is said to imply "an incapacity to change and to improve," probably awakened a particularly sympathetic response in his audience.[80] Two years earlier, in 1897, Riegl had found space in his lectures to draw a parallel between the first Christian era and modern-day socialism, praising the latter because "at least in its fundamental manifestations, it proposes to improve this world here below."[81] This passage has been seen as an allusion to the Christian Socialists, whose leader, the anti-Semite Karl Lüger, had just been elected mayor of Vienna.[82] I cannot say whether or how far Riegl indeed accepted the anti-Semitic tenets of the Christian Socialist Party. However, his tendency to regard race and style as coterminous entities emerges in a footnote to his book *Spätrömische Kunstindustrie*: the divergence between late pagan and proto-Christian art has often been exaggerated, he says, and is in itself scarcely credible, given that pagans and Christians belonged to the same race.[83]

12. Wilhelm Worringer, who did more than anyone else to spread Riegl's ideas (albeit in much cruder terms), did not hesitate to set them in an explicitly racist framework.[84] In his *Formprobleme der Gotik* (Formal problems of Gothic) of 1911, Worringer repeatedly links different levels of stylistic purity to an ethnic hierarchy:

> [It] may be said that France created the most beautiful and most living Gothic buildings but not the purest. The land of pure Gothic culture is the Germanic North . . . It is true that English

architecture is also tinged with Gothic, in a certain sense; it is true that England, which was too self-contained and isolated to be so much disturbed in its own artistic will [*Kunstwollen*] by the Renaissance as was Germany, affects Gothic as its national style right down to the present day. But this English Gothic lacks the direct impulse of German Gothic.[85]

Hence Worringer's conclusion:

For Gothic was the name we gave to that great phenomenon irreconcilably opposed to the classical, a phenomenon not bound to any single period of style, but revealing itself continuously through all the centuries in ever new disguises: a phenomenon not belonging to any age but rather in its deepest foundations an ageless racial phenomenon, deeply rooted in the innermost constitution of Northern man, and, for this reason, not to be uprooted by the levelling action of the European Renaissance.

In any case we must not understand race in the narrow sense of racial purity: here the word race must include all the peoples, in the composition [*Rassenmischung*] of which the Germans have played a decisive part. And that applies to the greater part of Europe. Wherever Germanic elements are strongly present, a racial connection in the widest sense is observable which, *in spite of* racial differences in the ordinary sense, is unmistakably operative. . . . For the Germans, as we have seen, are the *sine qua non* of Gothic.[86]

The years that have passed since these words were written in 1911 have given them a sinister feel. Of course, one should avoid anachronistic readings. Nevertheless, hearing this talk of race "in the widest sense"—so wide that it would go beyond limited notions of "racial purity"—one is inevitably reminded of the Nuremberg laws with their minutely detailed ordinances concerning various levels of *Rassenmischung*. Worringer's stylistic club is open to peoples of all kinds, so long as they have a sufficient percentage of German blood in their veins.

13. Our discussion so far will have established an appropriate context in which to consider the role attributed to style by an influential contemporary philosopher of science, Paul Feyerabend.

In an essay titled "Science as Art," Feyerabend seeks to apply to the sciences Riegl's theory of art, which he distinguishes from Vasari's approach.[87] In a note in *Against Method* (1970), Feyerabend had remarked that if one considered both science and art as approaches to solving problems, then no important difference would remain between them: it would be possible to speak of "styles and predilections in the first case, and progress in the second case."[88] With typical mischievousness, Feyerabend invokes Gombrich (mentioned in the immediately preceding note) against Popper. However, the equivalence proclaimed here between science and art turned out to be no more than a step along the road leading to "Wissenschaft als Kunst," "Science as Art"—the title of Feyerabend's essay on Riegl and also of the volume in which it was subsequently republished. Riegl was a perfect choice: his work involved (a) a coherent attack on positivism, based (b) on a vision of history as consisting of series of artistic impulses (*Kunstwollen*), discrete and self-contained, which led to a rejection of the notions of (c) decadence and (d) progress. This last point regarding progress in fact seems quite unconvincing, in that it ignores the Hegelian, teleological aspect of Riegl's work.[89] However, the other points justify Feyerabend's conclusion: "In the light of this modern conception of art [i.e., Riegl's conception], the sciences are arts."[90] Riegl's relativistic approach, based on the idea that every age creates its own artistic universe governed by laws specific to it, offered unlooked-for support to a relativistic view of science: it allowed the elimination of referentiality, truth, and reality, all of which could be placed, so to speak, in quotation marks. We are not surprised when Feyerabend proclaims that Riegl, along with a handful of others, has "understood the process of the acquisition of knowledge and of change in the sphere of knowledge better than most modern philosophers."[91]

Feyerabend must have discovered Riegl in the early 1980s.[92] However, his posthumous autobiography *Killing Time* (1995) shows that much earlier, at the time of his intellectual formation in Vienna, Feyerabend had been caught up in what we might call the by-products of Riegl's ideas.

Killing Time is presented as an unusually frank and sincere account—terms to be regarded with a certain caution, as always in the case of autobiography.[93] The section on the war, in which the young Feyerabend took part as a volunteer, fighting on the Russian front and reaching the rank of lieutenant, seems markedly reticent: of his military career, he writes, "This is what my army records say; my mind, however, is a blank."[94] Perhaps the past that has been

erased from the author's memory (or at any rate from his narrative) emerges again in the deliberate ambiguity of the book's title: "passing the time," and "a time to kill." However, the pages on the war do include a striking passage drawn from some lectures that the author gave to other officers in 1944, in Dessau Rosslau. The argument of these lectures was closely connected to the theme I have been examining. Feyerabend's summary is full of extracts (here indicated by italics) from his notes of fifty years earlier:

> People have different professions, different points of view. They are like observers looking at the world through the narrow windows of an otherwise closed structure. Occasionally they assemble at the centre and discuss what they have seen: *"then one observer will talk about a beautiful landscape with red trees, a red sky, and a red lake in the middle; the next one about an infinite blue plane without articulation; and the third about an impressive, five-floor-high building; they will quarrel. The observer on top of their structure* [me] *can only laugh at their quarrels—but for them their quarrels will be real and he will be an unworldly dreamer."* Real life, I said, is exactly like that. *"Every person has his own well-defined opinions, which color the section of the world he perceives. And when people come together, when they try to discover the nature of the whole to which they belong, they are bound to talk past each other; they will understand neither themselves nor their companions. I have often experienced, painfully, the impenetrability of human beings—whatever happens, whatever is said, rebounds from the smooth surface that separates them from each other."*
>
> My main thesis was that historical periods such as the Baroque, the Rococo, the Gothic Age are unified by a concealed essence that only a lonely outsider can understand. Most people see only the obvious . . . Secondly, I said, it is a mistake to assume that the essence of a historical period that started in one place can be transferred to another. There will be influences, true; for example, the French Enlightenment influenced Germany. But the trends arising from the influence share only the name with their cause. Finally, it is a mistake to evaluate events by comparing them with an ideal. Many writers have deplored the way in

which the Catholic Church transformed Good Germans during the Middle Ages and later and forced them into actions and beliefs unnatural to them. . . . But Gothic art produced harmonic units, not aggregates. This shows that the forms of the Church were not alien forms (*artfremd*, a favorite term at the time), and the Germans of that period were natural Christians, not unwilling and cowardly slaves. I concluded by applying the lesson to the relations between Germans and Jews. Jews, I said, are supposed to be aliens, miles removed from genuine Germans; they are supposed to have distorted the German character and to have changed the German nation into a collection of pessimistic, egotistic, materialistic individuals. But, I continued, the Germans reached that stage all by themselves. They were ready for liberalism and even Marxism. " *Everybody knows how the Jew, who is a fine psychologist, made use of this situation. What I mean is that the soil for his work was well prepared. Our misfortune is our own work, and we must not put the blame on any Jew, or Frenchman, or Englishman.*"[95]

At a number of points in his autobiography, Feyerabend speaks of the Jews, of his attitude toward them, of his Jewish friends, of anti-Semitism, of different ways of playing Shylock. A certain ambivalence and embarrassment is often perceptible in these remarks.[96] No doubt he must have been pleased to discover that in 1944 he had taught other officers that the Jews were not to blame for Germany's corruption. However, the text of the lectures reveals a more complex chain of reasoning. The examples of visual art chosen to illustrate the difficulties of human communication (at the time, Feyerabend wanted to become a painter) put one in mind of the *blaue Reiter* group—Marc, Kandinsky, and Feininger—whose works had been put on show in the exhibition of degenerate art held at Munich in 1937.[97] All of the examples suggest the idea of another world, different, coherent and self-contained, comparable to the larger-scale worlds of the Gothic, the baroque, and the rococo. The "hidden essence" that unites each period (or each civilization) is, of course, style. We detect a faint echo of Riegl's aesthetic attitude toward history, his way of seeing it as a succession of self-enclosed civilizations each based on particular *Kunstwollen* or styles.[98] In the intervening years, however, Riegl's insistence on style as a coherent and cohesive phenomenon, with its own criteria, had acquired a new meaning, one that can already be sensed in Worringer's work. The connection between style and race had reached a wider audience through the works of crude ideologists like H. F. K. Günther (*Rasse und Stil* [Race and Style], 1926), who during the Nazi period became an influential expert on racial questions.[99] Style had become a most effective tool of exclusion. Adolf Hitler spoke as follows at a party meeting held on 1 September 1933 (the "Victory Congress"):

> It is a sign of the horrible spiritual decadence of the past epoch that one spoke of styles without recognizing their racial determinants. . . . Each clearly formed race has its own handwriting in the book of art, as far as it is not like Jewry, devoid of any creative artistic ability. The fact that a people can imitate an art which is formally alien to it [*"artfremde Kunst"*] does not prove that art is an international phenomenon.[100]

Feyerabend's paraphrase of his notes from 1944 reads thus: "Gothic art produced harmonic units, not aggregates, [which] shows that the forms of the Church were not alien forms (*artfremd*, a favorite term at the time)." It is clear that the lecture Feyerabend gave to his fellow officers echoed Nazi ideas on race, culture, and style. If every civilization is a homogeneous entity, from both the stylistic and the racial point of view, then Jews and foreigners can have no proper role to play in the development of the German nation, since they are excluded from it by birth. The implications of these ideas, from Auschwitz to the former Yugoslavia, from "racial purity" to ethnic cleansing, are well known.

14. Race plays no role in the works of Feyerabend's maturity. However, a relation does exist between what he said in his 1944 lectures and certain leading themes of his mature work. As a young man, Feyerabend had regarded the difficulty of communicating between one world and another as a regrettable condition, which not even the solitary observer, equipped with privileged access to reality, was in a position to overcome. These early observations on the "impenetrability of human beings" may have constituted a psychological stimulus to Feyerabend's later theoretical reflections.[101] Be that as it may, in his mature work he allotted himself a position in some ways close to that of the "unworldly dreamer": comparing one (scientific) universe with

another, he emphasized their incommensurability. Cicero had expressed himself in somewhat similar terms; however, he had made it clear that the impossibility of establishing a hierarchy applied as between—and only as between—works that had all achieved artistic excellence: a conception quite distinct from the attitude that "anything goes" (however that motto may be interpreted).[102]

The Latin word *interpretatio* means "translation." An interpreter who compares various styles of thought, with the aim of highlighting the intrinsic differences between them, is carrying out a kind of translation. The term seems readily adapted to such a context: the comparison between styles and languages (suggested by that between styles and writing) generally leads to the recognition that both are diverse.[103] However, translation is also the most powerful argument against relativism. To be sure, each language constitutes a different world, and these worlds are to a certain extent incommensurable: but translations *are possible*. Our capacity to understand diverse styles can illuminate our capacity to understand other languages and other styles of thought, and vice versa.

15. I shall conclude this essay with an exercise in translation, which suggests the possibility of dialogue between three people who so far as I am aware never in fact entered into dialogue, direct or indirect, with one another.

The first is Simone Weil. In 1941, two years before her death, she made an entry in her *Notebooks* commenting on a passage in the *Timaeus* (28a):

> When a thing is perfectly beautiful, as soon as we fix our attention upon it, it represents unique and single beauty. Two Greek statues: the one we are looking at is beautiful, the other is not. So it is with Catholic faith, Platonic thought, Hindu thought, etc. Whichever one is looking at is beautiful, the others are not.

For Weil, the impossibility of comparison—often invoked, as we have seen, in relation to works of art—applies also not only to philosophy but to religion too:

> Each religion is alone true, that is to say, that at the moment we are thinking on it we must bring as much attention to bear on it

as if there were nothing else; in the same way, each landscape, each picture, each poem, etc., is alone beautiful. A "synthesis" of religions implies a lower quality of attention.[104]

The second is Adorno. One of the aphorisms in *Minima Moralia* (written in 1944) reads, in part, as follows:

> *De gustibus est disputandum.*—Even someone believing himself convinced of the non-comparability of works of art will find himself repeatedly involved in debates where works of art, and precisely those of highest and therefore incommensurable rank, are compared and evaluated one against the other. The objection that such considerations, which come about in a peculiarly compulsive way, have their source in mercenary instincts that would measure everything by the ell, usually signifies no more than that solid citizens, for whom art can never be irrational enough, want to keep serious reflection and the claims of truth far from the works. This compulsion to evaluate is located, however, in the works of art themselves. So much is true: they refuse to be compared. They want to annihilate one another. Not without cause did the ancients reserve the pantheon of the compatible to Gods or Ideas, but obliged works of art to enter the *agon*, each the mortal enemy of each. . . . For if the Idea of Beauty appears only in dispersed form among many works, each one nevertheless aims uncompromisingly to express the whole of beauty, claims it in its singularity and can never admit its dispersal without annulling itself. Beauty, as single, true and liberated from appearance and individuation, manifests itself not in the synthesis of all works, in the unity of the arts and of art, but only as a physical reality: in the downfall of art itself. This downfall is the goal of every work of art, in that it seeks to bring death to all others. That all art aims to end art, is another way of saying the same thing. It is this impulse to self-destruction inherent in works of art, their innermost striving towards an image of beauty free of appearance, that is constantly stirring up the aesthetic debates that are apparently so futile.[105]

Paul Valéry compared works of art in a museum to a "tumult of frozen creatures, each of which demands in vain the non-existence of all the others."[106] Adorno alludes implicitly to this passage, and brings it within the Hegelian concept of the "death of art": every work of art tends toward the truth and thus toward self-destruction, inasmuch as it partakes of the intolerance that is the nature of truth. By a different and even opposite route, Adorno's intellectualism arrives at a conclusion paradoxically close to that reached by Weil's mysticism: every work of art creates an empty space around itself, and we therefore need to perceive it in isolation.

This very position was Roberto Longhi's polemical target in his essay "Proposte per una critica d'arte" (1950):

> And so this is the moment to crush the lingering metaphysical flotsam and jetsam constituted by the principles of the absolute masterpiece and of its splendid isolation. The work of art, from the vase made by the Greek craftsman to the vault of the Sistine chapel, is always an exquisitely "relative" masterpiece. The work never stands alone; it is always a relationship. In the first place, it is at the least a relationship with another work of art. A work that stood alone in the world could never be understood as a human production, but would be regarded with veneration or with horror as a piece of magic, a taboo, the work of God or of a sorcerer rather than of man. And we have already suffered more than enough from the myth that artists are divine or super-divine beings rather than simple humans.[107]

In reading those clashing passages one is reminded of the distinction between _simpliciter_ and _secundum quid_ that Vasari took from Aristotelian and Scholastic tradition.[108] Weil and Adorno both insist (even though their starting points are different) that we must approach works of art as absolute and unrelated entities. Longhi, like Vasari before him, argues that works of art must be seen in a historical and relational perspective, _secundum quid_. Both of these positions seem to me indispensable, even while they are mutually incompatible: we cannot adopt them _simultaneously_. It is like the well-known figure of the duck-rabbit: the duck and the rabbit are both there, but you cannot see them both at the same time.[109] However, the two perspectives are united in an asymmetrical relationship. The "simple," direct, absolute vision can be expressed in the language of history, but the reverse is not the case.

7

Distance and Perspective

TWO METAPHORS

In 1994, an essay by Alan Sokal, professor of theoretical physics at New York University, was published in the journal *Social Text*. Sokal's long and densely referenced essay was titled "Transgressing the Boundaries: Toward a Transformative Hermeneutics of Quantum Gravity." Some time later, Sokal himself revealed that the essay had been a savage parody of the radically relativist positions nowadays fashionable among philosophers, anthropologists, literary critics, and historians (including historians of science). The episode had wide international repercussions, ending up on the front pages of the *New York Times* and *Le Monde*. Paul Boghossian, who teaches philosophy at New York University, contributed an article to the *Times Literary Supplement* (under the title "What the Sokal Hoax Ought to Teach Us") in which he included an example to illustrate the kind of target Sokal was aiming at in his parody of postmodern relativism. To a postmodernist, Boghossian wrote, the views of archaeologists concerning the origins of the first peoples to live on the American continent are no more or less true than the myths current among Native American peoples such as the Zuñi. Boghossian argued thus:

> [The] suggestion would be that the Zuñi and archaeological versions are equally true. . . . This is impossible, since they contradict each other. One says, or implies, that the first humans in the Americas came from Asia; the other says, or implies, that they did not, that they came from . . . a subterranean world of spirits. How could a claim and its denial both be true? If I say that the earth is flat, and you say that it is round, how could we both be right?
>
> Postmodernists like to respond to this sort of point by saying that both claims can be true because both are true relative to some perspective or other, and there can be no question of truth outside of perspectives. Thus, according to the Zuñi perspective, the first humans in the Americas came from a subterranean world; and according to the Western scientific perspective, the first humans in the Americas came from Asia.
>
> Since both are true according to some perspective or other, both are true.[1]

I should say at the outset that I am as critical as Sokal and Boghossian of the skeptical positions arrived at by the postmodernists. However, Boghossian's way of presenting their point of view seems to me to be simplistic. The argument that affirms a connection between truth and perspective deserves a more serious analysis, paying heed both to its metaphorical aspect and to its history—which of course begins long before postmodernism.[2] I shall look especially at three crucial episodes, the first dating from late antiquity and the other two from the modern age.

I

In recent decades, the relationships among history, memory, and forgetting have been discussed much more intensively than they ever were in the past. As many people have remarked, there are several reasons for this: the members of the last generation of witnesses to the extermination of European Jewry are reaching the end of their lives; nationalisms new and old are surfacing in Africa, Asia, and Europe; there is growing dissatisfaction with a dryly scientific approach to history; and so on. None of this can be denied, and it sufficiently justifies the attempt to situate memory within a less narrow historiographical vision than currently holds sway. However, memory and historiography do not necessarily converge. Here I shall insist on a different and even opposite theme: the irreducibility of memory to history.

In his book *Zakhor*, Yosef Yerushalmi has analyzed the link between memory and history, asking how "the command to remember [is] related to the writing of history" and noting that "historiography, an actual recording of historical events, is by no means the principal medium through which the collective memory of the Jewish people has been addressed or aroused."[3]

The Jews have engaged in a vital relationship with the past on one hand by way of the prophets, with their exploration of the meaning of history, and on the other (writes Yerushalmi) by way of a collective memory transmitted through ritual, which hands down

> not a series of facts to be contemplated at a distance, but a series of situations into which one could somehow be existentially drawn. This can perhaps be perceived most clearly in that quintessential exercise in Jewish group memory which is the Passover Seder . . . a symbolic enactment of an historical scenario whose three great acts structure the Haggadah that is read aloud: slavery—deliverance—ultimate redemption.

Yerushalmi concludes that the ahistorical, if not indeed frankly antihistorical, attitude so markedly characteristic of biblical and rabbinical tradition "did not inhibit the transmission of a vital Jewish past from one generation to the next, and Judaism lost neither its link to history nor its fundamentally historical orientation."[4]

"History" here means *res gestae*, not *historia rerum gestarum*: a lived experience of the past, not a detached knowledge of the past. In the ceremony of the Seder, Yerushalmi pointedly writes that "memory . . . is no longer recollection, which still preserves a sense of distance, but reactualization."[5]

This conclusion does not of course apply solely to Jewish tradition. In any culture, collective memory conveyed through rituals, ceremonies, and similar events reinforces a link with the past of a kind that involves no explicit reflection on the distance that separates us from it. We usually regard such reflection as becoming possible only with the emergence of historiography, a literary genre that aims among other things to record and preserve information about events worth remembering. It is not contingent that the term "history" derives from the Greek word *historia*, "inquiry." Thucydides was for long considered the first practitioner of history as scientific inquiry, and his narrative of the Peloponnesian Wars was seen as the supreme example of a neutral, objective approach. More recently, however, attention has been drawn to his role as an observer caught up in the events he was recounting. One essay on Thucydides' historical perspective maintains, for instance, that the famous passage (1.10.2), in which Thucydides anticipates the day, far in the future, when Athens and Sparta will be destroyed, results from the viewpoint that the historian adopted in much of his work as a consequence of the Athenians' defeat in 404. This defeat taught Thucydides that cities were not imperishable.[6]

It might be somewhat pedantically objected that the ancient Greeks had no word corresponding to "perspective," and no practice equivalent to that which was invented and theorized in fifteenth-century Florence.[7] There is certainly nothing to prevent our applying the term "perspective" to the passages in which Thucydides suggests, as a rule implicitly, his own subjective involvement in what appears to be a detached narrative. However, even these passages have very little in common with the postmodern idea that Boghossian criticizes, according to which either of two accounts of the origins of the first inhabitants of the Americas can be true "because both are true relative to some perspective or other." The distant origins of such a way of thinking may be traced back, as I shall attempt to show, to a tradition that was neither Jewish nor Greek.

Let us return to memory and ritual: more precisely, to a case in which the connection between these two elements is especially explicit. Celebrating the Passover before his death, Jesus says: "This is my body which is given for you; do this as a memorial of me" (Luke 22:19). These words, as has been pointed out, were certainly in accordance with Jewish tradition.[8] However, when Paul quoted them, in a slightly altered form, in the first letter to the Corinthians,

he radically reinterpreted them, transforming the body of Jesus into
what would much later come to be defined as the *corpus mysticum*,
the mystical body in which all believers were incorporated:

> When we bless "the cup of blessing," is it not a means of sharing
> in the blood of Christ? When we break the bread, is it not a
> means of sharing in the body of Christ? Because there is one loaf,
> we, many as we are, are one body; for it is one loaf of which we
> all partake. (1 Corinthians 10:16 ff.)

"All" meant, as we read in Galatians 3:28, everyone; it implied the
disappearance of every ethnic, social, or sexual distinction: "There is
no such thing as Jew and Greek, slave and freeman, male and female;
for you are all one person in Christ Jesus."[9]

In this universalist perspective, the relationship with the past, and
more especially with the Jewish past, took on new forms. Saint
Augustine defines the question in general terms in a passage of *De
Trinitate* (14.8.11) where he discusses the presence of seeds of the
divine image in the human soul:

> There are things . . . which are either in their own proper places,
> or have passed in time; although those that have passed no longer
> exist themselves, but only certain signs of them as passed, and
> these signs, when they are either seen or heard, indicate what was
> and what has passed. Such signs are either located in certain
> places, as the tombs of the dead and the like; or they are in reli-
> able books, as is all history of weight and approved authority; or
> they are in the minds of those who already know them.[10]

The power that governs signs in our minds is memory, the faculty
that Augustine treats with such wonderful profundity in the tenth
book of the *Confessions*. However, as has been pointed out, *"memoria"* in Augustine's writings had meanings different from—and to us,
less obvious than—those of the term as we use it. To him it denoted
the tombs of the martyrs or (as in the passage just cited) of the dead
in general; relics and reliquaries; and liturgical commemorations.[11]
All these signs and meanings were linked to the *Ecclesia sanctorum*,
the church of the saints, which Augustine defined as follows in the
Ennarationes in Psalmos (149.3):

The church of the saints is that which God first prefigured [*praes-ignavit*] before it was seen, and then set forth that it might be seen. The church of the saints was heretofore in writing, now it is in nations. Heretofore, the church of the saints was only read of; now it is both read of and seen. When it was only read of, it was believed; now it is seen, and is spoken against![12]

144

DISTANCE AND

PERSPECTIVE

Two Metaphors

Ecclesia sanctorum erat antea in codicibus, modo in gentibus. One of Augustine's contemporaries, Nicetas of Aquileia (ca. 340–414), gave even clearer emphasis to the continuity between the Old and the New Testaments, between what might be read in holy books and what might be experienced in reality:

> What else is the Church but the congregation of all the Saints? From the beginning of the world, the Patriarchs Abraham, Isaac and Jacob; the apostles; the martyrs; and the other just who were and are and will be, are one Church, because sanctified by one faith and conversation, signed by one Spirit, they are made into one body; the head of which is Christ, as it is written.[13]

In Augustine's thought, the Jewish and the Christian past are connected through the notion of *figura*.[14] In his treatise *De doctrina Christiana*, Augustine used this as a means to clarify several passages from the Gospels that are difficult to understand. For instance, the apparently monstrous words of John 6:53—"unless you eat the flesh of the Son of Man and drink his blood you can have no life in you"—are said to be "a figure of speech directing that we are to participate in the Lord's passion and treasure up in grateful and salutary remembrance the fact that His flesh was crucified and wounded for us."[15]

Elsewhere in *De doctrina Christiana*, however, Augustine points out that figurative interpretations of the Bible can be taken to excess. He warns against projecting into the Bible the customs of the time and place in which we, its readers, live:

> Since human nature is inclined to appraise sins not by the measure of their malice, but, instead, by the measure of its own customs, it often happens that a man considers as reprehensible only those acts which the men of his own country and age usually protest against and denounce; and he holds as acceptable and

commendable only those allowed by the usage of those with whom he lives. The result is that, if Scripture either teaches something which is at variance with the custom of its listeners, or censures what is not at variance, they consider it a figurative expression, provided that the authority of its word has a hold upon their minds. But, Scripture commands only charity.[16]

This principle implies that "we must prudently take into account what is proper for places, circumstances, and persons [*quod igitur locis et temporibus et personis conveniat*], so that we may not indiscreetly convict them of sin."[17]

There are cases, Augustine observes, where we must read the Bible at once literally and figuratively, because customs have changed since those times:

> Upright men of former times represented and foretold the kingdom of heaven under the guise of an earthly kingdom. Since it was in order to provide sufficiently numerous descendants, the practice of one man having several wives at the same time was unobjectionable. . . . And anything of that kind that is there related [i.e., in Scripture] is understood not only in its historical and literal application, but also in its figurative and prophetic implication [*non solum historice ac proprie, sed etiam figurate ac prophetice acceptum*], and must always be interpreted toward that purpose of charity, whether it pertains to God, our neighbour, or both.[18]

We are obliged to read the Bible at once prophetically and historically, because God has accommodated himself to the history of the human race.[19] The attitude that Augustine adopted toward the sacrifices of the Jews was inspired by the need, here articulated in respect of the polygamy of the patriarchs, to judge customs according to time and circumstance. The Roman senator Volusianus once posed a provocative question, asking how it was that God had found the new sacrifices of the Christians acceptable and had rejected the old sacrifices: perhaps God had changed his mind? In his reply, sent to Imperial Commissioner Flavius Marcellinus, Augustine again invoked the idea of God's accommodation to the human race.[20]

Augustine wrote as follows:

Anyone can see what a wide application this principle has, if he relies on and does not fail to observe the difference between beauty and fitness, which is spread far and wide, so to speak, in the generality of things. For, beauty is looked upon and praised for its own sake, and its contrary is ugliness and unsightliness. But fitness, whose opposite is unfitness, depends on something else, and is, in a sense, fastened to it; it is not prized for its own value, but for that to which it is joined. Doubtless, the words "suitable" and "unsuitable" are synonyms, or are so considered. Let us now apply what we said before to this point under discussion. The sacrifice which God had commanded was fitting in those early times, but now it is not so. Therefore, He prescribed another one, fitting for this age, since He knew much better than man what is suitably adapted to each age [*novit quid cuique tempori accommodate adhibeatur*], and, being the unchangeable Creator as well as Ruler of the world of change, He knows as well what to give and when to give, to add to, to take away, to withdraw, to increase, or to diminish, until the beauty of the entire world, of which the individual parts are suitable each for its own time, swells, as it were, into a mighty song of some unutterable musician, and from thence the true adorers of God rise to the eternal contemplation of His face, even in the time of faith.[21]

To understand this fundamentally important passage, we must remember that Augustine's first piece of writing was a treatise, *De pulchro et apto* (On the beautiful and the fitting), dedicated to a Roman orator who had been born in Syria and educated in Greece (*Confessions* 4.13.20). In his *Confessions* (4.15.4), Augustine refers to the contents of this treatise, already lost then and never since recovered, and with hindsight criticizes the Manichean viewpoint he had adopted in it. From the title, and from Augustine's concise reference, we can see that the treatise must have turned on the difference between the beautiful and the fitting or suitable ("*pulchrum*" as against "*aptum*" or "*accommodatum*").[22] Plato discusses this distinction in the *Greater Hippias*, and it had undoubtedly entered into the traditions of Platonism. Augustine's knowledge of Greek was slight, however, and he must have come upon these themes indirectly, by way of the writings of Cicero, which he read passionately in his youth.[23] In the passage we have just noted, Augustine is echoing a long argument developed by Cicero in his *De oratore*. This begins by referring deferentially to Plato, but soon takes a decidedly anti-Platonic turn.[24] Cicero starts by remarking that there is in nature "a multiplicity of things that are different from one another and yet are esteemed as having a similar nature."[25]

This apparently innocuous principle was applied first to the arts (visual and verbal), and then to rhetoric, leading to the point where the notion of literary or rhetorical genre was transformed into something close to what we call individual style.[26] Poets such as Aeschylus, Sophocles, and Euripides each have their own incomparable excellence; all artists achieve perfection in the way particular to them. All in all, says Cicero, "if we could scrutinize all the orators from every place and every time, would we not conclude that there are as many genres as there are orators?" (3.34).

There is no single perfect kind, Cicero concludes: it is for the orator to choose, from time to time, whichever is suitable to the circumstances.

Augustine had learned—first as a student, and later as a professor of rhetoric—to employ technical terms such as *"aptum"* and *"accommodatum,"* which are Latin translations of the Greek word *"prepon."*[27] His development and exposition of Christian theology was strongly influenced by this education in rhetoric. This applies especially to his notion of divine accommodation, whose specifically rhetorical origin is plainly evident in his indirect answer to the Roman senator Volusianus. In his analysis of the relationship between Christians and Jews, Augustine drew on a conceptual schema derived from his youthful reflections on the relation between *pulchrum* and *aptum*— between what is universally beautiful and what is fitting. Cicero had insisted that in the realm of the visual and verbal arts, excellence and diversity are not incompatible. His arguments, however, despite a reference to orators "present and past," were essentially achronic. Augustine made use of the same model, but extended its application into the dimension of time. Nature, like the activity of humans, "change according to the needs of times by following a certain rhythm, but this does not affect the rhythm of their change."[28] Here Augustine turns to the time of history, describing God, "the unchangeable Creator as well as Ruler of the world of change," as being like an "unutterable musician."[29] Cicero's reflections on the nature of art and poetry had opened the way that led Augustine to praise the beauty of the course of human experience (*"universi saeculi pulchritudo"*), comparing it to a melodious song: a metaphor that allowed him to reconcile divine immutability and historical change, the truth of Jewish sacrifices in their own time and the truth of the Christian sacraments that had replaced them.

Although the ancient historians, from Thucydides to Polybius, had emphasized that human nature was invariable, they had understood that institutions and customs change. This was something of which Augustine was also aware. In *De doctrina Christiana* (3.12.19), he remarks: "It was a disgrace among the ancient Romans to wear tunics that reached to the ankles and had long sleeves; now it is unseemly for those of noble birth, when they wear tunics, not to have that kind"—by no means a banality, since this example of historical change follows, and reinforces, the justification he offers for the polygamy practiced by the Patriarchs.[30] Augustine generally regarded the Jewish past as a special case, linked to the Christian present by a typological rather than an analogical relationship.[31] However, in order to express the idea that constituted the cornerstone of figurative reading—namely, that the Old Testament was at once true and superseded—Augustine had recourse to Cicero's argument that artistic excellence is intrinsically resistant to comparison.

"If Herodotus was the father of history," Yerushalmi reminds us, "the fathers of meaning in history were the Jews."[32] However, neither the Greeks nor the Jews ever entertained anything comparable to the notion of historical perspective with which we are familiar.[33] Only a Christian such as Augustine, reflecting on the destined relationship between Christians and Jews, and between the Old and New Testaments, could have formulated the idea that became, by way of the Hegelian concept of *Aufhebung*, a crucial element of our historical consciousness: namely, that the past must be understood both on its own terms and as a link in the chain that in the last analysis leads up to ourselves.[34] I am proposing that we can see, in this ambivalence, a secularized projection of the Christian ambivalence toward the Jews.

II

The beauty of the course of human experience, *universi saeculi pulchritudo*, is compared by Augustine to a melody based on a harmonious variety of sounds. He wrote in *De vera religione* that the succession of the centuries might be likened to a song that no one is able to hear in its entirety.[35] We are at once reminded of the importance of music in the reflections on time set forth in the *Confessions*. Faith is based on hearing *("fides ex auditu")*: in this way, Augustine was able to counterpose human history, the time of faith and of listening, to eternity, the timeless contemplation of God.[36]

Today, however, we are irresistibly drawn to translate Augustine's acoustic metaphors into visual metaphors that turn on distance and perspective. It is obvious enough why this sensory shift has taken place. Printing has made images and books infinitely more accessible and has played its part in what has been called the triumph of vision or, more recently, the "scopic regime of modernity."[37] I wonder, however, whether such a vague category as this can really explain our propensity for visual metaphors. Far more thought-provoking is the parallel, often emphasized by Panofsky, between the invention of linear perspective in the Italian Renaissance and the emergence at the same time of a critical attitude toward the past.[38] To be sure, this is no more than a convergence, though a suggestive one. However, Gisela Bock, in a most perceptive essay, has identified a specific link between the two terms, in a place—the dedication of Machiavelli's *Il Principe* (The Prince)—where no one had looked for it.[39]

The Prince was written in 1513–1514, and published in 1532, five years after Machiavelli's death. It at once achieved fame, success, and notoriety. The "little work" *(opusculo)*, as its author called it, was originally dedicated to Giuliano de' Medici; when he died, it was dedicated instead to Lorenzo di Piero de' Medici, Duke of Urbino and nephew of Lorenzo the Magnificent. The posthumous printed edition of *The Prince*, produced in the Medici circle, still carried this dedication to the Duke of Urbino, who had died in 1519.[40] Short but densely written, it is centrally concerned with Machiavelli's awareness that, as a private citizen of humble birth, he was showing considerable audacity in setting forth rules for the exercise of princely power. He defends himself against possible criticism as follows:

Nor I hope will it be considered presumptuous for a man of low and humble status to dare discuss and lay down the law about how princes should rule; because, just as men who are sketching the landscape put themselves down in the plain to study the nature of the mountains and the highlands, and to study the low-lying land they put themselves high on the mountains, so, to comprehend fully the nature of the people, one must be a prince, and to comprehend fully the nature of princes one must be an ordinary citizen.[41]

It has been convincingly argued that we should see in this passage an allusion to Leonardo, who made maps and drew "landscape."[42] Between October and December 1502, Machiavelli was the official ambassador of the Republic of Florence at the court of Cesare Borgia, Duke of Romagna, in Imola. While there, he may well have met Leonardo, whom Borgia had engaged as a military engineer. A few months later, the map of Imola that Leonardo produced offered exceptional evidence of his ability to depict landscape from above.

In May 1504, Machiavelli, in his capacity as secretary to the Chancellery of the Republic, approved the payment of an advance to Leonardo. This was toward the sum payable for a fresco that would represent, on the walls of the Palazzo della Signoria, the battle of Anghiari, an episode in Florentine history. The fresco was never completed, and has not survived. In Leonardo's *Codex Atlanticus*, we find a brief description of the battle written in the hand of Machiavelli's secretary Agostino Vespucci. We may speculate, but it is unfortunately impossible to assemble these scraps of evidence into a coherent whole. Still, Machiavelli's passion for "things as they are in real truth," like his contemptuous judgment on authors who describe ideal, purely imaginary republics (see chapter 15 of *The Prince*), may have been strengthened, even if it was not inspired, by Leonardo's detached, analytical attitude to reality.[43]

It is in chapter 15 of *The Prince* that Machiavelli famously writes that "a man who wants to act virtuously in every way necessarily comes to grief among so many who are not virtuous." The tragic awareness that reality is as it is—so often interpreted as cynicism—derived from an impassioned advocacy of analytical detachment. Here is where we find the parallel with those who "sketch the landscape," and implicitly (by way of the insistence on point of view) with the practice of perspective. Machiavelli was suggesting that different points of view produced different representations of political reality. The representations derived from the respective positions of the prince and the populace were equally limited: objectivity was attainable only by one who observed reality from outside, from a distance, from a peripheral, marginal position—such (we may add) as Machiavelli occupied in 1513–1514.

It can be seen that we are a very long way from the Augustinian model, and not only because Machiavelli's cognitive metaphor was based on sight rather than on hearing. Far more important is the difference between a model based on divine accommodation, in which truth (Judaism) leads to a higher truth (Christianity), and a purely secular model, based on conflict.[44] The contrast between representations of political reality derives from the nature of things, which is inherently conflictual: Machiavelli's awareness of this came, as he wrote in the dedication to *The Prince*, from "a long acquaintance with contemporary affairs [*cose moderne*] and a continuous study of the ancient world."[45] His involvement in political struggle and his study of Roman history suggested to Machiavelli the entirely new thesis, expounded in chapter 1, 4 of the *Discourses* (and later developed in the *Storie Fiorentine*), that "the disunion of the Plebs and the Roman Senate made that republic free and powerful."[46]

The Prince achieved such great and wide fame and success (and was the subject of such condemnation and refutation)[47] that it may seem a waste of time to search for specific echoes of the passage in the dedication where Machiavelli likens himself to "men who are sketching the landscape." We might think that we need look no further than "the scopic regime of modernity." However, a less hasty investigation turns out to produce unexpected results.

In 1646, over a century after its posthumous publication, *The Prince* was the central subject of an exchange of letters between Descartes and his devoted pupil Elizabeth, Princess of the Palatinate. After reading and commenting on a draft of the *Traité des passions de l'âme*, Elizabeth asked Descartes what his thoughts were concerning *la vie civile*—political and social life, as we might put it nowadays.[48] The two (one in Holland, the other in Berlin) then decided that they should read Machiavelli's *Prince* together. In August or September 1646, Descartes sent Elizabeth a detailed commentary on various passages in *The Prince*, without mentioning the book's title or its author. This caution was understandable, since *The Prince*, listed in the index of prohibited books, was regarded by Catholics and Protestants alike as an impious and heretical work (not to mention unsuitable for a princess). In order to conceal the

fact that they were corresponding on such a scandalous topic, Elizabeth asked Descartes to address these letters to her younger sister,

Sofia, who was an adolescent. Descartes complied with the request,
and at the end of his letter suggested prudently that in future, Elizabeth should write to him in code.[49]

We shall shortly see the pertinence of these details. For the
moment, let us just note that the passage on the drawing of landscape is among those that Descartes quotes (in French) from *The
Prince* and discusses. Here as in some other places, he expresses his
disagreement:

> Now the pencil represents only such things as can be seen from a
> distance; but the main reasons for the actions of princes often lie
> in circumstances so special that they are not to be imagined
> except by one who is himself a Prince or has long been a sharer
> of their secrets.[50]

Thus Descartes, by emphasizing the special position of princes,
reinstates the social and cognitive hierarchy denied by Machiavelli's
symmetrical metaphor.[51]

The correspondence between Descartes and Elizabeth remained
in the possession of Sofia, who later became Electress of Hanover.
Some decades later it was to be discovered by her protégé Leibniz, a
zealous seeker-out of Descartes' manuscripts and letters.[52] Leibniz,
who of course knew *The Prince* very well,[53] must have been struck by
Descartes' comments on the passage concerning the depiction of
landscape. This conjoint reading of Descartes and Machiavelli
underlies a famous passage in the *Monadology*:

> And as the same town, looked at from various sides, appears
> quite different and becomes as it were numerous in aspects [*per-*
> *spectivement*]; even so, as a result of the infinite number of simple
> substances, it is as if there were so many different universes,
> which, nevertheless, are nothing but aspects [*perspectives*] of a sin-
> gle universe, according to the special point of view of each
> Monad.[54]

For Leibniz as for Machiavelli, the metaphor of perspective allowed
the development of a model of cognition based on a plurality of

points of view. However, whereas Machiavelli's model had been based on conflict, Leibniz's was based on the harmonious coexistence of an infinite multiplicity of substances. Such coexistence implied, in the last analysis, the nonexistence of evil. In the *Theodicy*, Leibniz draws a comparison between apparently shapeless images— "those inventions using perspective, in which certain beautiful drawings seem nothing but confusion, until they are restored to the correct point of view, or looked at by way of a certain mirror or lens"— and "the apparent deformities of our little Worlds [which] are reunited in beauty in the great world": that is, in God.[55] In the various versions of historicism, echoes of these theological themes may be heard. The theologian and philosopher Johann Martin Chladenius, who developed Leibniz's thought along original lines, stands right at the beginning of this intellectual tradition.[56] Historical sources, when they are the product of human intentions, and the writings of historians are both bound up, according to Chladenius, with particular "points of view" (*Sehe-Punckte*): an expression that, Chladenius observes, Leibniz was probably the first to use in a general as opposed to a strictly optical sense.[57] However, Chladenius, when he insists that the accounts of any historical event must diverge, as well as on the idea that they can ultimately be harmonized, reveals that he had read Leibniz with Machiavelli in mind: "A loyal subject, a rebel, and a foreigner, a courtier, a city-dweller and a peasant, will each have their own way of perceiving a rebellion."[58]

Chladenius's observation, which seems banal enough to us (but which for a long time was anything but banal), formulated anew Machiavelli's counterposition of the populace's view of the prince and the prince's view of the populace. This example shows that the cognitive models we are discussing can be adequately evaluated only in a long-term perspective: an expression I employ not for the sake of a silly play on words but for reasons I shall soon explain.

Simplifying, we may say that the three models developed by Augustine in the fifth century, by Machiavelli in the sixteenth, and by Leibniz in the seventeenth can be placed under the signs, respectively, of accommodation, of conflict, and of multiplicity. A few examples will be enough to illustrate the lasting influence that all three have had. Hegel's philosophy of history combines Machiavelli's conflictual model with a secularized version of Augustine's model, based on accommodation.[59] It is plain enough that we find in

Marx, who greatly admired Machiavelli, a reworking of the latter's conflictual model.[60] We need hardly remind ourselves that in Nietzsche's battles against positivistic objectivity, perspectivism performed a crucial role.[61] Metaphors connected with distance and perspective have played and still do play an important part in our intellectual tradition.

III

I ended the first section of this essay by noting the ambivalence felt by Christians toward the Jews. This ambivalence goes to the roots of Christianity, right from its beginnings. In using this arboreal metaphor, I am of course making an allusion to Paul's letter to the Romans (11, 16 ff.). Here Paul, the Jewish "apostle to the Gentiles," compares the Gentiles converted to Christianity to a wild olive tree, grafted onto a cultivated olive tree (the Jews) whose branches have been cut off because of their "unbelief"—that is, because they have not recognized Jesus as the Messiah. This same attitude, combining distance and continuity, subsequently expressed itself in the Christians' claim to be *"verus Israel"* (the true Israel): a polemical self-definition aimed on one hand at the Jews and on the other at those Christians who, like Marcion in the second century, sharply opposed Jesus, the benevolent God, and the malevolent God of the Old Testament.[62] Marcion's ideas have never completely disappeared from Christian culture, or subculture, even if they have never succeeded in gaining predominance. Marcion's defeat is symbolized in the Christian Bible, where the physical contiguity of the two testaments (even if the "old" is allotted merely the position of precursor to the "new") is displayed in a single volume or *codex*.[63]

It was a defeat that had incalculable consequences. Continuity and distance, nearness and hostility, continued to characterize the relationship—which is perhaps unique in the history of the great religions—between Christians and Jews. All this is obvious. Less obvious are the consequences, beginning with the argument developed by Augustine to demonstrate that Jewish ceremonies were at once true and superseded—a conclusion that must have seemed quite simply absurd to a learned heathen such as Volusianus, the Roman senator whose questions it was intended to answer.

In *De civitate Dei* (12.4.1), Augustine rejects the cyclical theory of history together with the dictum in *Ecclesiastes* that "there is nothing new under the sun." We know, he declares, that Plato taught once and once only, at Athens, because we know that Jesus Christ died once, and once only, for our sins.[64] The insistence on the uniqueness of the Incarnation gave rise to a new perception of human history. The kernel of the current historiographical paradigm is a secularized version of the model of accommodation, to which may be added a variable dose of conflict and multiplicity. Metaphors such as perspective, point of view, and so on vividly express this attitude toward the past. I myself, the reader will have remarked, have not been able to forgo the use of such metaphors: one small proof that they are omnipresent in current historiographical discourse. However, their secular garb should not conceal their origin, which goes back to Augustine. Our way of knowing the past is imbued with the Christian attitude of superiority toward the Jews. In other terms: the phrase *"verus Israel"* (the true Israel), inasmuch as it is the self-definition of Christianity, is also the matrix of the conception of historical truth that remains—and here I deliberately use an all-embracing term—our own.

This discovery made me very uneasy: a feeling that others, Jewish or not, may perhaps share. In the end, however, the context in which ideas originate only partly determines the uses to which they are later put. In *De doctrina Christiana*, Augustine takes the action of the sons of Israel in plundering the gold and silver jewels of the Egyptians (Exodus 12:35–36) as a model of the attitude Christians should have taken to the heathen cultural inheritance. Every cultural inheritance, we well know, is subject to continuous appropriation and redevelopment. Who will plunder and appropriate our notion of history, possibly rejecting its conceptual core, embodied in the metaphor of perspective?

I have no answer to this question. One thing, however, is beyond doubt: two of the three models identified so far have recently been called in question, though in milieux of widely differing importance. Fundamentalists of every kind attack the model based on accommodation; the model based on conflict is contemptuously dismissed as a piece of antic by those who talk, or used to talk, about "the end of history."[65] The model based on multiplicity, by contrast, becomes ever more fashionable, albeit in a skeptical version that sees each social group, determined by gender, ethnic origin, religion, and so forth, as adhering to a set of values of which it is, in the last analysis, the prisoner. Perspective, we are told, is good, because it emphasizes the element of subjectivity; but it is also bad, because it emphasizes intellectual distance, rather than emotional closeness (or identification).[66] It is this anti-intellectualistic climate that has fostered the line of argument that I referred to at the start, according to which memory, being closer to lived experience, is better able than history to establish a vital relationship with the past.

An adequate discussion of these attitudes would require another essay.[67] I shall make just one remark here. Both fundamentalists and neo-skeptics reject or ignore, though each for their own different and opposed reasons, what has made perspective into such a powerful cognitive metaphor: the tension between subjective point of view and objective and verifiable truths, guaranteed by reality (as in Machiavelli) or by God (as in Leibniz). If this tension can only be kept open, the notion of perspective will cease to be a stumbling block between scientists and social scientists and become instead a space to meet—a square where we can converse, discuss, and disagree.

8

To Kill a Chinese Mandarin

THE MORAL IMPLICATIONS OF DISTANCE

The opposition between the laws of nature and history has been bequeathed to us, like so much else, by the ancient Greeks. In a famous passage of the *Rhetoric*, Aristotle wrote:

> Just and unjust actions have been defined in reference to two kinds of law and in reference to persons spoken of in two senses. I call law on the one hand specific, on the other common, the latter being unwritten, the former written, *specific* being what has been defined by each people in reference to themselves, and *common* that which is based on nature [*kata physis*]; for there is in nature a common principle of the just and unjust that all people in some way divine, even if they have no association or commerce with each other, for example, what Antigone in Sophocles' play seems to speak of when she says that though forbidden, it is just to bury Polyneices,

since this is just by nature: "For not now and yesterday, but always, ever / Lives this rule, and no one knows whence it appeared."[1]

The Moral

Implications

of Distance

Aristotle is analyzing the various branches of rhetoric: deliberative, judicial, and epideictic (intended, that is, to praise or to reprove). It is in his discussion of judicial rhetoric that he formulates the opposition between specific, written laws and the general unwritten law. Aristotle wastes no time demonstrating the existence of unwritten natural law: if it is natural, it self-evidently exists. One should note that the Loeb Classical Library translation (1926) ("as all *men* in a manner divine . . . no *man* knoweth") has to our ears an undertone of sexism that is not in the original Greek. The point is not unimportant: both Aristotle and Sophocles use neuter terms (*"oudeis,"* no one"; *"pantes,"* everyone) in passages that refer directly to female characters like Antigone, or invoke such characters as examples. These neuter terms remind us that natural law includes both women and men. Antigone speaks in the voice of the universal; the written (and masculine) law in whose name Creon prohibits Polyneices' funeral, by contrast, is—according to Aristotle—"a specific law" (*nomon ton men idion*).

Aristotle seems to want to tell us that what is "based on nature" (*kata physis*) is not confined to particular places and times. However, a different point of view is suggested in some passages in the second book of the *Rhetoric*. Here, Aristotle is analyzing the various emotions called into play by the orator as he seeks to convince his audience. For example (1386a), pity:

> Now those for whom people feel pity are the following and those like them. They pity their acquaintances, unless they are very closely connected to their own household, and in that case they feel for them as they feel about their own future suffering . . . [For] the dreadful is something different from the pitiable and capable of expelling pity . . . for people no longer feel pity when something dreadful is near themselves. And they pity those like themselves in age, in character, in habits, in rank, in birth; for in all these cases something seems more to apply also to the self; for in general, one should grasp here, too, that people pity things happening to others in so far as they fear for themselves. And since

sufferings are pitiable when they appear near at hand and since people do not feel pity, or not in the same way, about things ten thousand years in the past or future, neither anticipating nor remembering them, necessarily those are more pitiable who contribute to the effect by gestures and cries and display of feelings and generally in their acting; for they make the evil seem near by making it appear before [our] eyes either as something about to happen or as something that has happened, and things are more pitiable when having just happened or going to happen in a short space of time.

159

TO KILL A

CHINESE MANDARIN

The Moral

Implications

of Distance

We encounter a similar argument in the section devoted to envy (1388a):

[People] envy those near to them in time and place and age and reputation, whence it has been said that "Kinship, too, knows how to envy." And [they envy] those they rival; for they rival those mentioned, [feeling] the same way toward them and on the same grounds, but no one rivals people ten thousand years in the future or dead nor those who live at the Pillars of Heracles nor those they or others regard as inferior or much superior.[2]

Aristotle takes it as obvious that the emotions analyzed in the second book of the *Rhetoric* are "based on nature," *kata physis*. Nonetheless, he ends up setting both historical and geographical limits to them. According to the myth recounted by Plato, the kingdom of Atlantis flourished nine thousand years before Solon's time.[3] Aristotle uses a still larger number, "ten thousand years" (*murioston*), to convey the idea of an immensely distant time, past or future, which would preclude any possibility of our identifying positively or negatively with the emotions of the human beings who lived in it. Something more or less similar is implied by the allusion to the Pillars of Heracles: legendary traditions (which would be one day connected to Aristotle's pupil Alexander the Great) held that the lands and seas that lay beyond the limits of the Mediterranean were peopled by savages or monsters.

What Aristotle says about the chronological and geographical limits of pity and envy cannot be reduced to an opposition between reality and myth. Mythical beings, especially when they appeared on the stage, could arouse deep feelings. Aristotle remarked in the *Poetics* that tragedy deals with "incidents that awaken fear and pity" (*phoberon kai eleeinon*) (1452b), and he went on to add that deeds

160

TO KILL A

CHINESE MANDARIN

The Moral

Implications

of Distance

regarded as fearful or pitiable must of course involve people who are either friends to one another, or enemies, or neither. Now if a man injures his enemy, there is nothing pitiable either in his act or in his intention, except in so far as suffering is inflicted; nor is there if they are indifferent to each other. But when the sufferings involve those who are near and dear, when for example brother kills brother, son father, mother son, or son mother, or if such a deed is contemplated, or something else of the kind is actually done, then we have a situation of the kind to be aimed at.[4]

"Out of sight, out of mind," as the English say; as the Italians say, "*Fratelli, coltelli*"—where there are brothers, there are knives. These two proverbs help us to grasp the contradiction implicit in the passages we have just quoted from the *Rhetoric* and the *Poetics*. Too great a distance gives rise to indifference; too great proximity may awaken compassion, or provoke murderous rivalry. This ambivalence, expressed with extraordinary vigor in Greek drama, was part of everyday experience in the society Aristotle lived in: a limited, confined society based on face-to-face relationships.

2. Let us turn now to a very different text, written two thousand years later. Diderot's *Entretien d'un père avec ses enfants, ou du danger de se mettre au-dessus des lois* (Conversation of a father with his children, or the danger of setting oneself above the law) was first published in 1773.[5] In a broken, frantic style, inspired by Sterne's *Tristram Shandy*, Diderot describes a conversation that takes place one calm winter's evening in his father's house. People come and go, all of them telling of events and memories that bear on a single problem: the relationship between the written code of the law and moral principles— between, as Aristotle would have put it, "specific" laws and the "common" law, which are represented respectively by Diderot *père* and Diderot *fils*.[6] Do we have the right to break the written code in order to protect the general principles of morality? Is it allowable for a doctor to refuse to treat a wounded criminal? Is it morally legitimate to destroy an unjust will that would deprive a group of poor people of

their inheritance to the sole benefit of a rich egoist? When he reworked the text of the *Entretien*, subsequent to its original 1773 publication, Diderot inserted a digression that is not very well linked to the main text. A hatmaker arrives and tells his story. For eighteen years he tended to his sick wife; when she died, and he found himself penniless, he appropriated the dowry that by law should have gone to her relatives. Has his action been right or wrong? A discussion begins, in which Diderot *père* insists that the hatter should restore what he has wrongfully taken. To this advice the hatter replies brusquely:

161

TO KILL A

CHINESE MANDARIN

The Moral

Implications

of Distance

> "No, sire, I shall go away to Geneva."
> "And do you suppose you will leave your remorse behind here?"
> "I do not know, but I shall go to Geneva."
> "Go where you will, your conscience will await you there."

The hatmaker departed; and our talk turned to his strange response. We agreed that distance in place and time perhaps to some extent weakened feeling and awareness of all kinds, even the consciousness of crime. The murderer transported to the coast of China is too far away to make out the corpse he has left bleeding on the banks of the Seine. Perhaps remorse is engendered less by our horror at ourselves than by our fear of others, less by the shame we feel over our deeds than by our knowledge that blame and punishment would be the consequence should they be discovered.[7]

In the *Supplement to the Voyage da Bougainville*, Diderot was to maintain that sexuality, since it is a natural faculty, should be subject to no kind of legal constraint. In the *Entretien d'un père avec ses enfants*, he seems to suggest the same thing about murder. Diderot's uncompromising observation that "distance in place and time perhaps to some extent weakens feeling and awareness of all kinds" seems a word-for-word echo of the passage quoted earlier from Arisotle's *Rhetoric*; but here Aristotle's thought is taken to its logical extreme. There is nothing strange in this. In his earlier *Discourse on Dramatic Poetry* (1758), Diderot had described Aristotle as a philosopher who proceeded in an orderly manner and formulated general principles, leaving it to others to draw their consequences and apply them.[8] One instance of such a consequence would be Diderot's own move here, where he transforms the lack of compassion, which Aristotle had seen as a result of "distance in place or time," into the presumptive lack of remorse for murder, which might follow from the same causes. Human beings who are far apart and unable to communicate turn themselves into split egos—the theme that inspired two of Diderot's finest works, *Rameau's Nephew* and *The Paradox of Acting*.

162

TO KILL A

CHINESE MANDARIN

The Moral

Implications

of Distance

This turning inward takes place across a geographical space—the distance from France to China—infinitely wider than the Mediterranean world Aristotle wrote of. But why China? This mention of China in the discussion of a fictitious moral case has been thought to show that Diderot perhaps took the example he uses from a Jesuit casuistical treatise.[9] The hypothesis is attractive, though as yet unproven. Wherever he found the anecdote, Diderot made it the starting point for a moral experiment that may be compared to the one he had thought up twenty years earlier in the *Lettre sur les aveugles, à l'usage de ceux qui voient* (Letter on the blind, for the use of those who can see):

> I suspect that the blind in general lack humanity; for of all the outward signs that awaken compassion in us and convey the idea of pain, they are affected only by cries. To a blind person, what is the difference between a man urinating and a man who bleeds but does not cry out? Do not we too cease to feel compassion once distance, or the smallness of objects, produces the effect on us that the lack of sight produces on the blind? How greatly our virtues depend upon how we feel things and upon the degree to which we are affected by what is outside us! And so I doubt not that, but for the fear of punishment, many people would find it less hard to kill a man at a distance from which he appeared no larger than a swallow, than they would to slit a bullock's throat with their own hands. If we feel compassion for the sufferings of a horse, but have no scruples about squashing an ant, does not this same principle determine our feeling?[10]

There is an obvious analogy between the distance that separates France from China and the sensory deprivation that afflicts the blind.[11] The lack of humanity and compassion which (according to Diderot) results from either situation calls into question the presumption that morality has an eternally established character. As Diderot exclaimed to Mme de Puisieux, the dedicatee of the *Lettre sur les aveugles*, "Ah, Madam, the morality of the blind—how different it is from our own!"[12] Morality, in Diderot's view, is the result of physically and historically specific circumstances and constraints. The same two words *"crainte"* and *"châtiment,"* "fear" and "punishment," echo across a twenty-year gap, explaining both how a hypothetical murderer might quit Paris for China and how someone might kill a man who was placed at such a distance that he looked no larger than a swallow. And then, with a sudden shift typical of his mode of reasoning, Diderot allows this analogy to introduce a new theme that raises the question of a quite different kind of gap—that involved in human attitudes toward animals. Even when we look at animals, says Diderot, our perceptions of size and distance have an influence. He does not make clear what consequences are to be drawn from this apparently innocent principle; and they are far from obvious. Should we extend to the ants the pity we feel for a suffering horse? Or should we rather regard the horse's sufferings with the same lack of compassion that we, human beings, feel for ants?

There is no doubt that the former conclusion is more in harmony with Diderot's stress on the passions and sensibility—"that disposition," as he wrote (undoubtedly with himself in mind), "which accompanies constitutional weakness, and which results from the movements of the diaphragm, the liveliness of the imagination, the delicacy of the nervous organization; which is always ready to pity, to shudder, to wonder and to fear, to grow anxious and to weep," and so on.[13] However, one eighteenth-century reader explicitly drew the other, opposite conclusion, with its implication that our indifference to the sufferings of insects should be applied universally. Franco Venturi, the great historian of the European Enlightenment, acutely observed (in his youthful work *Jeunesse de Diderot*) that Sade was strongly influenced by the arguments against religion set forth in the *Lettre sur les aveugles*.[14] It may be that we should even go so far as to say that we cannot imagine Sade's philosophy without Diderot's *Lettre sur les aveugles*.[15] Here is how Sade defends the legitimacy of murder in *La Philosophie dans le boudoir*:

What is man, and how does he differ from the other plants and animals of nature? Not at all, surely. Placed like them by chance

163

TO KILL A

CHINESE MANDARIN

The Moral

Implications

of Distance

164

TO KILL A

CHINESE MANDARIN

The Moral

Implications

of Distance

in the world, he is born in the same manner; reproduces, grows and dwindles as they do; like them, he arrives at old age and falls into nothingness at the end of the term set by nature to the existence of every animal species, as a result of his organic constitution. If he is so close in kind that the eye of the philosopher is quite unable to discern any dissimilarity, then it must be fully as wrong to kill an animal as to kill a man, or rather there can be as little wrong in either case; and it is only the prejudice of our pride which sets the two apart. But nothing is more sadly absurd than the prejudice of pride. . . . If it is impossible in nature that creatures should live forever, then it is a law of nature that they must be destroyed. . . . At the moment when a large animal breathes its last, small animals are formed, and the life of these little animals is nothing but a necessary effect and consequence of the momentary sleep of the large one. Would you now dare to say that one is more pleasing than the other in the sight of nature?[16]

3. Sade has sometimes been regarded as the extreme but logical outcome of the Enlightenment—an argument that was suggested as early as 1801, by the reactionary writer Charles de Pougens.[17] However it was Diderot rather than Sade who was the obvious target in the eyes of the political and intellectual champions of the Restoration. François-René de Chateaubriand gave a new twist to the story of the assassin who leaves Europe for China in his extremely successful *Génie du Christianisme.* "Distance in place and time perhaps to some extent weakens feeling and awareness of all kinds, even the consciousness of crime," Diderot had written; and no such consciousness would arise in the absence of the fear of punishment. These words awakened the virtuous indignation of Chateaubriand:

O conscience! are you then perhaps nothing but a phantom of our imagination, or the fear of human punishment? I interrogate myself, I ask the question: If, merely by wishing it, you could kill a man in China and inherit his fortune in Europe, being assured by supernatural means that the deed would remain forever unknown, would you allow yourself to form that project? It is in vain that I exaggerate my poverty to myself; it is in vain that I seek to soften the murder by supposing that my wish would cause the

Chinaman to die suddenly and painlessly, that he has no heirs, or that his death would in any case mean the loss of his goods to the State; it is in vain that I imagine this stranger as one bowed down with sickness and grief; it is in vain that I tell myself that death would be a boon to him, that he himself calls out for it, or that he has but a moment left to live: all my poor subterfuges cannot silence the voice that speaks deep in my heart, and which forbids me so loudly even to entertain such a thought that I cannot for an instant doubt the reality of conscience.[18]

165

TO KILL A

CHINESE MANDARIN

The Moral

Implications

of Distance

It is plain that Chateaubriand was here responding both to the passage in Diderot concerning the murderer who flees to China and to Diderot's claim that many people would not hesitate to kill a human being at a distance. By combining the two passages he created a new story, in which the victim was Chinese and the murderer, who explicitly sought to gain a sum of money by his deed, was European. In this new version the story—misattributed to Rousseau—became famous. The mistaken attribution can be traced back to Balzac.[19] In *Père Goriot*, Rastignac spends a night considering the possibility of making a rich marriage that would involve him, at least indirectly, in a murder. Then he goes to the Luxembourg Gardens, where he meets a friend, Bianchon. Rastignac, declaring that he has been tormented by "temptations," asks Bianchon:

"Have you read Rousseau?"
"Yes."
"Do you remember the passage where he asks the reader what he would do if he could make a fortune by killing an old mandarin in China by simply exerting his will, without stirring from Paris?"
"Yes."
"Well?"
"Bah! I'm at my thirty-third mandarin."
"Don't play the fool. Look here, if it were proved to you that the thing was possible and you only needed to nod your head, would you do it?"
"Is your mandarin well-stricken in years? But, bless you, young or old, paralytic or healthy, upon my word—The devil take it! Well, no."[20]

4. The parable of the mandarin foreshadows how the character of Rastignac will develop. Balzac wants to show that in bourgeois society it is difficult to keep faith with moral obligations, including the most elementary ones. The series of relations in which we are all caught up may make any of us responsible, at least indirectly, for a crime. A few years later, in his novel *Modeste Mignon*, Balzac again used the figure of a mandarin to put forward a similar argument. The poet Canalis asks:

166

TO KILL A

CHINESE MANDARIN

The Moral

Implications

of Distance

> "If at this instant the most important mandarin in China were breathing his last, plunging the Empire into war, would you be so sad? In India, the English are killing thousands of people like ourselves; at this very moment, a delightful lady is being consigned to the flames; and yet have you not drunk your coffee just the same?"[21]

In a world where we know that the cruelty of backwardness and the cruelty of imperialism hold sway, our moral indifference is already a form of complicity.

When Rastignac's friend resists the idea of killing an unknown Chinese mandarin, we may see in this an implicit recognition of the fact that (as Aristotle had put it) "there is in nature a common principle of the just and unjust." Now, however, with the emergence of a global economic system, there would henceforth be real opportunities for people to grow rich across distances immeasurably greater than ever Aristotle had imagined or could imagine.

This connection had long been recognized. In the section of the *Treatise of Human Nature* titled "Of Contiguity and Distance in Space and Time," David Hume remarked that "a West Indian merchant will tell you, that he is not without concern about what passes in Jamaica."[22] As we shall see, however, Hume's subtle discussion ignores the moral and juridical implications of the question. Today, we are struck by this silence. We know that one person's economic gain may be the more or less direct cause of the sufferings of other human beings at a great distance, who are condemned to poverty, malnutrition, or even death. Economic relations, moreover, are but one of the means that progress makes available for influencing the lives of other human beings at a distance. The most widely known version of the story of the Chinese mandarin has him killed by the simple pressing of a button: a detail that puts us in mind of modern weapons of war rather than of Rousseau, the supposed author of the anecdote.[23] Airplanes and missiles have shown how right Diderot was to suppose that people might find it much easier to kill human beings if they looked no bigger than swallows. The progress of bureaucracy has run along a similar track, making it possible to treat large numbers of individuals as if they were mere numbers— another potent way of placing them at a distance.

167

TO KILL A

CHINESE MANDARIN

The Moral

Implications

of Distance

To release a bomb that kills hundreds of thousands of people may lead to remorse, as it did in the case of Claude Eatherly, the Hiroshima pilot. Bombs, however, do not require those who launch them to learn the dreadful particulars of human butchery. Even in the (frequent) cases where the requisite training succeeds completely, little malfunctions may still occur. This is shown in Christopher Browning's terrible book *Ordinary Men*, which gives a detailed account of the role played by a reserve battalion of the German police force in the extermination of the Jews in Poland.[24] When these normal German citizens who had been transformed into mass murderers chanced to come across Jews whom they had previously known, they proved incapable of carrying out their task in the expected manner. It was clearly far easier to project the stereotypes of Nazi propaganda onto dozens, hundreds, or thousands of Jews.

The clear-cut distinction between *us* and *them* that was at the center of the racial legislation of the Nazis was connected, at the level of theory, to an explicit rejection of the idea of natural laws. In this sense we may see the emergence, at the end of the Second World War, of the legal notion of "crimes against humanity" as a belated victory of Antigone. "Though forbidden, it is just to bury Polyneices, since this is just by nature": Aristotle regarded these words as implying the superiority of common laws over specific laws, of duties toward the human species over duties toward a particular community, and of distance over proximity. However, as Aristotle himself did not fail to point out, distance and proximity are ambivalent notions. As we have seen, distance, when pushed to extremes, may lead to an absolute lack of pity for other human beings. How then are we to draw the boundary between distance and excessive distance? To put this another way: what are the cultural boundaries of a putative natural feeling such as human compassion?

5. This is a difficult question, and I shall not try to give a direct answer. I shall attempt only to clarify some of its implications.

168

TO KILL A
CHINESE MANDARIN
The Moral
Implications
of Distance

The story of the mandarin involves distance in space only. Hume, in his *Treatise*, explored a much wider theme, "Contiguity and Distance in Space and Time," with which Aristotle, as we have seen, had already been concerned. Hume writes:

> Accordingly we find, in common life, that men are principally concerned about those objects that are not much removed either in space or time, enjoying the present, and leaving what is afar off to the care of chance and fortune. Talk to a man of his condition thirty years hence, and he will not regard you. Speak of what is to happen to-morrow, and he will lend you attention. The breaking of a mirror gives us more concern when at home, than the burning of a house when abroad, and some hundred leagues distant.

In his *Theory of Moral Sentiments* (1759), Adam Smith developed Hume's reflections, arguing that only the sense of equity and justice is capable of correcting the natural egoism of our sentiments. This egoism is evoked by Smith by way of a parable that recalls the Lisbon earthquake that had happened in 1755, shortly before he wrote. Diderot's story of the murderer escaped to China may have been one indirect inspiration for the parable:

> Let us suppose that the great empire of China, with all its myriads of inhabitants, was suddenly swallowed up by an earthquake, and let us consider how a man of humanity in Europe, who had no sort of connexion with that part of the world, would be affected upon receiving intelligence of this dreadful calamity. He would, I imagine, first of all, express very strongly his sorrow for the misfortune of that unhappy people, he would make many melancholy reflections upon the precariousness of human life, and the vanity of all the labours of man, which could thus be annihilated in a moment. He would too, perhaps, if he was a man of speculation, enter into many reasonings concerning the effects which this disaster might produce upon the commerce of Europe, and the trade and business of the world in general. And when all this fine philosophy was over, when all these humane

sentiments had been once fairly expressed, he would pursue his business or his pleasure, take his repose or his diversion, with the same ease and tranquillity, as if no such accident had happened. . . . If he was to lose his little finger tomorrow, he would not sleep tonight; but, provided he never saw them, he will snore with the most profound security over the ruin of a hundred millions of his brethren, and the destruction of that immense multitude seems plainly an object less interesting to him, than this paltry misfortune of his own.[25]

169

TO KILL A

CHINESE MANDARIN

The Moral

Implications

of Distance

Hume, for his part, makes no mention of sympathy, which he regards as strictly connected with morality. However, he introduces a distinction:

> Though distance, both in space and time, has a considerable effect on the imagination, and by that means on the will and passions, yet the consequences of a removal in *space* are much inferior to those of a removal in *time*. Twenty years are certainly but a small distance of time in comparison of what history and even the memory of some may inform them of, and yet I doubt if a thousand leagues, or even the greatest distance of place this globe can admit of, will so remarkably weaken our ideas and diminish our passions.

Hume then supports this view by citing the "West Indian merchant," concerned about events in Jamaica; whereas "few extend their views so far into futurity, as to dread very remote accidents." This asymmetry leads him to discuss a further distinction that can be made in respect of time: "*the superior effects of the same distance in futurity above that in the past.*"[26] Distance in the past weakens both our passion and our will. "This difference with respect to the will is easily accounted for," says Hume. "As none of our actions can alter the past, it is not strange it should never determine the will." He offers a much fuller discussion of the passions, concluding as follows:

> We conceive the future as flowing every moment nearer to us, and the past as retiring. An equal distance, therefore, in the past and in the future, has not the same effect on the imagination; and that because we consider the one as continually increasing, and

the other as continually diminishing. The fancy anticipates the course of things, and surveys the object in that condition to which it tends, as well as in that which is regarded as the present.

170

TO KILL A

CHINESE MANDARIN

The Moral

Implications

of Distance

Hume claims that his detailed analysis has enabled him to account for

three phenomena, which seem pretty remarkable. Why distance weakens the conception and passion: why distance in time has a greater effect than that in space: and why distance in past time has still a greater effect than that in future. We must now consider three phenomena, which seem to be in a manner the reverse of these: why a very great distance increases our esteem and admiration for an object: why such a distance in time increases it more than that in space: and a distance in past time more than that in future.

These two sets of contrasting arguments reveal, unless I am mistaken, a contradiction (of fact, rather than logic) that Hume, and the Enlightenment more generally, were unable to face up to. On the one hand, there was the tendency to make nothing of the power and prestige of tradition, to regard them as based on a mere irrational argument; on the other, there was the tendency to recognize the force that they undeniably exerted. In some of the sharp remarks he makes in comparing temporal distance with spatial distance, we overhear Hume the philosopher engaged in fruitful dialogue with Hume the historian:

Ancient busts and inscriptions are more valued than Japan tables: and, not to mention the Greeks and Romans, it is certain we regard with more veneration the old Chaldeans and Egyptians, than the modern Chinese and Persians; and bestow more fruitless pains to clear up the history and chronology of the former, than it would cost us to make a voyage, and be certainly informed of the character, learning and government of the latter.[27]

Hume's way of attempting to resolve the contradictions we have mentioned is disappointing, because he considers only individual psychology. He emphasizes the connection between what is distant and what is difficult, and between difficulty and the pleasure of over-coming obstacles, but this is not enough to explain the value attrib-uted in our civilization to distance and to the past—indeed to the very remote past. This is a specific phenomenon, bound up with par-ticular historical circumstances that have undergone profound change in the course of the twentieth century. Hume could still write confidently that "none of our actions can alter the past." Today, we might well add that human actions can, however, exert a profound influence on the way the past is remembered: they can dis-tort its traces, consign them to oblivion, and condemn them to destruction.

171

TO KILL A

CHINESE MANDARIN

The Moral

Implications

of Distance

6. The impulse to rescue the past from an incumbent menace has never been so poignantly articulated as in Walter Benjamin's "Theses on the Philosophy of History," written in the first months of 1940, in the aftermath of the Hitler-Stalin pact. "Even the *dead* will not be safe from the enemy if he wins," wrote Benjamin, who within a few months was to put an end to his own life.[28] The second thesis begins with a quotation from the nineteenth-century philosopher Hermann Lotze: "One of the most remarkable characteristics of human nature is, alongside so much selfishness in specific instances, the freedom from envy that the present displays toward the future."

Here we discern a distinct echo of Aristotle's *Rhetoric*, with its dis-cussion of the ambivalent relationship between the passions (in the case in point, envy) and temporal and spatial distance. Lotze saw the lack of envy we display toward those who will come after us as a "wonderful phenomenon" that

may well tend to confirm our belief that there is some unity of history, transcending that of which we are conscious, a unity in which we cannot merely say of the past that it is not—a unity rather in which all that has been inexorably divided by the tem-poral course of history, has a co-existence independent of time. . . . The presentiment that we shall not be lost to the future, that those who were before us though they have passed away from the sphere of earthly reality have not passed away from reality altogether, and that in some mysterious way the progress of his-tory affects them too—this conviction it is that first entitles us to speak as we do of humanity and its history.[29]

172

TO KILL A

CHINESE MANDARIN

The Moral

Implications

of Distance

The *Passagen-Werk*, Walter Benjamin's great unfinished work on nineteenth-century Paris, includes a number of quotations from and references to Lotze's *Microcosmus*, which enjoyed great popularity at the end of the nineteenth century. Lotze was an important, though long neglected, influence on Benjamin's thought.[30] One of the fundamental themes of Benjamin's "Theses on the Philosophy of History," the need to "brush history against the grain," takes up Lotze's observations about the redemption of the past, developing them in a perspective inspired by both Judaism and historical materialism. "Like every generation that preceded us," writes Benjamin, "we have been endowed with a *weak* Messianic power, a power to which the past has a claim."[31]

These words were written in 1940. In the light of what has happened since then, we may be tempted to say that the last two generations have been endowed, contrary to what Benjamin supposed, with a *strong*, if negative, Messianic power. The end of history—not in the metaphorical sense that has recently been in vogue, but in an absolutely literal sense—has become technically feasible during the last half century. The possibility that the human race may be destroyed, a possibility that in itself constitutes a decisive historical turning point, has exerted and will exert its influence respectively on the lives of every future generation and on the fragments of memory of every generation that passes or has passed; and this includes those of whom Aristotle wrote, "ten thousand years in the past or future." At the same time, the sphere of what Aristotle called "common law" seems to have become much broader. But to express compassion for those distant fellow humans would be, I suspect, an act of mere rhetoric. Our capacity to pollute and destroy the present, the past, and the future is incomparably greater than our feeble moral imagination.

9

Pope Wojtyla's Slip

I

The Catholic Church has asked for forgiveness from the Jews, and we can expect the discussions that this has sparked off to continue for a long time to come. Many people cannot accept such a turn of events, and it would certainly have been inconceivable to anyone until the last ten years or so. The first occasion on which the Church had the courage to acknowledge its responsibility for Christian anti-Semitism was, we have been reminded, the "now historic pilgrimage of John Paul II to the Synagogue in Rome."[1] This reminder unexpectedly prompted a doubt— one that I set out to resolve by reading, first of all, the account of this extraordinary event printed in the *Osservatore Romano* of 14–15 April 1986, and then the complete text of the speech that the pope gave at the time.

John Paul II's visit had been announced in advance, and

journalists from across the world stood among the crowd waiting for him to appear. The Chief Rabbi, Elio Toaff, and the leader of the Jewish community in Rome, Giacomo Saban, recalled the persecution that the Jews, especially those living in Rome, had been subjected to for centuries: humiliations, massacres, mourning. Then the pope spoke. His first words were: "Dear friends and brothers, Christian and Jewish." The applause, in the words of the *Osservatore Romano*, was "unforeseen and almost unpredictable, but it was long and warm." Further bursts of applause continued to interrupt the speech: one of these, the journalist continued, was "memorable," and greeted "another very beautiful expression of the Pope's: 'You are our dearest brothers and one might say, in a certain sense, our elder brothers.'"

Commentators seized upon these words, and in the eyes of international public opinion they seemed to sum up the meaning of the event, as not only a solemn condemnation of anti-Semitism but also and more generally the opening of a new period in relations between Christians and Jews, in which Christianity would acknowledge the indissoluble links between the two religions and the historical precedence of Judaism. The same two words (*"fratelli maggiori,"* elder brothers) were used by Rabbi Toaff as part of the title of his autobiography *Perfidi giudei fratelli maggiori* (Milan, 1987), conjointly with the notorious phrase referring to "perfidious Jews," which Pope John XXIII had had removed from the Catholic liturgy. Toaff seemed to imply that we have come a long way, in these last decades, toward a better understanding between Jews and Christians.

I do not know if anyone noticed (though I imagine that they did) that the words "elder brothers" echo a passage in Saint Paul's letter to the Romans (9:12). The significance of this concealed reference will soon become plain. At the start of Romans 9, Paul reminds us of the prophecy made by the Lord to Rebecca when she was pregnant with twins (Genesis 25:23): "The elder shall be servant to the younger." And this is exactly what came to pass: the younger brother, Jacob, bought the older brother Esau's birthright for a mess of pottage, and then tricked their old, blind father, Isaac, into giving him his blessing in Esau's stead. Paul applies the prophecy to the relationship between the Jews and those Gentiles who had been converted to Christianity: "The elder shall be servant to the younger," or in other words the Jews (Esau) will be placed below the converted Gentiles (Jacob). In Saint Jerome's Vulgate version, the verb *"serviet"* is used; the original Greek employs a still harsher term, *"douleusei,"*

which has connotations of degrading enslavement (see the entry for *"doulos"* in Kittel and Friedrich's New Testament *Lexicon*, for instance, columns 1417 and 1429). To emphasize how we are to read the phrase "'The elder shall be servant to the younger," Paul goes on to quote another phrase, the words attributed to the Lord by the prophet Malachi: "Jacob I loved and Esau I hated." For two thousand years this passage from the works of the converted Jew Paul has been invoked to legitimate Christians' hatred of the Jews, who have been regarded as the representatives of the letter as against the spirit and of the flesh as against the spirit. If a single text is the foundation of Christian anti-Semitism, then this is it.

And this is the text to which John Paul II referred on the solemn occasion of his pilgrimage to the synagogue at Rome. The fact is scarcely credible. How can we explain it? There are two possible answers. The first is that even as he was pronouncing the most explicit and grave condemnation of anti-Semitism in all its forms, the pope wished to remind the Jews that their condition was to remain one of subordination and inferiority. This was my initial hypothesis, improbable as I thought it, because it seemed to me still more improbable that the pope could have been unaware that the phrase he used in trying to define the relations between Christians and Jews was taken verbatim from so well-known and pertinent a text as Romans 9:12. However, when I read the complete text of the speech as it was published in the *Osservatore Romano*, I decided that the idea of deliberate quotation was quite untenable. The pope had insisted on the ties that bind the two religions together and on the fact that each of them "desires recognition and respect by virtue of its own identity, beyond any syncretism or any suggestion of appro- priation"; he had reminded his audience that "the fundamental dif- ference, from the beginning, has been that we as Christians adhere to the person and the teachings of Jesus of Nazareth, who is a son of your people," but had commented that "this adherence is a matter of faith, that is, of the free assent of the intelligence and the heart under the guidance of the Spirit, and can never be the object of any outward pressure, in one direction or the other." It seemed to me frankly absurd to suppose that as an introduction to statements of this nature the speaker could deliberately have picked out a quotation emphasizing the subordination of the Jews to the Christians. How, then, was this to be explained?

My second hypothesis remained, namely that when the pope, in his search for a definition of the relationship between Christians and Jews, had used the expression "elder brothers," he had done so without being aware of the fact that he was echoing Romans 9:12. In this regard it is worth observing that not even the full text of the speech as published in the *Osservatore Romano* records this reference to Paul, though it is generally scrupulous in noting all the scriptural quotations that punctuate the pope's speech—including two, a few lines further on, drawn from other passages of the letter to the Romans (2:6 and 11, 28 ff.). Perhaps the expression "elder brothers" was added at the last moment? I do not think we can rule out this possibility. The phrase is preceded in the speech by a reference to the conciliar document *Nostra Aetate*, dedicated to relations between Christians and Jews, which makes many references to the letter to the Romans (including chapter 9) while carefully avoiding its anti-Jewish passages. Here the pope said: "The Jewish religion is not 'extrinsic' to us, but in a certain kind of sense it is 'intrinsic' to our religion. And therefore our relationship with it is unlike the relationship we have with any other religion. You are our dearest brothers and one might say, in a certain sense, our elder brothers." The whole speech, as one would expect given the solemnity of the occasion, is very carefully worked, stylistically and rhetorically. The inelegant repetition, within a few lines, of the phrases "in a certain kind of sense," "in a certain sense," might reveal an extempore addition. The pope was looking for a definition: from the recesses of memory a definition— the traditional one—came into his mind. At the very moment when he was seeking to turn over a new leaf, the old texts reasserted their power over him.

We have learned from Freud to regard slips as the result of impulses that the conscious ego has censored. Often these impulses are aggressive ones. Some might take the view that the pope's slip reveals his true feelings about the Jews. I do not think this is at all the case. In my view the implications of the slip are far more serious. Jesus was not a Christian but a Jew (even the Vatican II Council has acknowledged this, in *Nostra Aetate*). Christianity is born with Paul, by way of differentiation from and opposition to Judaism. The eradication of Christian anti-Semitism requires more than the goodwill and courage of a single individual, even if that individual is a pope. In John Paul II's slip, tradition—not simply anti-Jewish tradition— returned for a moment and took its revenge. There is still a long way, a very long way, to go.

II

The above argument appeared in *La Repubblica* on 7 October 1997. The following day, Gian Franco Svidercoschi charged me (in an article in *L'Avvenire*) of dealing in a "light and superficial" manner with the questions raised by the pope's use of the expression "elder brothers" on the occasion of his visit to the Synagogue in Rome in 1986. I had seen the expression as containing an echo, which seemed and still does seem obvious to me, of the passage in the letter to the Romans (9:12) where Paul applies to the Jews and the Gentiles converted to Christianity the prophecy in Genesis (25:23) concerning Esau and Jacob: "The elder shall be servant to the younger." After weighing up the possibility that this was a conscious allusion— which would have had a somewhat unfortunate air, to say the least, in that place and those circumstances—I remarked that such a possibility was ruled out given the content of the pope's speech as a whole. The other possibility was that the pope had made a slip, which I tried to interpret.

According to Svidercoschi, I claimed that Pope Wojtyla made a "Freudian slip." Clearly he was deceived by the title—*"Il lapsus freudiano di papa Wojtyla"* (Pope Wojtyla's Freudian slip)—under which the article appeared in *La Repubblica*. All the same, as a journalist by profession, Svidercoschi should know that titles are supplied by editors. If he had read my article less hurriedly, he would have realized that I did indeed attribute the slip to unconscious causes, but that I refused to interpret it as Freud would have done in terms of individual psychology. I wrote:

We have learned from Freud to regard slips as the result of impulses that the conscious ego has censored [more accurately, that it has repressed]. Often these impulses are aggressive ones. Some might take the view that the pope's slip reveals his true feelings about the Jews. I do not think this is at all the case.

In other words, I explicitly ruled out the possibility that the slip revealed putative anti-Semitic feelings on the part of Pope Wojtyla.

I would never speculate in this vein, even in the light of the most unfortunate remarks that the pope made in Rio (2 October 1997) about there having been "many Holocausts"—remarks that seem almost to go against the attempt, begun with great courage in the speeches of Wojtyla himself, to acknowledge the particular responsibilities that Christian anti-Semitism must bear. Rather, I explained the slip by reference to the weight of the tradition, now almost two thousand years old, that goes back to the letter to the Romans.

> The pope was looking for a definition: from the recesses of memory a definition—the traditional one—came into his mind. At the very moment when he was seeking to turn over a new leaf, the old texts reasserted their power over him.

Svidercoschi rebukes me for not having even asked myself "whether the inspiration for this phrase might not have come to the pope by other ways rather than via Saint Paul." He then offers an alternative—seemingly authoritative—explanation: "On the contrary, *for all we know* [my italics], this phrase may have been drawn from the cultural network, the historical 'memory,' of the Polish fatherland, which the Pope brought with him when he entered into office." It may have come "from a kind of political manifesto . . . which was to be used in the constitutions of the future independent Slav states," a manifesto drawn up by the great Romantic poet Adam Mickiewicz, in which he speaks of "Israel" (that is, of the Jews), calling it "our older brother" to whom are due "esteem, and help upon the path to prosperity and welfare, and equal rights in all matters."

That in a speech such as this, given in the synagogue at Rome, and full of references to the letter to the Romans, the expression "elder brothers" used of the Jews should derive instead from Mickiewicz seems to me not "very probable" (as Svidercoschi writes), but very improbable; and in any case impossible to prove. Moreover, even if the pope himself were to affirm that it did, my argument would not be damaged in the least, for the simplest of reasons— namely, that Mickiewicz himself was obviously referring to the letter to the Romans. I say "obviously" because no one affected even minimally by Christian tradition can call the Jews "elder brothers" without alluding, consciously or unconsciously, to Romans 9:12. That Mickiewicz could have done so is completely implausible. The text that Svidercoschi draws to our attention is the *Simbolo politico polacco* (Polish Political Creed), a religio-political credo that Mickiewicz wrote simultaneously in Italian and Polish, dating it "Rome, 29 March 1848." "To Israel, our older brother . . . equality in all matters of civil-political rights": thus runs the Italian edition brought out in 1848 by the Propaganda Fide printing works (as we have seen, Svidercoschi, who presumably was making use of the Polish text, gives a slightly different version of these words: "equal rights in all matters"). This equality is linked, for Mickiewicz, with a messianic event: the national resurrection of Poland, which he compares, here and elsewhere, to the resurrection of Christ ("Poland rises up in the body in which it has suffered and in which it was placed in the sepulcher a hundred years ago"). Is it really true, as Svidercoschi tells us on good authority, that pope Wojtyla was thinking of Mickiewicz's *Simbolo politico polacco* while he was speaking in the synagogue in Rome? The opening phrases of the *Simbolo* make it clear what kind of framework would enclose the political-civil rights that the Jews were to enjoy:

1. The Christian spirit in the Holy Roman Catholic faith to manifest itself in free actions.
2. The Word of God, as given in the Gospels, to be the law of states—their civil and social law.
3. The Church to be custodian of the word.

As we can see, this is a most instructive text. It can be read in full (it is very short) in the collection of Mickiewicz's *Political Writings* edited by M. Bersano Begey (*Scritti politici* [Turin 1965], pp. 359 f.).

Mickiewicz takes us back, then, to Paul and to the expression "elder brothers." This alludes, by way of the passage from the letter to the Romans in which it is contained, to the subordination of/the Jews to the Christians. That this tradition surfaced involuntarily in the words of someone seeking to break with it, as Pope Wojtyla was, gives his slip a tragic aspect.

Svidercoschi accuses me of being someone who "drags along behind him an ancient remorse, full of rancor and suspicion, which prevents him from seeing the 'new thing' that is happening."

I shall not respond to this charge, whose tone I find unpleasant. I shall simply say that what I presented was not a suspicion, but an interpretation. I still await its refutation. As for the "new thing," there are very many of us who will be delighted if ever it succeeds in appearing.

NOTES

1. MAKING IT STRANGE: THE PREHISTORY OF A
LITERARY ÐEVICE

I have presented this essay in Helsinki, Venice (at a seminar in memory of Manfredo Tafuri), Pisa, Maastricht, and at the Getty Center in
Santa Monica. I am grateful for comments made by Perry Anderson,
Jan Bremmer, and Francesco Orlando; I thank John Elliott for drawing my attention to Guevara's travesty of Marcus Aurelius; and I
acknowledge the assistance of Pier Cesare Bori and the useful criticisms of those who took part in the seminar that I conducted in 1995
as visiting scholar at the Getty Center.

1. The passage is quoted by P. Steiner in *Russian Formalism. A
Metapoetics* (Ithaca, N.Y., 1984), p. 45.

2. In later years, their relationship soured. In the introduction
he wrote to T. Todorov's anthology *Théorie de la Littérature* (Paris,
1965), Jakobson poured scorn on Shklovsky's "silly" ideas about
estrangement (p. 8). A further polemical reference in the same
essay is discussed by V. Strada in *Strumenti critici* 1 (October 1966):
100.

3. V. Shklovsky, *Theory of Prose*, trans. Benjamin Sher with an introduction by Gerald L. Bruns (Elmwood Park, Ill., 1991), pp. 5 f. [Translators' note: We have added the gloss "or defamiliarizing" to the "estranging" of Sher's English version, as "defamiliarization" is the term employed elsewhere in the present chapter.]

4. Quoted in ibid., p. 7.

5. Ibid., p. 11.

6. Ibid., p. 6.

7. See F. Orlando, *Illuminismo e retorica freudiana* (Turin, 1982), p. 163. This is a revised edition of Orlando's *Illuminismo barocco e retorica freudiana* (Turin 1979).

8. My discussion here is indebted to Pierre Hadot's essays on Marcus Aurelius (*Exercices spirituels et philosophie antique* [Paris, 1987]), esp. pp. 119–154 of the Italian translation (*Esercizi spirituali e filosofia antica* [Turin, 1988]).

9. See Hadot, *Esercizi spirituali*, pp. 135–154.

10. *The Meditations of Marcus Aurelius*, trans. with a commentary by A. S. L. Farquharson (Oxford, 1944) [occasionally modified by the present translators].

11. See L. Tolstoy, *Für alle Tage*, ed. E. H. Schmitt and A. Skarvan (Dresden, 1906–1907).

12. See A. Aarne, *Vergleichende Rätselforschungen* (Helsinki 1918–1920), ff. 26–28 (Communications). On riddles in Latin culture, cf. Pauly-Wissowa, *Real-Enzyklopädie*, s.v. "Rätsel," esp. 116–122 (Weissbach). See also A. Jolles, *Einfache Formen* (1930) (see pp. 103–119 of the French translation, *Formes simples* [Paris, 1972]); and the perceptive essay by S. Levi Della Torre, "Ermeneutica Vinciana," *Achademia Leonardi da Vinci* 6 (1995): 228–231.

13. See the remarks of Joly in his introduction to the edition he prepared (*Pensées de l'empereur Marc-Aurèle-Antonin ou leçèon de la vertu que ce Prince philosophique se faisoit a lui-même, nouvelle traduction du grec . . .* [Paris, 1770], p. xix). Joly's edition was the first to be based on ms. Vatican 1950, which Winckelmann had discovered.

14. Prolegomena to *Marci Antonini imperatoris, de se ipso et ad ipsum libri xii, Guil. Xylander Augustanus graece et latine primus edidit, nunc vero [. . .] notas emendationes adjecit Mericus Casaubonus* (London, 1643).

15. P. Bayle, *Dictionnaire historique et critique*, 3rd ed. (Rotterdam 1720), 2:1339–1340. Bayle vigorously rejects the skeptical remarks passed by Guevara on the criticisms of his work made by the Spanish antiquarian Pedro de Rhua; on this exchange of letters, see *Biblioteca de autores españoles* (Madrid, 1872), pp. 229–250, and also the entry "Rua, Pierre" in Bayle's *Dictionnaire*. As early as 1548, Fausto da Longiano expressed the view that Guevara's book was "a complete fiction"; see H. Vaganay, "Antonio de Guevara et son oeuvre dans la littérature italienne," *La Bibliofilia* 17 (1915–1916): 339.

The followers of Erasmus made no comment on the matter, which M. Bataillon (*Erasmo y España* [Mexico–Buenos Aires, 1950], 2:222) interprets as a verdict of guilty against Guevara.

16. A. de Guevara, *Il terzo libro di Marco Aurelio con l'Horologio de' Principi* (Venice, 1571), 6v–7v. [Translators' note: Excerpts from Guevara's work, amounting only to about one-tenth of the original, are published in K. N. Colville, ed., *The Diall of Princes, by Don Antony of Guevara, translated by Sir Thomas North* . . . (London, 1919). In the present work, all passages from Guevara are translated from the Italian of Ginzburg's text.]

17. See A. de Guevara, *El Villano del Danubio y otros fragmentos*, with an introduction by A. Castro (Princeton, 1945), p. xv. L. Spitzer, however, makes some cogent criticisms of Castro's interpretation in his *Sobre las ideas de Américo de Castro a propósito de "El Villano del Danubio" de Antonio de Guevara* (Bogotà, 1950). Guevara's work receives no mention in G. Gliozzi's important book *Adamo e il nuovo mondo* (Florence, 1977).

18. Guevara, *Il terzo libro*, 9r.

19. Ibid., 6r.

20. See A. Castro, in his introduction to Guevara's *El Villano del Danubio*, p. xxiii.

21. See *El dyalogo di Salomon e Marcolpho* (Venice, 1502), reprinted in P. Camporesi's edition (Turin, 1978) of G. C. Croce, *Le sottilissime astuzie di Bertoldo. Le piacevoli e ridicolose semplicità di Bertoldino*, p. 208.

22. The Latin text (see the edition of W. Benary [Heidelberg, 1914], pp. 1–2) reads as follows:

Statura itaque Marcolphi erat curta et grossa. Caput habebat grande; frontem latissimum, rubicundum et rugosum; aures pilosas et usque ad medium maxillarum pendentes; oculos grossos et lipposos; et labium subterius quasi caballinum; barbam sordidam et fetosam quasi hirci; manus truncas; digitos breves et grossos; pedes rotundos; nasum spissum et gibbosum; labia magna et grossa; faciem asininam; capillos veluti spinule ericiorum; calciamenta pedum eius rustica erant nimis; et cingebat renes eius dimidius gladius; vaginam quoque mediam habebat crepatam et in summo capite repalatam; capulum de tilia factum erat et cum cornu hircino ornatum.

With reference to the confusion between the porcupine and the hedgehog (Latin *"ericius,"* Italian *"riccio"*), characteristic of other European languages as well as of Italian, see the entries for *"riccio"* and *"porcospino"* in Salvatore Battaglia's *Grande dizionario della lingua italiana*, particularly the quotations from Vincenzo Maria di S. Caterina and Lazzaro Spallanzani.

23. "Et hic fortasse est quem fabulose popularium narrationes Marcolfum vocant, de quo dicitur quod Salomonis solvebat aenigmata et ei

respondebat, aequipollenter et iterum solvenda proponens" (see Croce, *Le sottilissime astuzie di Bertoldo*, p. 169). On the medieval precursors of these stories, see R. J. Menner, ed., *The Poetical Dialogues of Solomon and Saturn* (New York, 1941).

24. Croce, *Le sottilissime astuzie di Bertoldo*, p. 10. On the echoes of the *Contadino del Danubio* in *Bertoldo*, see P. Camporesi, "Mostruosità e sapienza del villano," in *Agostino Gallo nella cultura del Cinquecento*, ed. M. Pegrari, pp. 193–214, esp. pp. 193–197.

25. M. Bakhtin, *Rabelais and His World*, trans. Hélène Iswolski (Bloomington, 1984).

26. Compare the passage from Augustine's *De civitate dei*, 4, in Aquinas's *De regimine principum* (Parmae, 1578), 2.5.112r–112v: "Remota iustitia quae sunt ipsa regna, nisi quaedam latrocinia? . . . introducit autem ad suum probandum intentum exemplum de quodam pyrata, qui vocabatur Dionides: qui cum fuisset captus ab Alexandro, quaesivit ab eo cur mare haberet infestum? Ipse libera contumacia respondit: Quid tibi, ut orbem terrarum? Sed quia ego exiguo navigio id facio, latro vocor, tu vero, quia magna classe, diceris imperator."

27. See Michel de Montaigne, *Essais*, ed. A. Thibaudet (Paris, 1950), p. 379 (II, ii, "De l'yvrongnerie"). Montaigne's judgment on Guevara's *Letters* was negative; see I, essay xlviii.

28. Michel de Montaigne, *The Essays of Michel de Montaigne*, ed. and trans. M. A. Screech (London, 1993), pp. 240 f.

29. For a general discussion of this issue, see G. Celati's preface to the Italian edition of Swift's *Gulliver's Travels* (*I viaggi di Gulliver*) (Milan, 1997).

30. J. de La Bruyère, "De l'Homme," in *Caractères*. See the *Oeuvres Complètes*, ed. J. Benda (Paris, 1978), p. 333. [Translators' note: We translate from the French original. A recent English version is La Bruyère, *Characters*, trans. J. Stewart (Harmondsworth, 1970).] This passage is translated into Italian and briefly discussed by G. della Volpe in *Rousseau e Marx* (Rome, 1962), pp. 163 f.; my interest in the theme I am discussing here dates back many years to my first reading of those pages.

31. Voltaire, *Essai sur les moeurs*, ed. R. Pomeau (Paris, 1963), pp. 22 f.

32. See A. Prosperi's important essay, " 'Otras Indias': Missionari della Controriforma tra contadini e selvaggi," in *Scienze, credenze occulte, livelli di cultura* (Florence, 1980), pp. 205–234; and see the same author's recent *Tribunali della coscienza: Inquisitori, confessori, missionari* (Turin, 1996), pp. 551 ff.

33. See C. Ginzburg, *History, Rhetoric, and Proof* (Hanover and London, 1999), pp. 71–91.

34. Shklovsky, *Theory of Prose*, 63. In his diary, the young Tolstoy noted, using phrases that seem to recall the passage by Voltaire we have just cited, that "to turn a person into a beast, all you need is a uniform, separation

from the family, and beating on a drum"; R. F. Gustafson quotes this in *Leo Tolstoy: Resident and Stranger* (Princeton, 1986), p. 347.

35. A document from late in Tolstoy's life (1907) is the short introduction he provided to an anthology of passages from La Bruyère and other French moralists, prepared by his disciple Rusanov; see N. Gareth Jones, ed., *I Cannot Be Silent: Writings on Politics, Art, and Religion* (Bristol, 1989), pp. 200 f. (this passage was brought to my notice by Pier Cesare Bori). Here Tolstoy compares the moralists—among whom he names the "extraordinary" Montaigne, saying that his work is in some respects an instance of the genre—to the systematic thinkers, displaying a clear preference for the former.

36. Cf. R. Pomeau's introduction to his edition of Voltaire's *Essai sur les moeurs*, 1:15: "Among all his works, it was this *Philosophy of History*, open even at that time to so many objections from a scientific point of view, which had the most pronounced influence on the imaginations of revolutionaries and romantics."

37. In his *Illuminismo e retorica freudiana* (a book from which I have learned much), F. Orlando has argued that the defamiliarization of the Enlightenment is to be clearly distinguished from that of the nineteenth and twentieth centuries (though he makes a partial exception of Brecht): see esp. p. 163. The perspective I am outlining here suggests, to the contrary, that on one hand, a substantial continuity links pre-Enlightenment and Enlightenment defamiliarization with that of Tolstoy, while on the other, there is a substantial break between the latter and Proustian defamiliarization.

38. L. Tolstoy, *Resurrection*, trans. Louise Maude (Moscow, 1985), p. 176.

39. See V. Bulgakov, *Leone Tolstoj nell'ultimo anno della sua vita* (Foligno, 1930), p. 431 (this passage, too, was brought to my notice by Pier Cesare Bori).

40. Proust, *À la recherche du temps perdu*, ed. P. Clarac and A. Ferré (Paris, 1960), 1:653 f. [Translators' note: We translate from the French. The standard English translation is *Remembrance of Things Past*, translated by C. K. Scott Moncrieff—with later revisions by Terence Kilmartin—and Andreas Mayor (London, Chatto and Windus, 1981).] Proust omits a phrase in his quotation from the *Letters*: Madame de Sévigné writes of "linen thrown here and there, black men, other men buried upright": see Madame de Sévigné, *Correspondance*, ed. R. Duchêne (Paris, 1974), 2:970 (letter of 12 June 1680).

41. Later critics have ignored the penetrating remarks made by Samuel Beckett in his *Proust* (London, 1965; first publ. 1931), pp. 85–87): see, for instance, J.-L. Backés, "Le Dostoïevski du narrateur," *Cahiers Marcel Proust*, n.s., 6, *Études Proustiennes* 1 (1973):95–107; A. Labat, "Proust's Mme de Sévi-

gné," *L'Esprit créateur* 15, nos. 1–2 (Spring–Summer 1975): 271–285; M. Pejovic, *Proust et Dostoïevski: Étude d'une thématique commune* (Paris, 1987).

42. See Shklovsky, *Theory of Prose*, p. 6. See also R. F. Gustafson's analysis, in his *Leo Tolstoy: Resident and Stranger* (p. 248), of the passage in *War and Peace* that depicts Prince Nesvitsky's arrival on the field of battle.

43. Cf. J. Monnin-Hornung's diligent account, *Proust et la peinture* (Geneva and Lille, 1951), pp. 72–101.

44. Proust, *À la recherche*, 1:838 f.

45. See M. Merleau-Ponty, *Sens et non-sens* (Paris, 1948), "Le doute de Cézanne," pp. 27–44, esp. p. 30: "We live in the midst of objects made by men, among tools, houses, streets, towns, and most of the time we see them only through the human actions in which they may be caught up. We become habituated to the idea that all this necessarily exists and is unshakable. Cézanne's paintings suspend this state of habit and reveal the background of inhuman nature upon which men have established their presence. This is why these figures are strange, as if seen by a being of another species." [Translators' note: We translate from the French. *Sens et non-sens* is translated into English by Hubert L. Dreyfus and Patricia Allen Dreyfus: *Sense and Non-Sense* (Evanston, Ill., 1964)] Merleau-Ponty does not mention Proust in this essay.

46. See F. Orlando's spendid essay "Proust, Sainte-Beuve e la ricerca in direzione sbagliata," published as the introduction to the Italian edition of *Contre Sainte-Beuve* (*Contro Sainte-Beuve* [Turin, 1974]).

47. See F. Moretti's brilliant analysis in *Opere mondo: Saggio sulla forma epica dal "Faust" a "Cent'anni di solitudine"* (Turin, 1994).

48. Proust, *À la recherche*, 3:378.

49. Cf. L. Spitzer, "Sullo stile di Proust," in Spitzer, *Marcel Proust e altri saggi di letteratura francese* (Turin, 1959), pp. 309 f.; and B. G. Rogers, *Proust's Narrative Techniques* (Geneva, 1965), pp. 160 ff.

50. Proust, *À la recherche*, 3:982 f.

51. See Proust, *La prisonnière*, p. 379; and Proust's article "Sentiments filiaux d'un Parricide," which appeared in *Le Figaro*, 1 February 1907 (this is reprinted in the Italian collection of Proust's journalistic and critical writings, *Scritti mondani e letterari*, ed. M. Bongiovanni Bertini [Turin, 1986], pp. 205–214). Proust's half-concealed identification with Henri de Blarenberghe, the young man who had killed his own mother, became especially explicit in the censored final pages of the article (p. 694). In an earlier passage, Proust had referred to his own feelings of guilt about the sufferings his mother had had to bear. All the same, it may be that at a deeper level his attitude was more ambivalent, and had more of the sadistic impulses expressed in the great scene "auprès de Montjouvain." It is significant that the latter ends with a clearly autobiographical phrase, which echoes the passage just

mentioned from "Sentiments filiaux d'un parricide": "That indifference to the sufferings we cause . . . which is, whatever other names we may give it, the terrible and permanent form of cruelty" (À la recherche, Du côté de chez Swann, p. 165).

2. MYTH: DISTANCE AND DECEIT

I must thank Perry Anderson, Pier Cesare Bori, Page DuBois, Amos Funkenstein, Alberto Gajano, Vyacheslav Ivanov, and Stefano Levi Della Torre for their suggestions; and, for pointing out some errors, Saverio Marchignoli and Cristiana Natali.

1. Representative studies include G. Nagy, *The Best of the Achaeans: Concepts of the Hero in Archaic Greek Poetry* (Baltimore, 1979); H. Blumenberg, *Arbeit am Mythos* (Frankfurt am Main, 1979) [*Work on Myth,* trans. R. M. Wallace (Cambridge, Mass., and London, 1985)]; M. Detienne, *L'invention de la mythologie* (Paris, 1981); P. Veyne, *Les Grecs ont-ils cru à leurs mythes?* (Paris, 1983); and C. Calame, ed., *Métamorphoses du mythe en Grèce antique* (Geneva, 1988).

2. This is M. Detienne's thesis, in his *L'invention de la mythologie* (see, for instance, pp. 282 ff.). Among those who have criticized it, see A. Momigliano, in *Rivista storica italiana* 94 (1982): 784–787; L. Brisson, *Platon les mots et les mythes* (Paris, 1982); and L. Edmunds, "The Practice of Greek Mythology," in the collection edited by him, *Approaches to Greek Myth* (Baltimore and London, 1990), pp. 1–20. Momigliano draws attention to the difference between Detienne's views and those of J.-P. Vernant, and this is confirmed, despite the claim made to the contrary, by the introduction to the new impression of *Les maîtres de la vérité dans la Grèce antique* (Paris, 1994); see esp. pp. 22 ff.

3. [Translators' note: Quotations from the *Republic* are from the version by F. M. Cornford (Oxford, 1941).] Aristotle, on the other hand, when he characterizes Homer as a master of the fictitious (*Poetics* 24), refers to the sphere of logic, rather than that of morality—so much so that he makes his point by citing a paralogism.

4. [Translators' note: Quotations from the *Timaeus* are from the version by Desmond Lee (Harmondsworth, 1971); from the *Phaedrus,* from the version by C. J. Rowe (London, 1986), modified in places.] E. Cassirer, in *Sprache und Mythos,* Studien der Bibliothek Warburg 6 ((Hamburg, 1923), pp. 1 ff., makes this passage from the *Phaedrus* his starting point; see also M. Detienne in *L'invention de la mythologie,* pp. 157 f.

5. Plato, *Phaedrus,* pp. 26 f.

6. Dionysus of Halicarnassus, *Essay on Thucydides,* Italian version by G. Pavano (Palermo, 1952), pp. 33 f. [Translators' note: The English text here is

based on this Italian edition.] In the following paragraph, Dionysus insists on the localistic aspect of such traditional tales, a point emphasized by L. Edmunds in his *Approaches to Greek Myth*, p. 5.

7. We find the same opposition in the first paragraph of Plutarch's *Lives*, where "reason" (*logos*) is contrasted with "myth" (*mythodes*). See W. Trimpi, *Muses of One Mind: The Literary Analysis of Experience and Its Continuity* (Princeton, 1983), p. 292.

8. See L. Brandwood, *The Chronology of Plato's Dialogues* (Cambridge, 1990), esp. pp. 245–247. On the composition of the *Republic*, and the possibility that there were two editions, see the introduction by A. Diès to the "Belles Lettres" ed. (Paris, 1989), pp. 122–128; Diès proposes an earlier date (no later than 375).

9. Here, and elsewhere in what follows, I develop some points briefly noted in the essay "Representation," which forms the third chapter of the present book. I have learned much from N. Denyer's *Language, Thought, and Falsehood in Ancient Greek Philosophy* (Cambridge, 1993), and have taken account of Denyer's discussion in my own argument.

10. [Translators' note: Quotations from the *Sophist* are from the version by A. E. Taylor, ed. R. Klibansky and E. Anscombe (Folkestone and London, 1971).] Aristotle argues similarly in the *Metaphysics*, 1051b.

11. Cf. L. M. de Rijk, *Plato's Sophist: A Philosophical Commentary* (Amsterdam, 1986), pp. 304 f. In the *Cratylus*, Plato had argued that nouns too possess truth-value (this is discussed in ibid., pp. 277–282). In "The Philosophy of Logical Atomism" (1918), Bertrand Russell remarks that it was only thanks to his pupil Wittgenstein that he realized the "obvious" fact that propositions (and not nouns) can be bearers of truth or falsehood; see B. Russell, ed. R. C. Marsh, *Logic and Knowledge: Essays 1901–1950* (London, 1966), p. 187, and the discussion in N. Denyer, *Language, Thought, and Falsehood*, pp. 15 and 214 n. 2.

12. [Translators' note: Quotations from *On Interpretation* are in the version by J. L. Ackrill: Aristotle, *De Interpretatione* (Oxford, 1963).]

13. M. Zanatta, the editor of the Italian edition of the *De Interpretatione* (*Dell'interpretazione* [Milan, 1992]), refers at this point (p. 146) to the work of V. Sainati.

14. Aristotle, *Posterior Analytics*, trans. H. Tredennick (London and Cambridge, Mass., 1960). [Translators' note: Tredennick renders "*tragelaphos*" as "unicorn," which we have replaced by "goat-stag."] On the general question, see G. Sillitti, *Tragelaphos: Storia di una metafora e di un problema* (Naples, 1980).

15. On this passage, see the interesting speculations of A.-J. Festugière, *La révélation de Hermès Trismégiste* (Paris, 1981), 4:14–16.

16. See Sillitti, *Tragelaphos*, pp. 11 f. and *passim*.

17. See L. M. de Rijk's suggested textual emendation, in his essay "On Boethius' Notion of Being," in L. M. de Rijk, *Through Language to Reality*, ed. E. P. Bos (Northampton, 1989), p. 27 n. 43.

18. Anicii Manlii Severini Boethii, *Commentarii in librum Aristotelis Peri Hermeneias* . . . , *pars posterior*, ed. C. Meiser (Lipsiae, 1880), 2:49–52:

> Maximam vero vim habet exempli novitas et exquisita subtilitas. Ad demonstrandum enim quod unum solum nomen neque verum sit neque falsum, posuit huiusmodi nomen, quod conpositum quidem esset, nulla tamen eius substantia reperiretur. Si quod ergo unum nomen veritatem posset falsitatemve retinere, posset huiusmodi nomen, quod est hircocervus, quoniam omnino in rebus nulla illi substantia est, falsum aliquid designare, sed non designat aliquam falsitatem. Nisi enim dicatur hircocervus vel esse vel non esse, quamquam ipsum per se non sit, solum tamen dictum nihil falsi in eo sermone verive perpenditur. . . . Hoc vero idcirco addidit, quod in quibusdam ita enuntiationes fiunt, ut quod de ipsis dicitur secundum substantiam proponatur, in quibusdam vero hoc ipsum esse quod additur non substantiam sed praesentiam quandam significet. Cum enim dicimus deus est, non eum dicimus nunc esse, sed tantum in substantia esse, ut hoc ad inmutabilitatem potius substantiae quam ad tempus aliquod referatur. Si autem dicimus dies est, ad nullam diei substantiam pertinet nisi tantum ad temporis constitutionem. Hoc est enim quod significat est, tamquam si dicamus nunc est. Quare cum ita dicimus esse ut substantiam designemus, simpliciter est addimus, cum vero ita ut aliquid praesens significetur, secundum tempus. Haec una quam diximus expositio. Alia vero huiusmodi est: esse aliquid duobus modis dicitur: aut simpliciter, aut secundum tempus. Simpliciter quidem secundum praesens tempus, ut si quis dicat hircocervus est. Praesens autem quod dicitur tempus non est, sed confinium temporum: finis namque est praeteriti futurique principium. Quocirca quisquis secundum praesens hoc sermone quod est esse utitur, simpliciter utitur, qui vero aut praeteritum iungit aut futurum, ille non simpliciter, sed iam in ipsum tempus incurrit. Tempora namque (ut dictum est) duo ponuntur: praeteritum atque futurum. Quod si quis cum praesens nominat, simpliciter dicit, cum utrumlibet praeteritum vel futurum dixerit, secundum tempus utitur enuntiatione. Est quoque tertia huiusmodi expositio, quod aliquotiens ita tempore utimur, ut indefinite dicamus: ut si qui dicat, est hircocervus, fuit hircocervus, erit hircocervus, hoc indefinite et simpliciter dictum est. Sin vero aliquis addat, nunc est, vel heri fuit, vel cras erit, ad hoc ipsum esse quod simpliciter dicitur, addit tempus.

I know of no analytical discussion of this passage. G. Nuchelmans mentions it in *Theories of the Proposition: Ancient and Medieval Conceptions of the Bearers of Truth and Falsity* (Amsterdam and London, 1973), p. 133.

19. J. L. Ackrill gives cautious support to this interpretation in his commentary on *De Interpretatione* (Oxford, 1963), p. 115.

20. L. M. de Rijk points this out in his "On Boethius' Notion of Being," p. 14.

21. Boethius (*Commentarii*, pp. 52, 65) translates Aristotle thus: "Nomen ergo est vox significativa secundum placitum sine tempore . . . verbum autem est quod consignificat tempus." The terms "absolutely" and "indefinitely" denote Aristotle's *"haplous"* and *"aoriston"* (16a.30, 16a.18). It is, however, notable that in his commentary on the *Peri Hermeneias*, Boethius renders the expression *"onoma aoriston"* as "nomen infinitum," rather than "nomen indefinitum": "et nomen hoc, quod nihil definitum designaret, non diceretur simpliciter nomen, sed nomen infinitum. Cuius sententiae Aristoteles auctor est, qui se hoc ei vocabulum autumat invenisse" (1.2.63). On "simpliciter," see also L. M. de Rijk, *La philosophie au moyen age* (Leiden, 1985), pp. 164–166 (in connection with Aquinas's interpretation of Exodus 3:14).

22. See J. Shiel, "Boethius' Commentaries on Aristotle," *Medieval and Renaissance Studies* 4 (1958): 217–244. L. M. de Rijk follows Shiel and offers further evidence, in "On the Chronology of Boethius' Works on Logic," *Vivarium* 2 (1964): 1–49, 125–152.

23. Augustine, *Confessiones* 11.20: "Tempora sunt tria, praesens de praeteritis, praesens de praesentibus, praesens de futuribus."

24. Boethius, *Quomodo Trinitas unus Deus*, in Migne's *Patrologia Latina*, 63:1253; and see also the *Proem* (ibid., 64:1249). C. Leonardi draws attention to the distance between Boethius and Aquinas on this point in "La controversia trinitaria nell'epoca e nell'opera di Boezio," *Atti del Congresso internazionale di studi Boeziani*, ed. L. Obertello (Rome, 1981), pp. 109–122. On the absence of any distinction between *aeternitas* and *sempiternitas* in Augustine, see *De Trinitate* 5.15 f. (*Patrologia Latina*, 42:921 f.).

25. L. M. de Rijk offers some reflections on this atemporal present in "Die Wirkung der neuplatonischen Semantik auf das mittelalterliche Denken über das Sein," in *Akten des VI internationalen Kongresses für mittelalterliche Philosophie* . . . (Berlin and New York, 1981), 1:19–35, esp. p. 29.

26. Boethius, *Commentarii* 2.22: "Sunt enim intellectus sine re ulla subiecta, ut quos centauros vel chimaeras poetae finxerunt." This is the passage L. M. de Rijk alludes to when he uses the English phrase "poetical fabrications" (*On Boethius' Notion of Being*, p. 16). My argument here advances further arguments for such a translation.

27. Macrobius, *Commento al "Somnium Scipionis,"* ed. M. Regali (Pisa, 1983), 1.2.11; 2.10.11.

28. See de Rijk, *"On the Chronology of Boethius' Works on Logic,"* esp. the tables on pp. 159 and 161.

29. Boethius, introduction to *De hypotheticis syllogismis*, ed. L. Obertello, 1.1.3–5, pp. 206 f.

30. The suggestion is L. M. de Rijk's and is supported by Obertello (see p. 135 of the latter's edition of *De hypotheticis syllogismis*).

31. *De hypotheticis syllogismis*, 3.6.6–7, pp. 356 f.

32. Gaius, *Institutiones*, ed. J. Reinach (Paris, 1950).

33. See M. Lipenius, *Bibliotheca realis juridica* (Lipsiae, 1757), 1:511; A. Dadin de Hauteserre (Dadinus de Alteserra), "De fictionibus juris" (Paris, 1679), in *Opera omnia*, vol. 6 (Naples, 1777); F. Pringsheim, "Symbol und Fiktion in antiken Rechten," *Gesammelte Abhandlungen* (Heidelberg, 1961), 2:382–400; E. Kantorowicz, "The Sovereignty of the Artist: A Note on Legal Maxims and Renaissance Theories of Art" [1961], in *Selected Studies* (Locust Valley, N.Y., 1965), pp. 352–365, esp. p. 354 f.; L. L. Fuller, *Legal Fictions* (Stanford, 1967).

34. See the contributions collected under the title "Platonic Insults" that appeared in *Common Knowledge* 2 (Fall 1993), in particular S. Toulmin's introduction (pp. 19–23) and the entry for "Rhetorical," by D. McCloskey (pp. 23–32).

35. W. Trimpi refers to Vaihinger's book in *Muses of One Mind*, emphasizing the importance of "fictiones" in literary theory. (Vaihinger wrote the work in 1876–1878, but it was first published only in 1911; it was reprinted in Hamburg, 1986.)

36. See J. Isaac, *"Le Peri Hermeneias" en Occident de Boèce à St Thomas* (Paris, 1953). (The illustration on page 36 shows clearly the spread of manuscripts of the work.)

37. *Peter Abelards Philosophische Schriften*, vol. 1, *Die Logica "Ingredientibus," 3, Die Glossen zu "Peri Hermeneias,"* ed. B. Geyer (Münster, 1927), p. 333.

38. See D. F. Blackwell, *Non-Ontological Constructs: The Effects of Abaelard's Logical and Ethical Theories on His Theology: A Study in Meaning and Verification* (Berne, 1988), esp. pp. 132–141.

39. See de Rijk, *La philosophie au moyen age*, p. 98.

40. See G. Paparelli, "Fictio," *Filologia Romanza* 7, nos. 3–4 (1966): 1–83: Paparelli emphasizes the etymology but does not draw attention to the word's juridical meaning (partly because he has not taken account of Kantorowicz's essay). See also A.-M. Lecoq, " 'Finxit': Le peintre comme 'fictor' au XVIème siècle," *Bibliothèque d'Humanisme et Renaissance* 37 (1975): 225–243.

41. See Saint Augustine, *Quaestionum evangeliorum libri duo*, 51 (*Patrologia Latina*, 35:1362), cited by Aquinas in the *Summa Theologiae*, 3, q.55, a.4: "Cum autem fictio nostra referetur ad aliquam significationem, non est men-

dacium, sed aliqua figura veritatis. Alioquin omnia quae a sapientibus et sanctis viris, vel etiam ab ipso Domino figurate dicta sunt, mendacia reputabantur quia, secundum usitatum intellectum, non subsistit veritas in talibus dictis." This passage, on which Kantorowicz remarks in his "The Sovereignty of the Artist" (p. 355), should be considered alongside those discussed by E. Auerbach in his crucial essay "Figura," in his *Scenes from the Drama of European Literature* (New York, 1959), pp. 11–76, 229–237; the discussion of Augustine is on pp. 37–43.

42. Cf. A. Funkenstein, *Theology and the Scientific Imagination* (Princeton, 1986), pp. 208–289 (on the idea of "accommodation").

43. D. W. Robertson Jr. cites this passage (see *Patrologia Latina*, 122:146) in "Some Medieval Literary Terminology, with Special Reference to Chrétien de Troyes," *Studies in Philology* 48 (1951): 669–692. See p. 673 (referring to Petrarch, *Familiares* 10.4).

44. See Petrarch, *Familiares* 10.4 (V. Rossi's Italian edition [Florence, 1934]), 2:301 ff.

45. G. Boccaccio, *Trattatello in laude di Dante*, first version, ed. P. G. Ricci, in Boccaccio's complete works (*Tutte le opere*, ed. V. Branca [Milan, 1974]), 3:475.

46. Ibid., p. 469.

47. See M. D. Chenu, " 'Involucrum': Le mythe selon les théologiens médiévaux," *Archives d'Histoire Doctrinale et Littéraire du Moyen Age* 22 (1955): 75–79; E. Jeauneau, "L'usage du notion d' 'integumentum' à travers les notes de Guillaume de Conches," *Archives d'Histoire Doctrinale et Littéraire du Moyen Age* 32 (1957): 35–100; B. Stock, *Myth and Science in the Twelfth Century: A Study of Bernard Silvester* (Princeton, 1972).

48. Here I develop some ideas put forward by Trimpi in *Muses of One Mind*; see also T. Pavel, *Univers de la fiction* (Paris, 1988).

49. Isidore of Seville, *Differentiarum Liber* 1.2.21; quoted by A.-M. Lecoq, " 'Finxit,'" p. 228.

50. See A. Chastel, "Le 'dictum Horatii quidlibet audendi potestas' et les artistes (XIIIème–XVIème siècles)," in A. Chastel, *Fables, formes, figures* (Paris 1978), 1:363–376.

51. This may also be true of some animal species: D. Lipset, in *Gregory Bateson* (Chicago, 1978), tells an anecdote concerning Bateson and a dolphin that relates closely to the themes we are considering here.

52. See C. Ginzburg, *The Cheese and the Worms*, trans. J. and A. Tedeschi (Harmondsworth, 1992), p. 49.

53. See G. Boccaccio, *Decameron*, ed. V. Branca (Turin, 1980), p. 82 (the third tale on the first day). On this theme, see U. Fischer, "La storia dei tre anelli: Dal mito all'utopia," in *Annali della Scuola Normale Superiore di Pisa, Lettere e Filosofia*, s. III (1973), 3:955–998. T. Todorov comments on the narra-

tive device in *Poétique de la Prose* (Paris, 1971) [*Poetics of Prose*, trans. R. Howard (Oxford, 1977)].

54. See T. Todorov, *La conquête de l'Amérique: La question de l'autre* (Paris, 1982) [*The Conquest of America: The Question of the Other*, trans. R. Howard (New York, 1984)]—a book from which I have learned a great deal, despite (and also because of) its rather unhistorical approach.

55. M. de Cervantes Saavedra, *Don Quijote de la Mancha*, ed. V. Gaos (Madrid, 1987), 2:1043 ("Para mí sola nació don Quijote, y yo para él . . . "); see *The Adventures of Don Quixote*, trans. J. M. Cohen (Harmondsworth, 1968; first publ. 1950), p. 940. Spitzer discusses some of these themes in his very fine essay "Linguistic Perspectivism in the *Don Quixote*," in his *Linguistics and Literary History* (Princeton, 1948), pp. 41–85: I read this only after writing these pages. Much to the present point is the way Spitzer draws attention in his essay to the "goat-stag" ("*tragelaphos*") and similar linguistic hybrids.

56. Cervantes, *Don Quijote*, p. 1045; *Don Quixote*, p. 940.

57. See J. Brown and J. H. Elliott, *A Palace for a King: The Buen Retiro and the Court of Philip IV* (New Haven and London, 1980), pp. 119 f. (Luca Cambiaso's *Susanna* was hung in the same room).

58. J. Gállego argues in the catalog, edited by A. Domínguez Ortiz and others, that the original measurements were the same; see *Velázquez* (New York, 1990), pp. 104 ff. J. Brown takes the view that they were not, claiming that the *Vulcan*, now 223 centimeters by 290 centimeters, was 33 centimeters narrower and the *Jacob*, now 223 centimeters by 250 centimeters, was 50 centimeters wider (*Velázquez, Painter and Courtier* [London and New Haven, 1986], p. 72). Brown makes his case regarding the *Jacob* by citing the *Descripción del Real Monasterio de San Lorenzo del Escorial* (Madrid, 1681), p. 66, though this gives only approximate information ("un cuadro casi de cuatro varas de largo, y de alto dos y media").

59. In his attribution to Velázquez of the painting in the Pallavicini Rospigliosi collection known as *La Riña en la embajada de España*, R. Longhi remarked that one of the figures in the work is based on a model used also in the *Vulcan* (see "Velázquez 1630: 'La rissa all'ambasciata di Spagna,'" in *"Arte italiana e arte tedesca" e altre congiunture fra Italia ed Europa* ([Florence, 1979], pp. 91–100). The figure in question is the young smith shown in profile (second from the right). J. López-Rey rejects the attribution in *Velázquez. A Catalogue Raisonné of his Oeuvre* (London, [1963]), p. 166 n. 3.

60. See the work of Justi, which E. Harris refers to in *Velázquez* (Oxford, [1982]), pp. 80 ff.

61. "One cannot deceive divine Wisdom, which sees the most hidden places of our hearts, which needs make no enquiry nor call any witnesses, since she knows everything about our secrets"; the quatrain is reproduced

2. MYTH

Distance and Deceit

in D. Angulo Iñíguez, "La fábula de Vulcano, Venus y Marte y 'La Fragua' de Velázquez," *Archivio Español de Arte* 23 (1960): 172 n. 10. The first to note the parallel with Tempesta's print was E. du Gué Trapier (*Velázquez* [New York, 1948], p. 162), who says, however, that the resemblance is "not very close."

62. In his essay "Aggiunte e marginalia," R. Longhi argues that the influence was direct: see *Arte italiana e arte tedesca*, pp. 97 ff.

63. E. Harris reproduces the *Calling of St Matthew*, citing it an instance of an imitation of nature that was "once revolutionary [but] now looks theatrical" when we compare it to Velázquez's Roman paintings. She observes that Velázquez nonetheless drew inspiration from Caravaggio much more than from the latter's pupils (*Velázquez*, p. 85, plate 76). Antonio Tempesta is discussed, and adjudged a banal imitator of received *Pathosformeln*, in E. Gombrich, *Aby Warburg: An Intellectual Biography*, new ed. (Chicago, 1986), pp. 230 ff. (referring to an unpublished paper by Warburg on Rembrandt's *Conspiracy of Claudius Civilis*).

64. In his comments on *The Forge of Vulcan*, C. Justi calls it a "critical turning point" ("kritische Wendepunkt") between two movements (*Diego Velázquez und sein Jahrhundert*, 2nd [rev.] ed. [Bonn, 1903], 1:255). Silvia Ginzburg drew my attention to Velázquez's debt to Domenichino.

65. Isidore of Seville, *Etymologiarum libri*, 1:16 (A.-M. Lecoq draws attention to the passage in her article "Finxit," p. 232). Cf. F. Pacheco, *Arte de la Pintura*, ed. F. J. Sánchez Cantón, 2 vols. (Madrid, 1956), index (however, this does not appear in the list published by Sánchez Cantón, "La libreria di Velásquez," in *Homenaje . . . a Menéndez Pidal* [Madrid, 1925], 3:379–406). In an imaginary speech that R. Longhi puts into Velázquez's mouth—Longhi is paying homage to Carl Justi's famous pastiches—the painter is made to say: "I feel that concentrated and focused memory of this kind issues in something that we call evidence: which is a fiction hardest of all to achieve" (*"Arte italiana e arte tedesca,"* p. 93).

66. See G. Celati, "Il tema del doppio parodico," in Celati's *Finzioni occidentali*, new ed. (1986; Turin, 1975), pp. 169–218, esp. p. 192: "Borges once insisted that if the character, Don Quixote, becomes the reader of the book, then this raises the suspicion that the reader in his turn might be a character" (it is this sensation, familiar to anyone who has looked at *Las Meninas*, which inspired Théophile Gautier's famous remark "Où est le tableau?"). In a footnote to the 1975 edition, Celati sums the point up thus: "Don Quixote incarnates the modern practice of writing as a mode of ordering the world at a remove, and thus of administering it bureaucratically or reinventing it novelistically (and here it is shown that these two things often amount to one)." I have been much stimulated in my own reflections both by these pages of Celati's book and by an essay of Italo Calvino's that is closely

linked to them (and that also discusses *Don Quixote* and meta-painting); see "I livelli della realtà in letteratura," written in 1978 and included in Calvino, *Una pietra sopra* (Turin, 1980), pp. 310–323; see esp. p. 315.

67. Plato, *Republic*, p. 76. See also Brisson, *Platon*, pp. 144–151 ("L'utilité des mythes").

68. This is the myth referred to by Karl Popper, in his depiction of Plato as a proto-Nazi, as the myth of Blood and Soil. See *The Open Society and Its Enemies*, 5th ed. (1966; first publ. 1945), 1:140.

69. Aristotle, *Metaphysics* 1074b, Oxford translation, ed. W. D. Ross, 2nd ed. (1928, reprint 1963). P. Veyne draws attention to this passage, calling it "sensational," in *Les Grecs ont-ils cru à leurs mythes?*, p. 153 n. 108; he refers to P. Aubenque, *Le problème de l'Etre chez Aristote* (Paris, 1962), pp. 335 ff.

70. The passage in question from Critias's *Sisyphus*, which is referred to by Sextus Empiricus (*Adv. math.* 9.54), is discussed in M. Untersteiner, *I sofisti*, new enlarged ed. (Milan, 1967), 2:205 ff.

71. See the evidence collected by M. Esposito, "Una manifestazione di incredulità religiosa nel Medioevo: Il detto dei 'Tre impostori' e la sua trasmissione da Federico II a Pomponazzi," *Archivio Storico Italiano*, s. 7, vol. 16, a. 89 (1931), pp. 3–48 (Esposito makes no mention of the passages from Plato and Aristotle discussed here). There is no adequate scholarly treatment of this topic.

72. Celsus, *Il discorso vero*, ed. G. Lanata (Milan, 1987), p. 65 (1:24, 26). On the fortunes of this text in the sixteenth century, see L. Febvre, *Origène et Des Périers* (Paris, 1942).

73. Esposito, "Una manifestazione," p. 40.

74. N. Machiavelli, *Discorsi sopra la prima deca di Tito Livio*, ed. C. Vivanti (Turin, 1983), pp. 68, 71 f. [Translators' note: We translate from the Italian. An English version is Machiavelli, *The Prince* and *The Discourses*, trans. M. Lerner (New York, 1940).]

75. The future plagiarist of Machiavelli's *Il Principe*, A. Nifo, had produced a rather drab commentary on the Aristotelian passage (1074b.1); see Nifo, *In duodecimum Metaphysices Aristotelis et Averrois volumen* (Venice, 1518), 32r.

76. This has been demonstrated by C. Dionisotti; see his *Machiavellerie* (Turin, 1980), p. 139.

77. See C. Nicolet, "Polybe et les institutions romaines," *Polybe* (Vandoeuvres and Geneva, 1973), *Entretiens Fondation Hardt* 20: 245 and bibliography. The echo from Polybius in Machiavelli was identified by O. Tommasini, as C. Vivanti notes in his edition of the *Discorsi*, p. 65 n. 1. [Translators' note: We translate from Ginzburg's Italian version of the text.]

78. A. Momigliano remarks (citing Mommsen to the same effect) that Polybius had little understanding of Roman religion; see "Polibio, Posidonio e l'imperialismo romano," in Momigliano, *Storia e storiografica antica*

(Bologna, 1987), pp. 303–315. As the passage quoted here shows, however, the outsider's vantage point can sometimes conduce to understanding.

79. On Polybius and Plato, see P. Friedländer, "Socrates Enters Rome," *American Journal of Philology* 66 (1945): 337–351; on Polybius and Aristotle, see I. Düring, *Aristotele* (Milan, 1976), p. 46.

80. Machiavelli, "Of the religion of the Romans," *Discourses*, 1:11 (pp. 66–70 of Vivanti's edition). M. C. Smith's "Opium of the People: Numa Pompilius in the French Renaissance," *Bibliothèque d'Humanisme et Renaissance* 52 (1990): 7–21, promises more than it delivers.

81. See Machiavelli, *Discourses*, 2:2, "What peoples the Romans had to fight with, and how tenaciously they defended their liberty" (pp. 223 f. of Vivanti's edition). On the debates occasioned by these pages, see A. Prosperi, "I cristiani e la guerra: una controversia fra '500 e '700," in *Rivista di storia e letteratura religiosa* (1994), pp. 57–83.

82. See R. Pintard, *Le libertinage érudit dans la première moitié du XVIIe siècle* (1943; new and enlarged ed. Geneva, 1983), p. 172. On this theme more generally, see also D. P. Walker, *The Decline of Hell: Seventeenth-Century Discussions of Eternal Torment* (London, 1964).

83. See C. Ginzburg, "The Dovecote Has Opened Its Eyes," in *The Inquisition in Early Modern Europe*, ed. G. Henningsen and J. Tedeschi (Dekalb, Ill., 1986), pp. 190–198.

84. "Oratius Tubero" (La Mothe La Vayer), "De la philosophie sceptique," in A. Pessel, ed., *Dialogues faits à l'imitation des anciens*, reprint ed. (Paris, 1988), p. 41: "Escrire des fables pour des veritez, donner des contes à la posterité pour des histoires, c'est le fait d'un imposteur, ou d'un autheur léger et de nulle considération; escrire des caprices pour des révélations divines, et des resveries pour des loix venuës du Ciel, c'est à Minos, à Numa, à Mahomet, et à leurs semblables, estre grands Prophetes, et les propres fils de Iupiter." T. Gregory quotes this passage in "Il libertinismo della prima metà del Seicento: Stato attuale degli studi e prospettive di ricerca," in Gregory, *Ricerche su letteratura libertina e letteratura clandestina nel Seicento* (Florence, 1981), pp. 26 f. La Mothe Le Vayer did not include the *Dialogues* in the collection that he made of his complete works.

85. "Oratius Tubero" (La Mothe Le Vayer), introduction to *Dialogues*: "Ma main est si genereuse ou si libertine, qu'elle ne peut suivre que le seul caprice de mes faintaisies, et cela avec une licence si independente et si affranchie, qu'elle fait gloire de n'avoir autre visée, qu'une naifve recherche des verités ou vray-semblances naturelles." The passage confirms that Valéry is correct in the interpretation of the term "*libertin*," which is quoted in G. Schneider's confused ragbag of a book *Il libertinismo* (Bologna, 1970), pp. 35 f.

86. La Mothe Le Vayer, *De la vertu des payens*, in *œîuvres*, 2 (Geneva, 1970) (a reprint of the Dresden edition of 1757), pp. 156 ff. (in the new pagination).

87. There is no in-depth scholarly treatment of this topic. For the subsequent period, a starting point is F. E. Manuel's *The Eighteenth Century Confronts the Gods* (Cambridge, Mass., 1959).

88. T. Hobbes, *Leviathan (1651)*, ed. A. D. Lindsay (London and New York: Everyman's Library, 1914), vol. 1, ch. 13, pp. 65, 64. [Translators' note: Spelling and capitalization have been modernized in this and subsequent quotations.] Hobbes lived in exile in Paris for some time. His *De Cive* was translated by Samuel Sorbière (Amsterdam, 1649): on this, see R. Pintard, *Le libertinage érudit*, pp. 552–558 and passim.

89. Hobbes, *Leviathan*, ch. 12, pp. 54–62. Hobbes draws a contrast between polytheism, which is the result of fear, and monotheism, which comes from "the desire men have to know the causes of natural bodies, and their several virtues, and operations": the latter, "as even the Heathen Philosophers confessed," leads to the notion of "one First Mover . . . a First, and an Eternal cause of things." On Hobbes's attitude to Aristotle, see L. Strauss, *The Political Philosophy of Hobbes* (1936; reprint, Chicago, 1973), pp. 30–43.

90. *Leviathan*, ch. 12, p. 62.

91. Ibid., ch. 32, p. 199.

92. On this aspect of the matter, see the convincing arguments of S. Landucci, *I filosofi e i selvaggi, 1580–1780* (Bari, 1972), pp. 114–142.

93. *Leviathan*, ch. 38, p. 240 (italics in original).

94. Ibid., ch. 17, p. 89: "This is the generation of that great Leviathan, or rather (to speak more reverently) of that mortal god."

95. Ibid., ch. 42, p. 269.

96. P. Bayle, *Pensées diverses sur la comète*, first published under a different title in 1682, and subsequently republished in an enlarged edition in 1683. See chapter 161. See also Bayle's "Réponse aux questions d'un provincial" in his *Oeuvres diverses*, 3, 2 (The Hague, 1737), p. 958, where Bayle invents an extraordinary dialogue between a Chinese mandarin and a Jesuit.

97. See *Trattato dei tre impostori: La vita e lo spirito del signor Benedetto de Spinoza*, ed. S. Berti and with a preface by R. Popkin (Turin, 1994). On the basis of various pieces of contemporary evidence, Berti attributes the work to Jan Vroesen.

98. In addition to a number of examples relating to Charron noted by Berti (pp. lxxiv–lxxvi), one notes how the *Traité* deals with the passage from La Mothe Le Vayer's "De la vertu des payens," which is quoted earlier in the present chapter (see note 86, above). The anonymous author of the *Traité* leaves out the phrases concerning the "great ignorance" of the pagans, skipping without comment from a passage comparing the fire caused by Phaeton with that which destroyed Sodom and Gomorrah to another in which Phaeton is compared with Elia ("For several have remarked the relation between Sampson and Hercules, Elia and Phaeton,"

etc.). The awkwardly concocted French text is made more awkward, in the Italian edition, by an error of translation.

99. *Trattato*, p. 71.

100. S. Berti rightly emphasizes this point in her introduction (ibid., p. lx).

101. Ibid., pp. 67, 69, 239.

102. I. Kant, *Critique of Pure Reason*, trans. J. M. D. Meiklejohn (London, Everyman's Library, n.d.), p. 2, Kant's footnote. The dropping of this from the preface to the second edition is noted by R. Koselleck, *Kritik und Krise: Ein Beitrag zur Pathogenese der bürgerlichen Welt* (1959); see p. 136 of the Italian translation, *Critica illuminista e crisi dela società borghese* (Bologna, 1972). Koselleck's book cleverly reworks the old conspiratorial thesis advocated by the Abbé Barruel.

103. See *Bisogna ingannare il popolo?* (Bari, 1968) (where Castillon's contribution is reprinted together with that of Condorcet), pp. 13, 53, 60–62. A fuller selection of the original texts is to be found in W. Krauss, ed., *Est-il utile de tromper le peuple?* (Berlin, 1966).

104. See G. L. Mosse, *The Nationalization of the Masses: Political Symbolism and Mass Movements in Germany from the Napoleonic Wars Through the Third Reich* (1974).

105. See p. 227 (fragment 884) of the Italian translation of Novalis, *Frammenti* (Milan, 1976).

106. The passage quoted is also quoted in part by E. Castelnuovo at the opening of his essay "Arte e rivoluzione industriale," in his *Arte, industria, rivoluzioni* (Turin, 1985), p. 85. See p. 43 of the Italian edition of Marx and Engels's *Works* (*Opere complete*, ed. N. Merker [Rome, 1986]).

107. K. Marx, *The Eighteenth Brumaire of Louis Bonaparte*, trans. E. and C. Paul (1926; third impression, London, 1943), p. 26.

108. Ibid., pp. 23–25.

109. Ibid., p. 3 (Marx's preface to the 1869 German edition). In a letter to Marx of 3 December 1851, Engels refers to the "travesty" and the "farce" of the Eighteenth Brumaire (Karl Marx and Friedrich Engels, *Selected Correspondence, 1849–1895*, trans. and with a commentary by D. Torr [London, 1943], pp. 49, 51).

110. *Eighteenth Brumaire*, p. 3. Marx notes that the term "Caesarism" was fashionable above all in Germany. Its origins were French: see A. Momigliano's two essays, republished in his *Sui fondamenti della storia antica* (Turin, 1984), pp. 378–392.

111. *The Eighteenth Brumaire* concludes with a reference to the "imperial mantle . . . [falling] on the shoulders of Louis Bonaparte" (p. 144).

112. Marx and Engels, *Selected Correspondence*, p. 299. The letter is dated 17 August 1870; the phrases "from the beginning" and "showman" are in English in the original.

113. Ibid., pp. 205 f. (letter of 13 April 1866).

114. For a general account, see D. Losurdo, *Democrazia o bonapartismo. Trionfo e decadenza del suffragio universale*, Turin, 1993.

115. [M. Joly], *Dialogue aux Enfers de Machiavel et Montesquieu, ou la politique de Machiavel au XIXe siècle par un contemporain* (Brussels, 1864), pp. 48 f. Shortly after its initial appearance, the work was republished (with Joly named as author) and translated into German (Leipzig, 1865); later, it was rediscovered and reprinted (Paris, 1948 and 1968).

116. A. de Tocqueville, *Democracy in America*, trans. G. Lawrence and ed. J. P. Mayer (London, 1994), pp. 691 f. (first publ. Paris, 1840).

117. Napoleon's words are mentioned and discussed in Losurdo, *Democrazia o bonapartismo*, pp. 56, 224.

118. On the sources of the forgery and the fortune it enjoyed, see N. Cohn's excellent book *Warrant for Genocide: The Myth of the Jewish World-Conspiracy and the Protocols of the Elders of Zion* (1967; London, 1996). Cohn justifies his use of the overworn term "myth" in a footnote (p. xii n. 2, in the 1967 edition). The connection with Joly's *Dialogue* was first revealed in an article in the *Times* in 1921. Another account of the work's fortunes is P.-A. Taguieff, (ed.), *Les Protocoles des Sages de Sion*, 2 vols. (Paris, 1992).

119. See the Italian edition of the *Protocols*, ed. G. Preziosi, republished as an appendix to S. Romano, *I falsi protocolli* (Milan, 1992), pp. 151, 153, 156, 163, 171, 176, 181, 205.

120. Ibid., p. 161.

121. See M. Confino, *Violence dans la violence: L'affaire Bakounine-Necaev* (1973); trans. into Italian as *Il catechismo del rivoluzionario, Bakunin e l'affare Necaev* (Milan, 1976), p. 123; and the references to the "system of the Jesuits" on pp. 150, 158 f., 171, 173, 200, 240. Confino cautiously attributes the *Catechism* to Nechaev and rules out the possibility that Bakunin may have contributed to it. V. Strada takes a different view in his introduction to A. Herzen, *A un vecchio compagno* (Turin, 1977); see the note on "revolutionary Jesuitism" on pp. xxxiii–xxxv.

122. Romano, *Falsi protocolli*, p. 161.

123. Hitler is said to have confided to Rauschning that his reading of the *Protocols* left him "perturbed." "How devious the enemy is, and how omnipresent! I realised at once that we must copy him, but in our own way, of course. . . . How they resemble us, and yet on the other hand how different from us they are! What a struggle there is between us and them! And the stakes are, quite simply, the destiny of the world" (H. Rauschning, *Hitler mi ha detto*, trans. G. Monforte [Milan, 1945], pp. 262 f.; English edition, *Hitler Speaks* [London, 1939]. N. Cohn quotes this in part in his *Warrant for Genocide*, p. 201 [translators' note: here we translate from the Italian]; and see also H. Arendt's comment, quoted in Cohn, *Warrant for Genocide*, p. 213). In

the same conversation, Hitler supposedly told Rauschning that he had "learned above all from the Society of Jesus. Besides, I seem to recall that Lenin did something similar" (*Hitler mi ha detto*, pp. 263 f.).

124. F. Nietzsche, *Die Geburt der Tragödie* (1872); trans. F. Golffing, in *The Birth of Tragedy and the Genealogy of Morals* (New York, 1956), pp. 108, 110 (translation slightly modified). L. Gossman quotes part of this passage in "Le 'boudoir' de l'Europe: la Bâle de Burckhardt et la critique du moderne," in *L'éternel retour: Contre la démocratie l'idéologie de la décadence*, ed. Z. Sternhell (Paris, 1994), p. 65. A little further on (p. 115), Nietzsche remarks that the conception of "primitive man as essentially good and artistic . . . has by degrees become a menacing and rather appalling *claim*, against which we who are faced with present-day socialist movements cannot stop our ears. The 'noble savage' demands his rights: what a paradisaical prospect!"

125. The original preface is dated December 1871 (*Birth of Tragedy and Genealogy of Morals*, p. 17). In the "Critical Backward Glance" written in 1886, Nietzsche refers to "the times in which (in spite of which)" the essay was composed: "1870–71, the turbulent period of the Franco-Prussian war" (ibid., p. 3). See Sorel's introduction (dated 1907) to *Réflexions sur la violence* (Paris, 1946), and also the section on Nietzsche (pp. 356–367).

126. See Nietzsche, *Birth of Tragedy*, pp. 16 f.

127. Both passages are quoted by V. Foa (who adds the italics) in Foa, *La Gerusalemme rimandata: Domande di oggi agli inglesi del primo Novecento* (Turin, 1985), p. 190 (and see the whole of this important book).

128. *Dialogues*, quoted in N. Cohn, *Warrant for Genocide*, p. 287.

129. The passage, from J. de Lignières, *Le centenaire de la presse* (June 1936), is quoted in W. Benjamin, *Das Passagen-Werk*, vol. 5, part 2 of Benjamin, *Gesammelte Schriften*, ed. R. Tiedemann (1982), p. 926.

130. Le Bon's *Psychologie des foules* is cited to this effect in Losurdo, *Democrazia*, pp. 83 f.; and see E. Gentile, *Il culto del Littorio: La sacralizzazione della politica nell'Italia fascista* (Rome and Bari, 1993), pp. 155 ff.

131. A. Hitler, *Mein Kampf*, quoted in D. Cantimori, "Appunti sulla propaganda" (1941), in Cantimori, *Politica e storia contemporanea: Scritti 1927–1942* (Turin, 1991), pp. 685 f. (and see the whole of this essay, pp. 683–699).

132. Cf. T. W. Adorno, *Minima Moralia*, trans. E. F. N. Jephcott (London, 1974), pp. 105 f., aphorism 69, "Little folk."

133. See T. W. Adorno and M. Horkheimer, *Dialektik der Aufklärung*, 1947; *Dialectic of Enlightenment*, trans. J. Cumming (London and New York, 1979; first published 1972), pp. 120–167; and G. Debord, *La société du spectacle* (1971); *The Society of the Spectacle*, trans. not named (Exeter, 1977); aphorism 43 (scarcely original, for all Debord's bombastic claims to the contrary).

134. *Birth of Tragedy*, p. 137.

135. Legitimation through myth is discussed in M. Frank, *Il dio a venire*

(Turin, 1994), in connection with the "new mythology" of the German Romantics. However, the idea that myth, *by virtue of being myth*, allows us access to a deeper truth is foreign to the line of thought that comes down from Plato. Such a (frequently unconscious) retrospective projection of Romantic views is what has hindered the apprehension of the nexus linking the *Phaedrus* and the *Sophist*, which is the starting point of the present essay.

136. On the question in general (considered from another point of view), see W. Rösler, "Die Entdeckung der Fiktionalität in der Antike," *Poetica* 12 (1980): 283–319.

137. See Detienne, *L'invention de la mythologie*, pp. 141–144.

138. On this passage, see Trimpi, *Muses of One Mind*, pp. 50 ff.

139. See Detienne, *L'invention de la mythologie*, p. 239 (quoting Athenaeus 6.22b.1–7).

140. This is argued by C. Calame, whose *Le récit en Grèce ancienne* (Paris, 1986), p. 155, is cited by N. Loraux in " 'Poluneikes eponumos': Les noms du fils d'Oedipe, entre épopée et tragédie," in the volume cited above, *Métamorphoses du mythe*, pp. 152–166, where the name is considered as the smallest mythic *énoncé* (p. 151). See also Nagy, *The Best of the Achaeans*. Unless I am mistaken, none of these studies cites H. Usener, *Götternamen* (1896). For an account of Usener, based in part on unpublished materials, see J. H. Bremmer's profile in *Classical Scholarship: A Biographical Encyclopaedia*, ed. W. W. Briggs and W. M. Calder III (New York, 1990), pp. 462–478.

141. The viewpoint suggested here allows us to reformulate, on slightly different premises, the notion of poetry as "neither true nor false" that was put forward by the English Romantics. See M. H. Abrams, *The Mirror and the Lamp* (Oxford, 1953; reprint, 1974), pp. 320–326.

142. See M. Proust, *Du côté de chez Swann* (Paris, 1954), 1:110. See also A. Henry, *Métonymie et métaphore* (Paris, 1971), pp. 44–46. Here, as elsewhere, Bloch is echoing other people's ideas. Maxime Du Camp recounts that Flaubert, having criticized Racine for his faults of language, went on to acknowledge that he had written "one line which is eternal, because it is so sublime. . . . [He] drew himself up to his full height and, in his most resounding tones, cried out: 'La fille de Minos et de Pasiphaé!'" (M. Du Camp, *Souvenirs littéraires*, with a preface by D. Oster [Paris, 1994], p. 443).

3. REPRESENTATION: THE WORD, THE IDEA, THE THING

1. See R. Chartier, "Le monde comme représentation," *Annales ESC* 6 (1989): 1514 f.

2. M.-J. Mondzain, *Image, icône, économie: Les sources byzantines de l'imaginarie contemporain* (Paris, 1996), at once denounces and symptomatically typifies this intellectual fashion.

3. See E. Lourie, "Jewish Participation in Royal Funerary Rites: An Early Use of Representation in Aragon," *Journal of the Warburg and Courtauld Institutes* 45 (1982): 192–194.

4. See R. E. Giesey, *The Royal Funeral Ceremony in Renaissance France* (Geneva, 1960), pp. 79–104. Giesey rejects, with convincing arguments, the theory that the first use of funeral effigies should be dated earlier, to the funeral ceremonies for Henri III in 1271; see on this also W. H. St. John Hope, "On the Funeral Effigies of the Kings and Queens of England, with Special Reference to Those in the Abbey Church of Westminster," *Archaeologia* 60 (1907): 526–528. Giesey makes a further contribution to the study of effigies in *Cérémoniale et puissance souveraine: France XVe–XVIe siècles* (Paris, 1987). There is now an account of the influence of these practices in Italy, in G. Ricci, "Le Corps et l'Effigie: Les Funérailles des Ducs de Ferrare à la Renaissance," in *Civic Ritual and Drama*, ed. A. F. Johnston and W. Hüsken (Amsterdam and Atlanta, Ga., 1997), pp. 175–201.

5. See St. John Hope, "On the Funeral Effigies," pp. 517–570; R. P. Howgrave-Graham, "Royal Portraits in Effigy: Some New Discoveries in Westminster Abbey," *Journal of the Royal Society of Arts* 101 (1953): 465–474 (I have not been able to consult this). A. Harvey and R. Mortimer, eds., *The Funeral Effigies of Westminster Abbey* (Woodbridge, 1994), surveys the most recent documentary evidence and includes many illustrations.

6. E. Kantorowicz, *The King's Two Bodies: A Study in Medieval Political Theology* (Princeton, 1957).

7. See La Curne de Sainte-Palaye, *Dictionnaire historique de l'ancien langage français*, vol. 9 (Paris, 1881), entry for "Représentation" (which refers to the funeral of the Count of Eu in 1388 and to the will of the Duc de Berry in 1415). A much older document (1225), which I have been unable to verify, refers to a payment made by a woman, of unspecified social status, for a *representacion* made of her husband after his death; see A. N. Zadok-Josephus Jitta, *Ancestral Portraiture in Rome and the Art of the Last Century of the Republic* (Amsterdam, 1932), p. 90, which refers to V. Gay, *Glossaire archéologique du Moyen Age et de la Renaissance* (Paris, 1928), 2:297.

8. Giesey, *The Royal Funeral Ceremony*, pp. 81 f., 99 f.

9. Ibid., p. 86.

10. See St. John Hope, "On the Funeral Effigies," pp. 530 f.; Kantorowicz, *The King's Two Bodies*, pp. 419 f. At the time of Edward II's death, a rumor was current (and was recorded in some contemporary chronicles) that he had been assassinated; if so, his corpse would then have been in no condition to be exhibited in the funeral cortège. Neither Giesey nor Kantorowicz records that one account, set down at the time by the papal notary Manuele del Fiesco, tells us Edward made a fool of his enemies by escaping from prison and that they then killed the doorkeeper in his place—which

would have made it absolutely impossible for the king's body to be exhibited; see A. Germain, *Lettre de Manuel de Fiesque concernant les dernières années du roi d'Angleterre Edouard II* (Montpellier, 1878); C. Nigra, "Uno degli Edoardi in Italia: favola o storia?," *La Nuova Antologia*, ser. 5, vol. 92 (1901): 403–425; C. P. Cuttino and T. W. Lyman, "Where Is Edward II?," *Speculum* 3 (1958): 522–544. However, this story, if true, would not explain why a figurine was used—still less why this practice lasted so long.

11. J. von Schlosser, "Geschichte der Porträtsbildnerei in Wachs," *Jahrbuch der kunsthistorischen Sammlungen des allerhöchsten Kaiserhauses* (1910–1911), 29:171–258, esp. pp. 202 f. (republished as *Tote Blicke: Geschichte des Porträtsbildnerei in Wachs*, ed. Th. Medicus [Berlin, 1993]).

12. Ibid., pp. 8 f.

13. Giesey, *The Royal Funeral Ceremony*, pp. 149 f. See pp. 145–154, 79 f., 170–174.

14. E. Bickerman, "Die römische Kaiserapotheose," *Archiv für Religionswissenschaft* 27 (1929): 1–34 (see Bickerman, "Consecratio, le culte des souverains dans l'Empire romain," in *Entretiens de la fondation Hardt*, vol. 19 [Vandoeuvres and Geneva, 1972], pp. 3 ff.). See also Giesey, preface.

15. See R. Hertz, *Mélanges de sociologie religieuse et de folklore* (Paris, 1928), pp. 1–98. So far as I can ascertain, this essay has never been made use of in discussions of royal funerals, with the single exception (and even here the reference is fairly superficial) of the book by R. Huntington and P. Metcalf, *Celebrations of Death* (Cambridge, 1979); see pp. 159 ff., on Kantorowicz and Giesey, on Hertz, p. 13.

16. Bickerman, "Die römische Kaiserapotheose," p. 4.

17. Hertz, *Mélanges*, p. 22.

18. F. Dupont, "L'autre corps de l'empereur-dieu," in *Le temps de la réflexion* (1986), pp. 231 f. (The theme of the volume was "Le corps des dieux").

19. Giesey, *The Royal Funeral Ceremony*, p. 152.

20. Ernest Cary's translation of Dio Cassius, quoted in Giesey, ibid., p. 149.

21. Giesey, *The Royal Funeral Ceremony*, pp. 147 f.

22. Ibid., p. 5 (drawing on Pierre du Chastel's account).

23. Ibid, pp. 172 ff., 189.

24. Ibid., p. 174.

25. Francisco Pizarro, *Relación del Descubrimiento y Conquista de los Reinos del Perú*, ed. G. Lohmann Villena (Lima, 1978), pp. 89 f., quoted in G. W. Conrad and A. A. Demarest, *The Dynamic of Aztec and Inca Expansionism* (Cambridge, 1984), pp. 112 f. (I must express my warm thanks to Aaron Segal for drawing this book to my attention.) See also pp. 51 f.

26. Ibid., p. 113 (I reproduce this account almost word for word).

27. Giesey, *The Royal Funeral Ceremony*, p. 190.

28. For discussion of an analogous problem, see the present author's *Storia notturna: Una decifrazione del sabba* (Turin, 1989), pp. 197 f., 205 (and the references to Bloch and Lévi-Strauss). The original edition of *Storia notturna* is available in English as *Ecstasies: Deciphering the Witches' Sabbath*, trans. R. Rosenthal (London, 1990).

29. Dupont, "L'autre corps," pp. 240 f.

30. M. Mauss, "Une catégorie de l'esprit humain: la notion de personne, celle de 'moi,'" in Mauss, *Anthropologie et sociologie* (Paris, 1960), pp. 352 f. See also M. Rambaud, "Essai sur certains usages funéraires de l'Afrique Noire et de la Rome antique," *Les Etudes Classiques* 46 (1978): 3–21, esp. pp. 12 f.

31. See Zadoks-Josephus Jitta, *Ancestral Portraiture*, pp. 97–110 (on the nonexistence of the so-called *jus imaginum* hypothesized by Mommsen).

32. Bickerman, "Die römische Kaiserapotheose," pp. 6 f.; Dupont, "L'autre corps," p. 240. On "funeral associations," see K. Hopkins, *Death and Renewal* (Cambridge, 1983), p. 211 (where *"funus imaginarium"* is translated "imaginary body").

33. P. Chantraine, "Grec *kolossos*," *Bulletin de l'Institut français d'archéologie orientale* 30 (1931): 449–452; E. Benveniste, "Le sens du mot *kolossos* et les mots grecs de la statue," *Revue de Philologie, de Littérature, et d'Histoire anciennes*, 3rd ser., 5 (1931): 118–135, esp. pp. 118 f. The discussion since then has included contributions from, among others, Ch. Picard ("Le cénotaphe de Midéa et les 'kolosses' de Ménélas," ibid. 7 [1933]: 341–354), J. Servais ("Les suppliants dans la 'loi sacrée' de Cyrène," *Bulletin de correspondance hellénique* 84 (1960): 112–147—a most useful overview), and J. Ducat, "Fonctions de la statue dans la Grèce ancienne: kouros et kolossos," ibid. 100 (1976): 239–251.

34. See J.-P. Vernant, *Figures, idoles, masques* (Paris, 1990), pp. 39, 72 ff. (and the entire volume is important).

35. P. Brown makes the same remark, in a different context, in "A Dark Age Crisis: Aspects of the Iconoclastic Controversy," in Brown, *Society and the Holy in Late Antiquity* (London, 1960).

36. See E. H. Gombrich, *Meditations on a Hobby Horse* (London, 1963), pp. 1–11 (see pp. 1, 3, 5, 9). The title essay dates from 1951. On its relationship with *Art and Illusion* (London, 1960), see *Meditations*, p. xi.

37. K. Pomian, "Entre et l'invisible: La collection," in Pomian, *Collectioneurs, amateurs et curieux* (Paris 1978), pp. 15–59; *Collectors and Curiosities: Paris and Venice, 1500–1800*, trans. E. Wiles-Portier (London, 1990), pp. 22, 24, 30.

38. J.-P. Vernant, *Mythe et Pensée chez les Grecs: Etudes de psychologie historique* (Paris, 1966); published in English (trans. unacknowledged) as *Myth and Thought Among the Greeks* (London, 1983). See chapter 13, "The Representation of the Invisible and the Psychological Category of the Double: The Colossos," pp. 308, 314 f.

39. See Vernant, *Figures, idoles, masques*; and also his "Psuché: Simulacre du corps ou image du divin?," *Nouvelle Revue de Psychanalyse* 44 (Autumn 1991): 223 ff., a special issue on the theme of *Destins de l'image*.

40. Dupont, "L'autre corps," pp. 234 f., 237.

41. J. Guyon, "La vente des tombes à travers l'épigraphie de la Rome chrétienne," *Mélanges d'archéologie et d'histoire: Antiquité* 86 (1974): 594, cited in P. Brown, *The Cult of the Saints* (Chicago, 1982), p. 133 n. 16.

42. Brown, *The Cult of the Saints*, pp. 3 f.

43. Much relevant material is brought together in H. Belting, *Bild und Kult* (Munich, 1990).

44. Our starting point must be the substantial evidence collected in D. Freedberg, *The Power of Images* (Chicago, 1989) (though the book's theoretical framework is not very convincing). M. Camille, *The Gothic Idol* (Cambridge, 1989), offers some stimulating ideas, much that is obvious, and a wealth of errors (see, for instance, the Latin quotations on pp. 21, 22, 221, 227, etc.).

45. See J. Seznec, *La survivance des dieux antiques* (London, 1940); F. Saxl, *Lectures* (London, 1957); E. Panofsky, *Renaissance and Renascences* (Stockholm, 1965).

46. See the critical edition of the *Liber miraculorum Sancte Fidis*, ed. and introd. L. Robertini (Spoleto, 1994). There is a discussion of the term "scholasticus" on pp. 319 f.; in Robertini's view it cannot be taken as a technical term referring to the master of a cathedral school. On the text, see A. G. Remensnyder, "Un problème de cultures ou de culture? La statue-reliquaire et les *joca* de sainte Foy de Conques dans le *Liber miraculorum* de Bernard d'Angers," *Cahiers de civilisation médiévale* 33 (1990): 351–379.

47. *Liber*, 1:13.

48. Brown, *Society and the Holy*, pp. 302–332, esp. pp. 318–321, 330; the quotation is from p. 330.

49. The chapter's title in full is *Quod sanctorum statue propter invincibilem ingenitamque idiotarum consuetudinem fieri permittantur, presertim cum nihil ob id de religione depereat, et de celesti vindicta.*

50. An important commentary on Bernard's chapter is B. Stock, *The Implications of Literacy* (Princeton, 1983), pp. 64–72.

51. Remensnyder, "Un problème de cultures," offers a different opinion. See also E. Bickerman, "Sur la théologie de l'art figuratif: A propos de l'ouvrage de E. R. Goodenough," in Bickerman, *Studies in Jewish and Christian History* (Leyden, 1986), 3:248, n. 7.

52. On this, see the excellent article by J. Taralon, "La majesté d'or de Sainte-Foy de Conques," *Revue del' Art* 40–41 (1978): 9–22, esp. p. 16; E. Dahl, "Heavenly Images: The Statue of St. Foy of Conques and the Signification of the Medieval Cult in the West," *Acta ad archaeologiam et artium historiam*

205

3. REPRESENTATION
The Word, the Idea, the Thing

pertinentia 8 (1978): 175–191; J. Wirth, *L'image médiévale* (Paris, 1989), pp. 171–194.

53. Taralon, "La majesté," p. 19.

54. See I. H. Forsyth, *The Throne of Wisdom* (Princeton, 1972).

55. See J. Wirth, "La représentation de l'image dans l'art du Haut Moyen Age," *Revue de l'Art* (1988), p. 15.

56. *Liber*, 1:1, 1:11, 1:14, 1:15, 1:17, 1:25, 1:26.

57. Ibid., 1:11.

58. Ibid., 1:13.

59. See R. Bugge's fine essay "Effigiem Christi, qui transis, semper honora: Verses Condemning the Cult of Sacred Images in Art and Literature," *Acta ad archaeologiam et artium historiam pertinentia* 6 (1975): 127–139.

60. See W. Durig, *Imago: Ein Betrag zur Terminologie und Theologie der römischen Liturgie* (Munich, 1952); R. Daut, *Imago: Untersuchungen zum Bildlegriff der Römer* (Heidelberg, 1975). See also E. Auerbach, "Figura," in Auerbach, *Scenes from the Drama of European Literature* (New York, 1959), pp. 11–76.

61. *Liber*, 1:5. A. Bouillet and L. Servières, in *Sainte Foy vierge et martyre* (Rodez, 1900), p. 458, translate the last phrase "Non dans l'abstraction, mais substantiellement incarné dans un corps." See also Stock, *Implications of Literacy*, p. 69: "Not in an image . . . but genuinely present in substance."

62. Saint Ambrose, *In psalmum 38*, n. 25 (see *Patrologia Latina*, 14:1051–1052), quoted in H. de Lubac, *Corpus mysticum* (Paris, 1949), p. 218 (and see pp. 217 ff. generally).

63. Dahl, "Heavenly Images," p. 191; de Lubac, *Corpus*, p. 275.

64. See Stock, *Implications of Literacy*, pp. 244 ff.

65. *Patrologia Latina*, 156:col. 631, quoted in Stock, *Implications of Literacy*, p. 250. See also J. Geiselmann, "Die Stellung des Guibert de Nogent," *Theologische Quartalschrift* 110 (1929): 67–84, 279–305.

66. Camille, *Gothic Idol*, p. 217.

67. P. Browe, "Die Hostienschändungen der Juden im Mittelalter," *Römische Quartalschrift für christliche Altertumskunde und für Kirchengeschichte* 34 (1926): 167–197; and the same author's "Die eucharistische Verwandlungswunder des Mittelalters," ibid. 37 (1929): 137–169.

68. See S. Levi della Torre, "Il delito eucaristico," in Della Torre, *Mosaico: Attualità e inattualità degli ebrei* (Rome, 1992), pp. 105–134; J. Cohen, *The Friars and the Jews: The Evolution of Medieval Anti-Judaism* (Ithaca, 1982). More recently, see G. I. Langmuir, "The Tortures of the Body of Christ," in S. Waugh and P. D. Diehl, eds., *Christendom and Its Discontents* (Cambridge, 1996), pp. 287–309.

69. Kantorowicz, *The King's Two Bodies*, pp. 196–206.

70. *Chronique du religieux de Saint-Denys* (Paris, 1839), 1:600. The author of the chronicle died between 1430 and 1435: see M. Nordberg, "Les sources

bourguignonnes des accusations portées contre la mémoire de Louis d'Or-
léans," *Annales de Bourgogne* 31 (1959): 81–98.

4. *ECCE*: ON THE SCRIPTURAL ROOTS OF CHRISTIAN
DEVOTIONAL IMAGERY

I have presented earlier versions of this chapter at two conferences: "Iconoclasm:
The Possibility of Representation in Religion," Heidelberg, 9–14 February 1997
(in honor of Moshe Barasch); and "Imagination und Wirklichkeit," Frankfurt,
14–16 June 1997. My thanks to all those who contributed to discussion, especially
Klaus Reichert. I am indebted, for other observations and criticisms, to Stephen
Greenblatt and, particularly, to Maria Luisa Catoni. A conversation with Jan Ass-
man (as ever) sparked off many ideas. Pier Cesare Bori's help was indispensable
at every stage of research. I take sole responsibility for the paper in its final form.

1. Here and below, the use of capitals is mine. [Translators' note: We use
the text of the New English Bible. This is modified here and when we quote
Luke 13:1 in that the word "behold" has been added; we also add it where
appropriate in later quotations. The Italian text used by CG is *La Bibbia di
Gerusalemme* (Bologna, 1980).]

2. See J. Coppens, "L'interprétation d'Is. VII, 14 à la lumière des études
les plus récentes," in *Lex tua Veritas: Festschrift für Hubert Junker*, ed. H. Gross
and F. Mussner (Trier, 1961), pp. 31–46. The alternatives *"parthenos"* and *"nea-
nis"* already constitute a topic of dissension in the dialogue between Justinus and his Jewish interlocutor Triphon (*Dialogue with Triphon*, 43); and see
P. Prigent, *Justin et l'Ancien Testament* (Paris, 1964), pp. 145 ff. More than a
thousand years later, the translators of the Jewish Bible into Ladino out-
flanked the censors of the Inquisition by printing different copies in which
the word *"'almah"* was rendered sometimes as *"virgen,"* sometimes as
"moça": see *The Ladino Bible of Ferrara (1553)*, critical edition, ed. M. Lazar
(Culver City, 1992), pp. xxii f.

3. Rendel Harris and others put forward fertile and trail-blazing—and
sometimes incautious—suggestions (see R. Harris and V. Burch, *Testi-
monies*, 2 vols. [Cambridge, 1916–1920]), as is recognized by C. H. Dodd, in
According to the Scriptures: The Sub-Structure of New Testament Theology
(London, 1952), p. 26 and passim. See also B. Lindars, *New Testament Apolo-
getic: The Doctrinal Significance of the Old Testament Quotations* (London,
1961).

4. The work's subtitle may be a later addition, as argued by C. H. Turner,
cited in J.-P. Audet, "L'hypothèse des Testimonia: Remarques autour d'un
livre récent," *Revue Biblique* 70 (1963): 381–405, esp. p. 382. Audet's tone is dis-
missive: in his view the supposed *testimonia*, including the fragments of
Qumrân (see pp. 391 f., 401) are probably unimportant "notes made while

reading" and "index-files of authors." The essay by Fitzmyer that we cite below offers a very different opinion.

5. J. A. Fitzmyer, SJ, " '4Q Testimonia' and the New Testament," *Theological Studies* 18 (1957): 513–537, esp. pp. 534 f.: "While the collections of *testimonia* that are found in patristic writers might be regarded as the result of early Christian catechetical and missionary activity, 4Q Testimonia shows that the stringing procedure of *OT* texts from various books was a pre-Christian literary procedure, which may well have been imitated in the early stage of the formation of the *NT*. It resembles so strongly the composite citations of the *NT* writers that it is difficult not to admit that *testimonia* influenced certain parts of the *NT*." The first editor of *4Q Testimonia* had noted: "It must now be regarded as more than a possibility that the first Christians were able to take over and use collections of Hebrew *testimonia* already current in a closely related religious community like this of Qumrân" (J. M. Allegro, "Further Messianic References in Qumrân Literature," *Journal of Biblical Literature* 75 [1956]: 174–187, esp. p. 186 n. 107).

6. See the survey (with bibliography) by F. Van Segbroeck, "Les citations d'accomplissement dans l'Evangile selon saint Matthieu d'après trois ouvrages récents," in *L'Evangile selon saint Matthieu: Rédaction et théologie*, ed. M. Didier (Louvain, 1972), pp. 108–130. More generally on the question of biblical references in the New Testament, see the review by I. H. Marshall, "An Assessment of Recent Developments," in *It Is Written: Scripture Citing Scripture. Essays in Honour of Barnabas Lindars*, ed. D. A. Carson and H. G. M. Williamson (Cambridge, 1988), pp. 1–21; and see the recent work C. M. Tuckett, ed., *The Scriptures in the Gospels* (Leuven, 1997).

7. The problem is of a general order and was put thus by Leo Strauss: "It is only naturally or humanly impossible that the 'first' Isaiah should have known the name of the founder of the Persian empire; it was not impossible for the omnipotent God to reveal to him that name" (*Spinoza's Critique of Religion* [1965; reprint, Chicago, 1997], introduction [1962], p. 28). Those who would reason on the basis of the second position would disqualify themselves from the research community.

8. K. Stendahl, *The School of St. Matthew and Its Use of the Old Testament* (Uppsala 1954), p. 204. G. M. Soares Prabhu, SJ, takes a contrasting view, arguing that the Gospel accounts of the infancy of Jesus were not "stimulated" by the Scriptures (a theory that might lead some to draw an analogy with the Hebrew tradition of midrashic commentary), "but by the event of Jesus Christ" (*The Formula Quotations in the Infancy Narrative of Matthew: An Inquiry into the Tradition History of Mt. 1–2* [Rome, 1976], pp. 15 f. n. 109).

9. See Stendahl, *School of St. Matthew*, p. 217 (pp. 207–217, the closing pages of the book, are devoted to a discussion of *testimonia*).

10. Stendahl writes in his introduction to the collection of essays that he edited titled *The Scrolls and the New Testament* (London, 1958, p. 16): "But it is hard to see how the authority of Christianity could depend on its 'originality,' i.e., on an issue which was irrelevant in the time when 'Christianity' emerged out of the matrix of Judaism, not as a system of thought but as a church, a community. But one may hope that the Christianity of today is spiritually and intellectually healthy enough to accept again the conditions of its birth." Stendahl, a professor at Harvard Divinity School, subsequently became Lutheran bishop of Stockholm.

11. W. Zimmerli, *Grande Lessico del Nuovo Testamento*, 9, cols. 333–334 (also Zimmerli in W. Zimmerli and J. Jeremias, *The Servant of God* [London, 1957], pp. 41 f.).

12. See J. Koenig, *L'herméneutique analogique du judaïsme antique d'après les témoins textuels d'Isaïe* (Leiden, 1982). H. M. Orlinsky compares the Septuagint's misinterpretation of Isaiah 7:14 with the identification of the "suffering servant" with Jesus, inasmuch as both exemplify ideas generated in a "non-Biblical hellenistic" ambiance ("Studies on the Second Part of the Book of Isaiah," in Orlinsky, *The So-Called "Servant of the Lord" and "Suffering Servant" in Second Isaiah* [Leiden, 1967], pp. 73 f.). Orlinsky denies that there is any relationship between the "suffering servant" and the Jesus of the Gospels.

13. See J. Bickerman, "Some Notes on the Transmission of the Septuagint" (1950), in Bickerman, *Studies in Jewish and Christian History* (Leiden, 1976), 1:137–176, esp. (for the date) p. 147.

14. The Vulgate reads: "Iesus autem sciens recessit inde, et secuti sunt eum multi, et curavit eos omnes. Et praecepit eis ne manifestum eum facerent, ut adimpleretur quod dictum est per Isaiam prophetam dicentem: 'Ecce puer meus, quem elegi, dilectus meus, in quo bene complacuit animae meae. Ponam spiritum meum super eum, et iudicium gentibus nuntiabit. Non contendet neque clamabit, neque audiet aliquis in plateis vocem eius; harundinem quassatam non confringet et linum fumigans non exstinguet donec eiciat ad victoriam iudicium. Et in nomine eius gentes sperabunt.'" [Translators' note: We have replaced "Here is my servant" (NEB text) with "Behold my servant."]

15. This is an instance of what has been called the *Reflexionszitate*, a formula that is characteristic of Matthew.

16. In this connection, see S. Levi Della Torre's densely argued commentary on the paradoxes of election, in his essay "L'idea del 'popolo eletto,'" in Della Torre, *Essere fuori luogo: Il dilemma ebraica tra diaspora e ritorno* (Rome, 1995), pp. 77–119.

17. J. Bickerman, "Utilitas Crucis," *Studies* 3 (1986): 137.

18. Zimmerli and Jeremias, *Servant of God*, p. 86 and passim. C. H.

Dodd—on the basis of somewhat different arguments—makes a similar case in *According to the Scriptures*. P. Benoît discusses a number of more recent studies in "Jésus et le serviteur de Dieu," in J. Dupont, ed., *Jésus aux origines de la christologie*, new enlarged ed. (Leuven, 1989), pp. 11–140, 419.

19. Jeremias, in Zimmerli and Jeremias, *Servant of God*, pp. 80 ff. See also R. Schnackenburg, *The Gospel According to St. John*, trans. K. Smith (Tunbridge Wells, 1984), p. 299. [Translators' note: The NEB text (John 1:36) has "Here is the Lamb of God," which we render below: "Behold the Lamb of God."]

20. This is pointed out by C. H. Dodd, *Historical Tradition in the Fourth Gospel* (Cambridge, 1963), pp. 42–44, 131 f. Dodd nonetheless concludes: "Surely the simpler hypothesis is that [John] has followed information received, and that it was the remembered facts that first drew the attention of Christian thinkers to the testimonium of Ps. XXXIII:21 rather than the other way round." Obviously this argument (formulated in general terms on p. 49) needs turning on its head. There is a full discussion in J. D. Crossan, *The Cross That Spoke: The Origins of the Passion Narrative* (San Francisco, 1988), pp. 161 ff.

21. See J. Henninger, "Zum Verbot des Knochenzerbrechens bei den Semiten," in *Studi orientalistici in onore di Giorgio Levi della Vida* (Rome, 1956), pp. 448–458; revised and enlarged in Henninger, "Neuere Forschungen zum Verbot des Knochenzerbrechens," *Studia Ethnographica et Folklorica in Honorem Béla Gunda* (Debrecen, 1971), pp. 673–702; and see also C. Ginzburg, *Storia notturna. Una decifrazione del sabba* (Turin, 1989), p. 228. The original edition of *Storia notturna* is available in English as *Ecstasies: Deciphering the Witches' Sabbath*, trans. R. Rosenthal (London, 1990).

22. See Dodd, *According to the Scriptures*, pp. 98 f. M. J. J. Menken argues convincingly in favor of the hypothesis of a preexisting *testimonium*—only to conclude, unexpectedly, by maintaining the opposite view—in "The Old Testament Quotation in John 19:36: Sources, Redaction, Background," in *The Four Gospels 1992: Festschrift Frans Neirynck*, ed. F. G. van Segbroeck et al. (Leuven, 1992), 3:2101–2118.

23. It is C. H. Dodd who remarks in *Historical Tradition* (p. 135), "You cannot 'see' a *theologoumenon*."

24. On the discussions to which this divergence has given rise, see C. H. Dodd, ibid., pp. 109 f. (who somewhat oddly denies that John was interested in the parallel between Jesus and the lamb of the Passover). Against this, cf. Schnackenburg, *The Gospel According to St. John*, p. 299: "The paschal lamb of the NT dies, according to the Johannine chronology, just when the paschal lamb of the Jews is being slaughtered in the Temple, and none of his bones are broken."

25. Papias, Bishop of Hierapolis (ca. 60–138 A.D.), cited by Eusebius of Caesarea (*Ecclesiastical History*, 3:39), says that the evangelist Matthew "col-

lected" ("*sunetaksato*") the *logia* "in Hebrew" (or "according to the Hebrew style"), "and translated them" (or "interpreted them") "as best he could." If, however, "*logia*" here means, as it does elsewhere, "oracles," "divine words" (see J.-E. Ménard, *L'Evangile selon Thomas* [Leiden, 1975], p. 75), then Papias is describing two phases of Matthew's editorial work—which makes it difficult to identify the *logia* with the Gospel, as is the intention of B. Orchard and H. Riley, *The Order of the Synoptics: Why Three Synoptic Gospels?* (Macon, Ga., and Leuven, 1988), pp. 169–195 (on Eusebius's chapter), esp. pp. 188 ff. The Gospel was presumably the outcome of the process.

26. J. D. Crossan, *The Historical Jesus: The Life of a Mediterranean Jewish Peasant* (San Francisco, 1992), p. 375.

27. Ibid, p. 372.

28. G. Vall, "Psalm 22:17B: 'The Old Guess,'" *Journal of Biblical Literature* 116 (1997): 45 f. [Translators' note: The NEB text has this as verse 16b rather than the 17b of AV.]

29. Such a *testimonium* is among those postulated by C. H. Dodd (*According to the Scriptures*, pp. 89 ff., esp. pp. 108–110). Dodd regards them as dating to a very early period, before the letters of Saint Paul, and attributes them in the final analysis to Jesus himself.

30. Stendahl, *School of St. Matthew*, pp. 196f; and see also D. Daube, "The Earliest Structure of the Gospels," *Neue Testamentliche Studien* 5 (1958–1959): 174–187.

31. I must thank Klaus Reichert for drawing my attention to this point, and Stefano Levi Della Torre for suggesting the interpretation proposed here.

32. See J.-E. Ménard, *L'Evangile selon Thomas* (a translation with commentary).

33. E. Bickerman, "The Septuagint as a Translation," in Bickerman, *Studies*, 1:167–200, esp. pp. 187 f.; and see also J. Coppens, "L'interprétation d'Is. VII," p. 39, and P. Fiedler, *Die Formel "Und Siehe" im Neuen Testament* (Munich, 1969) (which Pier Cesare Bori drew to my attention).

34. Fiedler, *Die Formel "Und Siehe,"* p. 13.

35. Ibid., pp. 43 f., citing M. Johannessohn, "Der Wahrnehmungsatz bei den Verben des Sehens in der hebräischen und griechischen Bibel," in *Zeitschrift für vergleichende Sprachforschung* 64 (1937): 145–260, esp. pp. 188 f.; and Johannessohn, "Das biblische *kai idou* in der Erzählung samt einer hebräischen Vorlage," in the same journal, 66 (1939): 145–195, and 67 (1942): 30–84.

36. I thank Pier Cesare Bori for drawing this point to my attention.

37. *Patrologia Latina*, 22:col. 543, letter 52 ("Ad Paulinum, de studio Scripturarum").

38. Eusebius of Caesarea, *Storia ecclesiastica*, trans. into Italian by M. Ceva (Milan, 1979), pp. 401 f. [Translators' note: We translate from the Italian.]

39. See E. von Dobschütz, "Christusbilder: Untersuchungen zur christlichen Legende," in *Texte und Untersuchungen zur Geschichte der altchristlichen Literatur*, ed. O. von Gebhardt and A. von Harnack, NF, III (Leipzig, 1899), pp. 31, 197 ff.; and A. von Harnack, *Die Mission und Ausbreitung des Christentums in den ersten drei Jahrhunderten* (Leipzig, 1902), p. 88.

40. See H. J. Geischer, *Der byzantinische Bilderstreit* (1968), pp. 15 ff. E. Clark argues in support of the text's authenticity in "Eusebius on Women in Early Church History," in *Eusebius, Christianity, and Judaism*, ed. H. W. Attridge and G. Hata (Leiden, 1992), pp. 256–269, esp. p. 261 (and there are references to recent studies). There is further discussion in M. V. Anastos, "The Argument for Iconoclasm as Presented by the Iconoclastic Council of 754," in K. Weitzmann, ed., *Late Classical and Medieval Studies in Honor of Albert Mathias Friend Jr.* (Princeton, 1955), pp. 181–188, esp. pp. 183 f.

41. See E. Dinkler, "Christus und Asklepios," *Sitzungensberichte der Heidelberger Akademie der Wissenschaften* 2 (1980): 12 and passim. Justinus explains in his first *Apologia*, after pointing out the parallels between the miraculous cures wrought by Jesus and by Aesculapius, that the latter deliberately imitated the former (22, 6; 54, 10).

42. I take the term "electricity" from T. F. Mathews, *The Clash of Gods: A Reinterpretation of Early Christian Art* (Princeton, 1993), pp. 61 ff., esp. p. 64.

43. I thank Stefano Levi Della Torre for suggesting this interpretation to me.

44. C. Nauerth, "Heilungswunder in der frühchristliche Kunst," *Spätantike und frühes Christentum, Ausstellung* . . . (Frankfurt, 1983), pp. 339–346, esp. p. 341, ill. 157; Nauerth tentatively identifies the kneeling woman in Latin sarcophagus 191 as the woman with the flow of blood. The fact that the woman is approaching Jesus from behind places this identification beyond doubt.

45. Mathews, *Clash of Gods*, p. 68. Of course this novelty is traceable back to the Gospels, as Erich Auerbach showed in some unforgettable pages in *Mimesis* (Berne, 1946; English translation by W. R. Trask [Princeton, 1953]). For a feminist discussion of the miracle of the woman cured of bleeding, see E. Moltmann-Wendel, "Das Abendmahl bei Markus," in *Wir Frauen und das Herrenmahl* (Stuttgart, 1996), pp. 50–55 (I thank Hildegard Cancik-Lindemaier for making it possible for me to read this). On the point in time or *punctum*, see R. Barthes, *La chambre claire: Note sur la photographie* (Paris, 1980) (*Camera Lucida: Reflections on Photography*, trans. R. Howard, [London, 1982]).

46. Mathews, *Clash of Gods*, p. 65.

47. K. Weitzmann, introduction to Weitzmann, ed., *Age of Spirituality: A Symposium* (New York, 1981), pp. 3 f.

48. E. Kitzinger, "Christian Imagery: Growth and Impact," in Weitzmann, ed., *Age of Spirituality*, p. 148.

49. See Mathews, *Clash of Gods*, pp. 116 ff.; and also G. Schiller, *Ikonographie der christlichen Kunst* (Gütersloh, 1971), 3:147, 183 ff.; and A. Grabar, *Christian Iconography: A Study of Its Origins* (Princeton, 1968), p. 44. [Translators' note: Again, the word "behold," not present in the NEB text, has been added and the text slightly modified.]

50. Daniel 7:13 ff.: "I was still watching in visions of the night and BEHOLD I saw one like a man coming with the clouds of heaven." [Translators' note: The NEB text has been modified by the interpolation of "BEHOLD".] Matthew 24:30: "Then will appear in heaven the sign that heralds the Son of Man. All the peoples of the world will make lamentation, and they will see the Son of Man coming on the clouds of heaven with great power and glory."

51. Mathews, *Clash of Gods*, p. 137. Cf. C. Diehl, "Une mosaïque byzantine de Salonique," *Comptes-rendus de l'Académie des Inscriptions et Belles-Lettres* (1927): 256–261; V. Grumel, "Dieu Sauveur au monastère du 'Latome' à Salonique," *Échos d'Orient* 33, no. 158 (April–June 1930): 157–175; J. F. Mitchell, "The Meaning of the *Maiestas Domini* in Hosios David," *Byzantion* 37 (1967): 143–152. [Translators' note: We alter "this is the Lord" (NEB) to "behold the Lord."]

52. See H. Belting, *Bild und Kult* (Munich, 1990), p. 162 and ill. 85. Belting cites K. Corrigan, "The Witness of John the Baptist on an Early Byzantine Icon in Kiev," *Dumbarton Oaks Papers* 42 (1988): 1–11: an icon dating from around the sixth century, originally from Mount Sinai and now in Kiev, shows the prophet not only holding a scroll bearing the words "Behold the Lamb of God" but also pointing to a medallion of Christ, to whom his prophecy refers.

53. See the very fine essay by A. von Harnack, "Die Bezeichnung Jesu als 'Knecht Gottes' und ihre Geschichte in der alten Kirche" (1926), in Harnack, *Kleine Schriften zur alten Kirche* (Leipzig, 1980), pp. 730–756. Figurative precedents in pagan art are discussed in Grabar, *Christian Iconography*, pp. 36 f. Here, however, I am concerned with a different theme, as the subtitle of this chapter indicates.

54. See C. Bertelli, "The Image of Pity in Santa Croce in Gerusalemme," in *Essays in the History of Art Presented to Rudolf Wittkower*, ed. D. Fraser et al. (London, 1967), pp. 40–55.

55. Belting, *Bild und Kult*, 462; and see also his *Bild und Publikum im Mittelalter* (Berlin, 1981).

56. [Translators' note: Again we have modified the NEB text, replacing "here is" by "behold."] The Vulgate (John 19:25–27) reads: "Stabant autem iuxta crucem Iesu mater eius et soror matris eius Maria Cleophae et Maria Magdalene. Cum vidisset ergo Iesus matrem eius et discipulum stantem quem diligebat, dicit matri suae: 'Mulier, ecce filius tuus'; deinde dicit dis-

cipulo: 'Ecce mater tua.'" On the use of *"ide"* in Jesus' utterances, see H. Schürmann, "Die Sprache des Christus," *Biblische Zeitschrift* 2 (1958): 54–84, esp. p. 64.

5. IDOLS AND LIKENESSES: A PASSAGE IN ORIGEN AND ITS VICISSITUDES

I thank Fernando Leal and Angelica Nuzzo for bibliographical suggestions; and Pier Cesare Bori, Alberto Gajano, and Mauro Pesce for their comments.

1. G. Ladner mentions the passage in "The Concept of the Image in the Greek Fathers and the Byzantine Iconoclastic Controversy," in Ladner, *Images and Ideas in the Middle Ages* (Rome, 1983), 1:91 n. 3 (and the whole essay is of fundamental importance); as also does P. C. Bori (who notes the "scholastic" nature of the distinction it draws) in *Il vitello d'oro: Le radici della controversia antigiudaica* (Turin, 1983), p. 64. To the best of my knowledge there has been no analytical discussion of the passage.

2. See Origen, *Werke*, ed. W. A. Baehrens, 6:1, *Die Homilien zu Genesis, Exodus, und Leviticus* (*Die griechischen Christlichen Schiftseller der ersten drei Jahrhunderte*) (Leipzig, 1920), pp. 221 f. The Latin is as follows:

Post haec videamus, quid etiam secundum videtur continere mandatum: "non facies tibi ipsim idolum neque omnem similitudinem eorum, quae sunt in coelo vel quae in terra vel quae in aquis subtus terram" [Exodus 20:4]. Longe aliud sunt idola et aliud dii, sicut ipse nos nihilominus Apostolus docet. Nam de diis dixit: "sicut sunt dii multi et domini multi" [1 Corinthians 8:5]; de idolis autem dicit: "quia uihil est idolum in mundo" [1 Corinthians 8:4]. Unde mihi videtur non transitorie haec legisse, quae lex dicit. Vidit enim differentiam deorum et idolorum et rursum differentiam idolorum et similitudinum; nam qui de idolis dixit quia non sunt, non addidit quia et similitudines non sunt. Hic autem dicit: "non facies tibi ipsi idolum neque similitudinem omnium" [Exodus 20:4]. Aliud ergo est facere "idolum," aliud "similitudinem." Et si quidem Dominus nos ad ea, quae dicenda sunt, illuminare dignetur, ego sic arbitror accipiendum, quod, verbi causa, si quis in quolibet metallo auri vel argenti vel ligni vel lapidis faciat speciem quadrupedis alicuius vel serpentis vel avis et statuat illam adorandam, non idolum, sed similitudinem fecit; vel etiam si picturam ad hoc ipsum statuat, nihilominus similitudinem fecisse dicendus est. Idolum vero fecit ille, qui secundum Apostolum dicentem quia: "idolum nihil est" [1 Corinthians 8:4], facit quod non est. Quid est autem, quod non est? Species, quam non vidit oculus, sed ipse sibi animus fingit. Verbi gratia, ut si qui humanis membris caput canis aut arietis formet vel rursum in uno hominis habitu duas facies fingat aut humano pectori postremas partes equi aut piscis adiungat. Haec et his similia qui facit, non similitudinem, sed idolum facit. Facit enim, quod non est nec habet aliquid simile sui. Et idcirco haec sciens Apostolus dicit: "quia idolum nihil est in mundo" [1 Corinthians 8:4]; non enim aliqua ex rebus exstantibus adsumitur species, sed quod ipsa sibi otiosa mens et curiosa reppererit. Similitudo vero [est], cum aliquid ex his, quae sunt "vel in coelo vel in terra vel in aquis," formatur, sicut superius diximus. Verumtamen non sicut de his, quae in terra sunt vel in mari, similitudinibus in promptu est pronuntiare, ita etiam de coelestibus; nisi si quis dicat de sole et luna et stellis hoc posse sentiri; et horum namque formas exprimere gentilitas solet. Sed quia Moyses "eruditus erat in omni sapientia Aegyptiorum" [Acts 7:22], etiam ea, quae apud illos erant in occultis et reconditis, prohibere cupiebat; sicut verbi causa, ut nos quoque appellationibus utamur ipsorum Hecaten quam dicunt aliasque daemonum formas, quae Apostolus "spiritalia nequitiae in coelestibus" [Ephesians 6:12] vocat. De quibus fortassis et propheta dicit quia: "inebriatus est gladius meus in coelo" [Isaiah 34:5]. His enim formis et similitudinibus invocare daemonia moris est his, quibus talia curae sunt, vel ad repellenda vel etiam ad invitanda mala, quae nunc sermo Deo universa complectens simul abiurat et abicit et non solum idolum fieri vetat, sed "et similitudinem omnium quae in terra sunt, et in aquis et in coelo" [Exodus 20:5].

3. On this see also R. Devreesse, *Les anciens commentateurs grecs de l'Octateuque et des Rois (Fragments tirés des chaînes)* (Vatican City, 1959), pp. 26 ff.; C. P. Hammond Bammel, *Der Römerbrieftext des Rufin und seine Origenes-Übersetzung* (Freiburg 1985), pp. 43–58.

4. See Migne, *Patrologia Graeca*, 12:353–354 (based upon F. Combefis, *Bibliothecae Graecorum Patrum auctarium novissimum*, 1 [Paris, 1672]): "Allo eidolon kai heteron homoioma. Homoioma men gar estin, ean poieis ikthuos e tetrapodou e theriou dia tekhnourgias e dia zographias homoioma. Eidolon de, hosa anatupousa psuche poiei, ouk eks huparkhonton prototupos. Hoion anamemigmenon to zoon apo anthropou kai hippou." Cf. L. Doutreleau, "Recherches autour de la Catena Romana de Combefis," in *Corona gratiarum (Miscellenea . . . Eligio Dekkers . . . oblata)* (Bruges, 1975), 2:367–388.

5. See Origen, *Die Homilien*, ed. Baehrens, pp. 221–223, and Baehrens's introduction, pp. xxvii–xxviii:

Ta men oon homoiomata ton onton eisin eikones zoon te kai somaton, ta de eidola anuparkton estin anaplasmata. Ou gar huparksis to eidolon. "Ouden gar eidolon en kosmo Paulos phesin. Hoion ei tis hippokentaurous e Panas e teratodeis tinas anaplasaito phuseis. Pan ara noema kata perileptiken phantasian en perinoia tes theias ginomenon phuseos eidolon plattei Theou, all'ou Theon kataggellei. Genoito d'an kai ton en ourano homoiomata graphonton e kai gluphonton tinon helion e selenen. Isos de kai peri ton kat'astrologian phesi dekanon. Allokotous gar tinas diagraphousi daimonas, haper isos "pneumatika tes ponerias en tois epouraniois" onomastai kata ton logon tou legontos Theou. "Hemethusthe he makhaira mou en to ourano." Toutous gar en pinaksin astrologikois katagraphousin en te phulakteriois apotreptikois daimonon e protreptikois, en hois an tis heuroi ta men homoiomata, ta de eidola.

I shall not comment on the second part of the passage, which does not fall within my area of concern in this essay. Migne, *Patrologia* Graeca, 87, 1, 605 ff. contains a Latin translation of this passage. Procopius of Gaza has often been regarded as the originator of the *catenae* as a literary genre; however, see F. Petit, *Catenae Graecae in Genesim et in Exodum*, vol. 1, *Catena Sinaitica* (Corpus Christianorum, Series Graeca) (Brepols and Turnhout, 1977), pp. xx f.

6. The quotations from Origen in the body of the chapter are translated from the Latin text printed in note 2 above.

7. See J.-C. Grenier, *Anubis Alexandrin et Romain* (Leiden, 1977).

8. See the entries "Mendes" and "Widder" in the *Lexikon der Aegyptologie* (W. Helck and E. Otto).

9. "*Eidos* Graece formam sonat; ab eo per diminutionem *eidolon* deductum atque apud nos formulam fecit" (Tertullian, *De Idololatria* 3.2–4, ed. J. H. Waszink and J. C. M. van Winden [Leiden, 1987], pp. 26 f.; see also pp. 10–13 on the date of the treatise). The editors remark on pp. 109 f. that Tertullian's etymology is incorrect. See, however, S. Saïd, "Deux noms de l'image en grec ancien: idole et icône," in *Académie des Inscriptions et Belles-Lettres, Comptes-rendus des séances de l'année 1987*, pp. 309–330, esp. p. 310.

10. The Vulgate has "*similitudinem*" in both Genesis 1:26 and Exodus 20:4; in Exodus 20:4, the Vulgate uses "*sculptile*" rather than the "*idolum*" of Vetus Latina.

11. See Ladner, "Concept of the Image," pp. 71 f., 84 ff.

12. See G. Ladner, *The Idea of Reform: Its Impact on Christian Thought and Action in the Age of the Fathers* (Cambridge, Mass., 1959), pp. 48–107, esp. p. 83 (on p. 94, Ladner remarks on the alternate usage of "*homoiosis*" and "*homoioma*" in Gregory of Nissa). See also J. Daniélou, *Origène* (Paris, 1948), p. 289.

13. See, in the *Theologisches Wörterbuch zum neuen Testament*, ed. G. Kittel and F. Gerhard, the article "Homoioma" (by J. Schneider).

14. See E. Cassirer, "Eidos und Eidolon," in *Vorträge der Bibliothek Warburg 1922–1923*, vol. 1 (1924), pp. 1 ff.; and also Saïd, "Deux noms de l'image" (which is very important).

15. Plato, *The Sophist*, trans. and intro. A. E. Taylor and ed. R. Klibansky and E. Anscombe (1961; reprint Folkestone and London, 1971), p. 123.

16. See W. S. Cobb, in R. S. Bluck and G. C. Neal, eds., *Plato's Sophist: A Commentary* (Manchester, 1975), p. 72.

17. Here I follow C. H. Kahn, "The Thesis of Parmenides," *Review of Metaphysics* 22 (1969): 700–724, esp. pp. 719 f. See also, in the same issue, the commentaries by H. Stein (pp. 725–734) and by A. P. D. Mourelatos (pp. 735–744), as well as Kahn's reply, "More on Parmenides," *Review of Metaphysics* 23 (1969): 333–340.

18. See Kahn, "More on Parmenides," pp. 338 f. Bluck (*Plato's Sophist*, pp. 61 f.) remarks that these kinds of being seem not to have been taken into account in Plato's argument, but he does not explain why.

19. See Sextus Empiricus, *Against the Logicians*, which alludes to Plato, *Timaeus*, 28a, and Origen, *Homilies* (*Die Homilien*, ed. cit., p. 222). [Translators' note: Our renderings of Sextus Empiricus are from the Italian edition used by CG, *Contro i logici*, ed. A. Russo (Rome and Bari, 1975).]

20. See F. H. Sandbach, "Phantasia Kataleptike," in A. A. Long, ed., *Problems in Stoicism* (London, 1971), pp. 9–21; G. Striker, "Kriterion tes aletheias," in *Nachrichten der Akademie der Wissenschaften in Göttingen, Phil.-hist. Kl.* (1974), 2:107–110; G. Watson, "Discovering the Imagination: Platonists and Stoics on Phantasia," in J. M. Dillon and A. A. Long, eds., *The Question of "Eclecticism": Studies in Later Greek Philosophy* (Berkeley and Los Angeles, 1988), pp. 208–233; G. Camassa, " 'Phantasia' da Platone ai Neoplatonici," in M. Fattori and M. Bianchi, eds., *Lessico intellettuale europeo: Phantasia-Imaginatio. V Colloquio internazionale* (Rome, 1988), pp. 23–56, esp. pp. 40–43. See also E. Elorduy, "El Enflujo estóico en Orígenes," in H. Crouzel et al., eds., *Origeniana* (Bari, 1975), pp. 277–288.

21. Origen, *Homilien*, pp. 221 f.

22. See A. Graeser, "A Propos *huparkein* bei den Stoikern," *Archiv für Begriffsgeschichte* 15, no. 2 (1971): 299–305. This is a critique of an article by P. Hadot, "Zur Vorgeschichte des Begriffs 'Existenz': *Huparkein* bei den Stoikern," *Archiv für Begriffsgeschichte* 13 (1962): 115–127.

23. Aristotle's *Posterior Analytics* is cited in the translation by Hugh Tredennick for the Loeb Classical Library edition (London and Cambridge, Mass., 1960). See A.-J. Festugière, *La révélation d'Hermès Trismégiste*, vol. 4, *Le Dieu inconnu et la gnose* (Paris, 1981), pp. 6–17, esp. the note on p. 11. C. H. Kahn, having formerly rejected this view, later acknowledged, implicitly, that Festugière was correct: see Kahn, "The Greek Verb 'to Be' and the Concept of Being," *Foundations of Language* 2 (1966): 245–265, esp. p. 259 n. 15, pp. 262–265 (postscript), and Kahn's subsequent book *The Verb "to Be" in Ancient Greek* (Dordrecht and Boston, 1973), pp. 300–306. J. Wirth discusses Aristotle's ideas on essence and existence in *L'image médiévale* (Paris, 1989),

a book with which I have often found myself disagreeing but that is full of suggestions: Wirth's exposition is inadequate, as is clear from the passages cited (p. 128) from the *Peri Hermeneias*.

24. [Translators' note: We have replaced Tredennick's "unicorn" with the literal "goat-stag."] Festugière does not consider this passage. For a general discussion, see G. Sillitti, *Tragelaphos: Storia di una metafora e di un problema* (Naples, 1980).

25. See also Diogenes Laertius, *Lives of the Philosophers*, 7:53 (cited by Watson, "Discovering the Imagination," p. 215).

26. H. Crouzel, *Origen*, trans. A. S. Worrall (Edinburgh, 1989), p. 162.

27. See Festugière, *La révélation*, 4:11n, where Festugière remarks that the insistence on *huparksis* was connected, in Philo and in the tradition descended from him, with the impossibility of knowing God. The fragment of the *Homily on Exodus* that Combefis published reads thus: *"ouk ex huparkhonton prototupos"* ("not made of things which originally existed").

28. For attempts to reconstruct Paul's debate with the Corinthians, see J. C. Hurd Jr., *The Origin of I Corinthians* (London, 1965), and R. A. Horsely, "Gnosis in Corinth: I Corinthians 8, 1–6," *New Testament Studies* 27 (1980): 32–51. C. K. Barrett argues in *Essays on Paul* (London, 1982), pp. 40–59, esp. p. 51, that there is a relationship between 1 Corinthians 8:4 and the text translated and edited by W. A. L. Elmslie, "The Mishna on Idolatry: Aboda Zara," *Texts and Studies* 8, no. 2 (Cambridge, 1911). At all events, the analogy between idolatry and "sacrifices to the dead" (pp. 31 ff.), which is insisted on in the Mishna, does not amount to the same thing as Paul's remarks on the nonexistence of idols, though it is compatible with it (and see also pp. 42 ff., "Excursus I: On the Deadness of the Idols"). Some interesting directions are indicated in R. M. Grant, "Hellenistic Elements in the 1 Corinthians," in *Early Christian Origins: Studies in Honor of Harold R. Willoughby*, ed. A. Vikgren (Chicago, 1961), pp. 60–66 (Grant does not comment on 1 Corinthians 8).

29. On the first pair of terms, see Saïd, "Deux noms," and Horsley, "Gnosis in Corinth," esp. p. 37; on the second, the works by Festugière and Kahn cited in note 23 above. The possibility that there is a Platonic echo in 1 Corinthians 8:4 is strengthened by the convergence between 1 Corinthians 3:9 and *Eutiphronis* 13e–14a, which W. K. C. Guthrie points out in *A History of Greek Philosophy* (Cambridge, 1975), 4:107 n. 1 (Alberto Gajano drew this note to my attention).

30. Origen, *I Principi*, ed. M. Simonetti (Turin, 1968), pp. 153 f. (Origen, *Traité des principes*, vol. 1, ed. H. Crouzel and M. Simonetti [Paris, 1968], in *Sources chrétiennes* 252, 126 ff.). [Translators' note: We translate from the Italian rendering.]

31. On the likeness between God and man, see Origen, *Homily on Genesis*, 1.13.

32. For general discussion of the point, see Ladner, *Images and Ideas*, 1:84 f.; H. Crouzel, *Théologie de l'image de Dieu chez Origène* (Paris, 1956), pp. 147–179, 217–245.

33. Cf. Ladner, *Images and Ideas*, 1:110: "Origen, in so many respects the father of Byzantine thought, both orthodox and heterodox."

34. *Patrologia Graeca*, 94:1376; G. Mercati, *Stephani Bostreni nova de sacris imaginibus fragmenta e libro deperdito* Katà Ioudaion, in *Opere minori* (Vatican City, 1937), 1:202–206; Ladner, *Images and Ideas*, 1:95–97.

35. *Patrologia Graeca*, 94:1376. See also John the Damascene, ibid., 94:1329.

36. As noted above, the *catena* of Procopius of Gaza remains unpublished. The Latin translation (*Commentarii in Exodum, Patrologia Graeca*, 87:1, 606—607) reads as follows: "Quidam quaerunt: Si adeo detestatur imagines, quare Cherubim fingi voluit? Respondetur: Non jussit fieri Cherubim ut adorentur; sed arca adoranda erat sub imaginibus vitulorum, quibus apud Aegyptios divinus deferebatur honor, ut sic cognoscerent se pariter Deum et numina Aegyptiorum colerent."

37. See J. Patrich, *The Formation of Nabatean Art: Prohibition of a Graven Image Among the Nabateans* (Jerusalem, 1990); G. W. Bowersock, *Hellenism in Late Antiquity* (Ann Arbor, 1990), ch. 1.

38. See Theodoretus of Cyrus, *Qaest. in Ex., Patrologia Graeca*, 80:264; Theodore of Studion, *Antirrheticus* 1.16, *Patrologia Graeca*, 99:345 C ff. (both mentioned in Ladner, *Images and Ideas*, 1:91 n. 73).

39. B. Smalley, *The Study of the Bible in the Middle Ages* (1940; reprint, Oxford, 1952), pp. 13 f. and note. Cf. Origen, *Homélies sur l'Exode*, ed. M. Borret (*Sources chrétiennes*, 321), p. 404, where Rabanus Maurus, *Comm. in Ex.* II, *Patrologia Latina*, 108:95, is cited; Jonas of Orleans, *De cultu imaginum*, *Patrologia Latina*, 106:321.

40. *Patrologia Latina*, 113:251–252.

41. J.-C. Fau, *Les chapiteaux de Conques* (Toulouse, 1956).

42. The Latin text is in *Patrologia Latina*, 182:914–916. The passage is quoted in M. Schapiro, "On Aesthetic Attitude in Romanesque Art," in Schapiro, *Romanesque Art* (London, 1977), pp. 1–25 (see esp. p. 6, but the whole essay should be consulted). [Translators' note: We reproduce Schapiro's English version, itself derived from the translation in G. Coulton, *Life in the Middle Ages* (New York, 1935).] See further C. Rudolph, *The "Things of Greater Importance": Bernard de Clairvaux's Apologia and the Medieval Attitude Towards Art* (Philadelphia, 1990), p. 283, and the comments on pp. 110–124; and also J. Adhémar, *Influences antiques dans l'art du Moyen Age français*, (London, 1939), p. 270 n. (which refers to a letter from Saint Nilus to Olympiodorus, *Patrologia Graeca*, 79:24). Unfortunately no reliance can be placed upon M. Camille's book *Image on the Edge: Margins in Medieval Art* (Cambridge, Mass., 1992). Camille begins by commenting

on the *incipit* of a manuscript—*Deus in adiutor* ("O Lord hear my prayer")—which reads in fact *Deus in adiutorium meum* ("O Lord, turn your eyes upon me to help me"), and this sets the standard for the rest of the work.

43. On textual transmissions, see A. Chastel, "Le *dictum Horatii quidlibet audendi potestas* et les artistes (XIIIème–XVIème siècles)," in Chastel, *Fables, formes, figures* (Paris, 1978), 1:363–376; on related images, see C. Villa, " 'Ut poesis pictura': Appunti iconografici sui codici dell'*Ars Poetica*," *Aevum* 62 (1988): 186–197.

44. See J. Leclercq, *Recueil d'études sur Saint Bernard et ses écrits* (Rome, 1987), 4:216 (*De arte poetica*, 139); and Leclercq, *Recueil d'études sur Saint Bernard et ses écrits* (Rome, 1966), 2:348 ff., esp. pp. 369–371 (letter to a monk named Evrard, identified as Evrard of Ypres).

45. See A. Wilmart, "L'ancienne bibliothèque de Clairvaux," *Collectanea ordinis Cisterciensium Reformatorum* 11 (1949): 101–123, 301–319, esp. pp. 117 f.; the catalogs and inventories prepared and edited by A. Vesnet, assisted by J.-F. Genest, titled *La Bibliothèque de l'abbaye de Clairvaux du XIIème au XVIIIème siècle* (Paris, 1979), 1:122 f. See also G. Hoquard, *Revue du moyen age latin* (1945), 1:192 f.; G. Bardy, "Saint Bernard et Origène," ibid., p. 420 f.; E. Gilson, *La théologie mystique de Saint Bernard* (Paris, 1947), pp. 27 f.; J. Leclercq, "Saint Bernard et Origène d'après un manuscrit de Madrid," in Leclercq, *Recueil d'études sur Saint Bernard et ses érits*, 2:373–385.

46. On Bernard and curiosity, see Schapiro, "On the Aesthetic Attitude," p. 7; Rudolph, *"Things of Greater Importance,"* pp. 10 ff. In his *Apologia* (12.28), Bernard opens his discussion of paintings and sculptures with a lukewarm acceptance of "curiosas depictiones" (Rudolph, p. 278).

47. Peter Abelard, *Sic et Non*, ed. B. B. Boyer and R. McKeon (Chicago, 1976–1977), pp. 204–210: XLV: "Quod Deus per corporales imagines non sit repraesentandus et contra." It seems that as a teacher, Abelard was much more explicit in attacking religious likenesses: cf. *Commentarius Cantabrigensis in Epistolas Pauli et Schola Petri Abaelardi*, ed. A. Landgraf (Notre Dame, Ind., 1939), 2:250 f. (on 1 Corinthians 8).

48. On this, see the third essay in the present volume.

49. See A. Reeve and M. A. Screech, eds., *Erasmus's Annotations on the New Testament: Acts—Romans—I and II Corinthians, Facsimile of the Final Latin Text with All Earlier Variants* (Leiden, 1990), p. 481:

> Thomas Aquinas adducit novam differentiam inter idolum et simulacrum, quod simulacrum sit effictum ad similitudinem alicuius rei naturalis: idolum contra, ut, inquit, si corpori humano addatur caput equinum. Quae distinctio vera sit, nec ne, iudicent alij: mihi lexico quod Catholicon inscribunt, non indigna videtur. Certe Ambrosius nullum novit discrimen inter idolum et simulacrum: nec ego ullum

video, nisi quod simulacrum est vox Latina a simulando dicta, idolon Graeca, ab *eidolon*, species, quod speciem et imaginem inanem prae se ferat, quum absit veritas. Unde quae nos spectra vocamus, Graeci vocant *eidola*.

50. See *Laurentii Valle Epistole*, ed. O. Besomi and M. Regoliosi (Padua, 1984), pp. 200 f. (letter to Giovanni Serra, 13 August 1440). Balbi's *Catholicon*, first published in Mainz in 1460, can be found in an anastatic reprint (Meisenheim/Glau, 1971).

51. G. Tortelli, *De Orthographia*, per Stephanum Koblinger, Vicentiae 1479: "Idolum . . . dici potest a nostris simulachrum. Et inde idololatria quasi simulachrorum cultura."

52. Saint Thomas Aquinas, *Super epistolas S. Pauli lectura*, ed. R. P. Cai, O.P. (Taurini-Romae, 1953), 1:314, 317: *"Idolum nihil est in mundo*, id est, nullius rei, quae sit in mundo habens similitudinem. Est enim differentia inter idolum, et similitudinem, quia simulachrum dicitur, quod fit ad similitudinem rei alicuius naturalis: idolum ad nullius rei est similitudinem, ut si corpori humano addatur caput equinum, *Esa. 40 cui similem fecistis Deum* etc."; "Contra, non potest artifex cogitare, vel formare nisi qualia non vidit, Responsio, non habet similitudinem in toto sed in partibus."

53. P. Glorieux, "Essais sur les Commentaires scripturaires de saint Thomas et leur chronologie," *Recherches de théologie ancienne et médiévale* 17 (1950): 237–266, esp. 254–258.

54. See Ammonius, *Commentaire sur le "Peri Hermeneias" d'Aristote, traduction de Guillaume de Moerbeke*, ed. G. Verbeke (Louvain and Paris, 1961). Verbeke suggests in his introduction (pp. lxvii ff.) that Aquinas's commentary on the *Peri Hermeneias* (the *editio princeps* was published in Venice, in 1526, by the heirs of O. Scoto) remained unfinished because Aquinas had to leave Viterbo before 12 September 1268, the date on which William of Moerbeke completed his translation (as we know from the colophon of *Vat. lat.* 2067).

55. Aristotle, trans. J. L. Ackrill, *De Interpretatione* (Oxford, 1963), pp. 43 (16a.9–18), 44 (16a.26–28). D. F. Blackwell points out some significant echoes of this in Abelard: see *Non-Ontological Constructs* (Berne, 1988), esp. pp. 133–141.

56. Ammonius, *Commentaire*, p. 60: "Accidet enim hanc quidem esse vocem significativam et litteratam, ut homo, hanc autem significativam et illitteratam ut canis latratus, hanc autem non significativam et litteratam ut blituri, hanc autem non significativam et illitteratam ut sibilus quae fit frustra et non gratia significandi aliquid aut vocis alicuius irrationalium animalium repraesentatio, quae fit non gratia repraesentationis (haec enim iam significativa), sed quae fit inordinate et sine intentione finis." Sextus Empiricus had noted the Stoics' interest in words without meanings (such as *"blituri," "skindapsos"*): see *Against the Logicians*, 2:133. On *"blituri," "blit-*

tri," "blictri," see the brilliant contributions of C. Giannelli, "Ancora a proposito di blittri," *Studi in onore di Angelo Monteverdi* (Modena, 1959), 1:269–277; and of G. Carabelli, "Blictri: Una parola per Arlecchino," *Eredità dell'Illuminismo,* ed. A. Santucci (Bologna, 1979), pp. 231–257 (it will be noted that the passage by Toland that is cited on p. 240 contains echoes of the passage in Aristotle's *Posterior Analytics* [89b.23–25] that is quoted, above, in the present chapter).

57. See E. Gombrich, *Art and Illusion* (London, 1960), pp. 154 ff.; H. W. Janson. "The 'Image Made by Chance' in Renaissance Thought," in *De Artibus Opuscula XL,* ed. M. Meiss (New York, 1961), 1:254–266.

58. A codified *system* of communication based on images, such as hieroglyphics, amounts to a separate case, and does not contradict the claim with which L. R. Horn begins his book *A Natural History of Negation* (Chicago and London, 1989), p. xiii: "All human systems of communication contain a representation of negation."

59. Leo Chen has pointed out to me that this is an observation made by S. Worth in *Studying Visual Communication* (Philadelphia, 1981), p. 179. It is a point that M. Foucault misunderstands in his essay *Ceci n'est pas une pipe: Deux lettres et quatre desseins de René Magritte* (Paris, 1973) (*This Is Not a Pipe,* trans. and ed. J. Harkness [Berkeley, 1983]). Foucault writes: "La vieille équivalence entre ressemblance et affirmation, Kandinski l'a donc congédiée dans un geste souverain, et unique; il a affranchi la peinture de l'une et de l'autre" (p. 59; cf. also pp. 77 ff.). For Kandinsky, to get rid of resemblances was the indispensable condition of the achievement of a fully affirmative painting: cf. S. Ringbom's important essay "Art in 'the Epoch of the Great Spiritual': Occult Elements in the Early Theory of Abstract Painting," *Journal of the Warburg and Courtauld Institutes* 29 (1966): 386–418.

6. STYLE: INCLUSION AND EXCLUSION

This essay was given as a paper at the conference "Histories of Sciences, Histories of Arts" at Harvard University in the autumn of 1995. For their suggestions and critical comments, I must thank Perry Anderson, Pier Cesare Bori, and Alberto Gajano.

1. See "Das älteste Systemprogramm des deutschen Idealismus." The text, dating from 1797, was first published by Franz Rosenzweig as a transcription, in Hegel's hand, of a text by Schelling, but is now generally agreed to be attributable to Hegel himself.

2. See Fulgenzio Micanzio, *Vita del padre Paolo (1552–1623),* in P. Sarpi, *Istoria del Concilio Tridentino,* ed. C. Vivanti (Turin, 1974), 2:1348 ff. See also *Stilus Romanae Ecclesiae* (n.p., n.d.) (the copy I have consulted in the Biblioteca Angelica is bound up with two writings by E. Buccella, *Dialogus cui titulus*

est religio and *In Constantini Imp. donationem, iuris utriusque praxis*, both published at Lucca in 1539); L. Prosdocimi, "Tra civilisti e canonisti del secolo XIII e XIV—a proposito della genesi del concetto di 'stylus,'" in *Bartolo da Sassoferrato* (Milan, 1962), 2:414–430; H. W. Strätz, "Notizen zur Stil und Recht," in *Stil. Geschichten und Funktionen eines kulturwissenschaftlichen Diskurselements*, ed. H. U. Gumbrecht and K. L. Pfeiffer (Frankfurt am Main, 1986), pp. 13–67 (and the whole volume is important). On the question in general, see first of all the extremely lucid and tightly packed entry "Stile" by C. Segre in *Enciclopedia Einaudi* (Turin, 1981), 13:549–565 (but note also the same author's *Notizie della crisi* [Turin, 1993], pp. 25–37). A useful overview is L. Grassi and A. Pepe, *Dizionario della critica d'arte* (Turin, 1978), pp. 565–568. See also E. H. Gombrich, "Style," in *The International Encyclopedia of the Social Sciences* (1968), 15:352–361; J. A. Schmoll gen. Eisenwerth, "Stilpluralismus statt Einheitzwang—Zur Kritik der Stilepochen Kunstgeschichte," in *Argo: Festschrift für Kurt Badt*, ed. M. Gosebruch and L. Dittmann (Cologne, 1970), pp. 77–95; W. Hager and N. Knopp, eds., *Beiträge zum Problem des Stilpluralismus*, Studien zur Kunst des 19. Jahrhunderts, no. 38 (Munich, 1977); J. Bialostocki, "Das Modusproblem in den bildenden Künsten" (1961), in *Stil und Ikonographie* (Cologne, 1981), pp. 12–42; W. Sauerländer, "From Stilus to Style: Reflections on the Fate of a Notion," *Art History* 6 (1983): 253–270; H. G. Gadamer, *Hermeneutik II, Wahrheit und Methode*, in *Gesammelte Werke* (Tübingen, 1986), "Excurs," 2:375–378.

3. See Cicero, *De oratore*, Loeb series, trans. H. Rackham (translation slightly modified).

4. It is significant that Cicero draws this comparison, for as a rule he includes oratory among the higher disciplines (*maximae artes*) such as war, politics, and administration, whereas poetry, painting, and sculpture are relegated to the lower disciplines (*mediocres artes*) such as mathematics or philosophy. See A. Desmouliez, *Cicéron et son goût* (Brussels, 1976), pp. 240 ff.

5. "Quid censetis si omnes, qui ubique sunt aut fuerunt oratores, amplecti voluerimus? nonne fore ut, quot oratores, totidem paene reperiantur genera dicendi?"

6. See M. Pohlenz, "*To prepon*. Ein Beitrag zur Geschichte des griechischen Geistes," in *Nachrichten von der Gesellschaft der Wissenschaften zu Göttingen aus dem Jahre 1933*, Phil.-Hist. Kl., n. 16, pp. 53–92, esp. pp. 58 ff.

7. S. Aurelii Augustini . . . , *Epistulae*, ed. A. Goldbacher (Vindobonae-Lipsiae, 1904), CSEL, vol. 44:3, letter 138, "Ad Marcellinum," 1. 5, p. 130; quoted in part by A. Funkenstein, *Theology and the Scientific Imagination* (Princeton, 1986), pp. 223 f. (and the whole of the chapter on accommodation is of great importance). On Volusianus, see P. Courcelle, "Date, source et genèse des 'Consultationes Zacchaei et Apollonii,'" *Revue de l'histoire des religions* 146 (1954): 174–193; A. Chastagnol, "Le sénateur Volusien et la con-

version d'une famille de l'aristocratie romaine au Bas-Empire," *Revue des études anciennes* 58 (1956): 241–253; P. Brown, "Aspects of the Christianisation of the Roman Aristocracy," *Journal of Roman Studies* 51 (1961): 1–11; and P. Brown, *Augustine of Hippo* (Berkeley and Los Angeles, 1969), pp. 300–303.

8. See chapter 7 in the present volume.

9. B. Castiglione, *Il Cortegiano*, ed. V. Cian (Florence, 1923), I, XXXVII, pp. 92f. (the editor rightly draws attention to the passage's allusion to Cicero). [Translators' note: We translate from the Italian. A recent English version is Castiglione, *The Courtier*, trans. G. Bull (London, 1976).] C. Dionisotti (*Appunti su arti e lettere*, [Milan, 1995], p. 121) has remarked of this passage that here for the first time artists are taken as authorities in a literary discussion. We should note, however, that Cicero's argument (*De oratore* 3.25 ff.) about diversity of style in fact starts by considering sculpture and painting. M. Kemp notes other passages more or less directly inspired by Cicero in " 'Equal Excellences': Lomazzo and the Explanation of Individual Styles in Visual Arts," *Renaissance Studies* 1 (1987): 1–26, esp. 5 f., 14.

10. G. Romano suggests that Mantegna was included in homage to Isabella d'Este, Duchess of Mantua (where Castiglione was born): see "Verso la maniera moderna," in G. Previtali and F. Zeri, eds., *Storia dell'arte italiana*, II, 2, 1 (Turin 1981), pp. 73 f. On the absence of Titian, see Dionisotti, *Appunti*, pp. 120–122.

11. E. H. Gombrich has used the term *"topos"* in reference to the passage from Cicero, of which he finds an echo in a text by Alamanno Rinuccini: see "The Renaissance Concept of Artistic Progress and Its Consequences," in Gombrich, *Norm and Form: Studies in the Art of the Renaissance* (London, 1966), pp. 139 f. n. 5. On Warburg's *Pathosformeln*, see E. H. Gombrich, *Aby Warburg: An Intellectual Biography* (London, 1970), pp. 178 ff.

12. E. Panofsky, "Das erste Blatt aus dem 'Libro' Giorgio Vasaris: Eine Studie über der Beurteilung der Gotik in der italienischen Renaissance . . ." The essay, published in 1930, is included in Panofsky, *Meaning in the Visual Arts* (Garden City, N.Y., 1955), pp. 169–235.

13. G. Vasari, *Le vite* (text of the 1568 edition), ed. G. Milanesi (Florence, 1906; anastatic reprint of 1973), 7:75.

14. Ibid., p. 76.

15. Panofsky, *Meaning in the Visual Arts*, p. 201.

16. Here I follow Funkenstein, *Theology*, p. 241, n. 69; but I have included Cicero, for the reasons given above.

17. G. Vasari, *Le vite . . . nell'edizione per i tipi di Lorenzo Torrentino, Firenze 1550*, ed. L. Bellosi and A. Rossi (Turin, 1986), p. 560.

18. Vasari, *Le vite* (1568 edition), 7:447 f., and the whole paragraph is relevant. See also ibid., p. 431, for a similar comment by Sebastiano del Piombo.

19. We can certainly dismiss C. Hope's suggestion that Michelangelo's comment "was perhaps provoked more by prudery than anything else" (*Titian* [New York, 1980], pp. 89 f.). The fact that *Danae* contains echoes of Michelangelo was already recognized by Cavalcaselle (G. B. Cavalcaselle, *Tiziano: La sua vita e i suoi tempi*, ed. J. A. Crowe [Florence, 1878; reprint, 1974], 2:57). Johannes Wilde pointed out, presumably in the 1950s, the relation between *Danae* and *Night*; see his lectures, posthumously published under the title *Venetian Art from Bellini to Titian* (Oxford, 1974), plate 149 (the caption should read *"Night"* instead of *"Dawn"*). F. Saxl argues that *Danae* derives from a sarcophagus depicting Leda (see "Titian and Aretino," in Saxl, *A Heritage of Images* [Harmondsworth, 1970], p. 81); this connection may be even more safely affirmed with respect to Michelangelo's lost *Leda* or to his *Night*. F. Valcanover links both of these to *Danae* (see the catalog *Da Tiziano a El Greco: Per la storia del Manierismo a Venezia* [Milan, 1981], pp. 108 f.). It is worth noting that the traditional identification of *Dawn* and *Night* in the Medici chapels is inverted by C. Gilbert, in *Michelangelo On and Off the Sistine Chapel* (New York, 1994), p. 45, plates 12 and 13; that this is an oversight is proved by (among other things) the words of the famous sonnet written at the time: *La notte, che tu vedi in sì dolci atti / dormir* ("Night, whom in such fair attitude thou seest asleep").

20. Vasari, *Le vite* (1568 edition), 4:92.

21. Ibid., 7:452. On this passage and its implications, see P. Sohm, *Pittoresco* (Cambridge, 1991), pp. 51 f.

22. In my view it is impossible, in the light of these passages, to maintain that "Vasari is interested in style rather than in the individual" (S. Leontief Alpers, "Ekphrasis and Aesthetic Attitudes in Vasari's *Lives*," *Journal of the Warburg and Courtauld Institutes* 23 [1960]: 190–215, esp. p. 210). It is true, on the other hand, that for Vasari "the means of art are gradually perfected while the ends remain constant" (p. 201); but I think it is excessive to charge such an approach, which is not unlike what we find in Castiglione and in Cicero before him (both are mentioned on p. 212), with being "frankly untheoretical."

23. L. Dolce, "Dialogo della pittura," in *Trattati d'arte del Cinquecento*, ed. P. Barocchi (Bari, 1960), 1:202 (on Titian's *Assumption*, in the church of Santa Maria Gloriosa dei Frari), 206. See also M. Warnke, "Praxis der Kunsttheorie: Über die Geburtswehen des Individualstils," *Idea: Jahrbuch der Hamburger Kunsthalle* 1 (1982): 54 ff.

24. On all this (and on Dolce), see D. Mahon, "Eclecticism and the Carracci," *Journal of the Warburg and Courtauld Institutes* 16 (1953): 303–341, esp. 311–313.

25. The labels used concealed a reality that was actually more complex, as is shown, for instance, by T. Puttfarken, "Composition, Perspective, and Presence: Observations on Early Academic Theory in France," in *Sight and*

Insight: Essays in Art and Culture in Honour of E. H. Gombrich, ed. J. Onians (London, 1994).

26. Roland Fréart sieur de Chambray, *Parallèle de l'architecture antique avec la moderne* (Paris, 1650), "Avant-Propos," pp. 1 f. We find the same key terms in Bellori's criticism of Rubens (G. P. Bellori, *Le vite de' pittori, scultori e architetti moderni*, ed. E. Borea [Turin, 1976], pp. 267 f.). On the parallels between Bellori's *Vite* and Fréart de Chambray's later *Idée de la perfection de la peinture*, see Previtali's introduction to Bellori (pp. xxiv–xxv).

27. Fréart de Chambray, *Parallèle*, p. 80.

28. R. Wagner-Rieger, "Borromini und Oesterreich," in *Studi sul Borromini* (Rome, 1967), 2:221 ff.

29. J. B. Fischer von Erlach, *Entwurf einer historischen Architectur in Abbildung unterschiedener berühmten Gebäude des Altertums und fremder Völker* (Leipzig, 1721):

Les dessinateurs y verront, que les goûts des nations ne diffèrent pas moins dans l'architecture, que dans la manière de s'habiller ou d'aprêter les viandes, et en les comparant les unes aux autres, ils pouront en faire un choix judicieux. Enfin ils y reconnoîtront qu'à la verité l'usage peut authoriser certaines bisarreries dans l'art de bâtir, comme sont les ornements à jour du Gothique, les voûtes d'ogives en tiers point, les tours d'Eglise, les ornements et les toits à l'Indienne, où la diversité des opinions est aussi peu sujète à la dispute, que celle des goûts.

The passage is quoted in part by Panofsky, *Meaning in the Visual Arts*, p. 180). See also A. Ilg, *Die Fischer von Erlach* (Vienna, 1895), pp. 522 ff.; J. Schmidt, "Die Architekturbücher der Fischer von Erlach," *Wiener Jahrbuch für Kunstgeschichte*, 1934, pp. 149–156, esp. p. 152; G. Kunoth, *Die historische Architektur Fischers von Erlach* (Düsseldorf, 1956); E. Iversen, "Fischer von Erlach as Historian of Architecture," *Burlington Magazine* 100 (1958): 323–325; H. Aurenhammer, *Johann-Bernhard Fischer von Erlach* (London, 1973), esp. pp. 153–159.

30. See P. Portoghesi, *Borromini nella cultura europea* (Bari, 1982), p. 152; and Portoghesi also refers to a conversation in similar vein between Bernini and an anonymous ecclesiastic (recorded by Baldinucci).

31. See R. Wittkower, "Francesco Borromini: Personalità e destino," in *Studi sul Borromini* (Rome, 1967), 1:33 (citing Borromini's *Opus*).

32. R. Wittkower maintains that Borromini may have been indirectly inspired by "ziggurats": see p. 178 of the Italian translation of his work *Arte e architettura in Italia, 1600–1750* (Turin, 1972).

33. This theme is explored in my essay "Alien Voices," in *History, Rhetoric, and Proof* (Hanover and London, 1999), pp. 71–91.

34. See Kunoth, *Historische Architektur*, and E. Iversen, "Fischer von Erlach." Borromini, who built the college De Propaganda Fide for the

Jesuits, left 500 *scudi* in his will for adornments to the altar of Saint Ignatius (Wittkower, "Francesco Borromini," p. 44).

35. See M. Tafuri, *La sfera e il labirinto* (Turin, 1980), p. 54.

36. *The World*, 27 March 1755, quoted by A. O. Lovejoy, in *Essays in the History of Ideas* (New York, 1960), p. 121 (but the whole of this essay, "The Chinese Origin of a Romanticism," should be read; as also the essay "The First Gothic Revival"; see pp. 99–135, 136–165). See also K. Clark, *The Gothic Revival* (1928; reprint, Harmondsworth, 1964), pp. 38–40; S. Lang and N. Pevsner, "Sir William Temple and Sharawadgi," *Architectural Review* 106 (1949): 391–393; O. Sirén, *China and the Gardens of Europe* (New York, 1950; 2d ed., Dumbarton Oaks, 1990).

37. The essay comprises pp. 11–51 of J. J. Winckelmann, *Il bello nell'arte*, ed. F. Pfister (Turin, 1973).

38. Ibid., p. 32.

39. See C. Justi, *Winckelmann*, 2d ed. (Leipzig, 1872), 3:167; cited in F. Meinecke, *Die Entstehung des Historismus* [1936], ed. C. Hinrichs (Munich, 1959): see p. 241 of the Italian translation, *Le origini dello storicismo* (Florence, 1973).

40. J. J. Winckelmann, *Geschichte der Kunst des Altertums*, ed. W. Senff (Weimar, 1964), p. 7.

41. Meinecke, *Die Enstehung*, Italian ed. (*Le origini*), pp. 232–246; F. Haskell, *History and Its Images* (New Haven and London, 1993), pp. 217–224.

42. Winckelmann, *Geschichte*, pp. 102 f. A faint echo of this passage is audible in a comment by O. J. Brendel on the "mother of Chianciano" (a work dating from c. 400 now kept in the Museo Archeologico in Florence): she "gazes in a void before her—gloomy ancestress of Michelangelo's sadly prophetic Madonna at Bruges" (*Etruscan Art* [Harmondsworth, 1978], p. 321).

43. See Justi, *Winckelmann*, 2:86–97 (here I take the argument in a slightly different direction).

44. A.-C.-P. comte de Caylus, *Receuil d'antiquités égyptiennes, etrusques, grecques, et romaines*, new ed. (1752; new ed., Paris, 1761), 1:7. [Translators' note: We translate this passage from CG's Italian rendering.]

45. In the dedication of his work to the Académie des Inscriptions et Belles-Lettres, Winckelmann wrote: "Until you were so gracious as to admit me among you, it was in a merely artistic light that I regarded these remains of learned Antiquity which had escaped the barbarism of the times; you have taught me to see in them an infinitely higher merit—the merit, I mean, of containing a thousand notable curiosities concerning the history, the religious practice, the manners and the customs of these renowned peoples." See the illuminating essay on Maffei and Caylus in K. Pomian, *Collectioneurs, amateurs et curieux* (Paris, 1978) (*Collectors and Curiosities: Paris and Venice, 1500–1800*, trans. E. Wiles-Portier [London, 1990]). The

importance of Caylus's antiquarian work has been stressed, independently, by Haskell, *History and Its Images*, pp. 180–186, and by G. Pucci, *Il passato prossimo* (Rome, 1993), pp. 108–118.

6. STYLE

Inclusion and
Exclusion

46. J. J. Winckelmann, *Lettere italiane*, ed. G. Zampa (Milan, 1961), p. 321; Justi, *Winckelmann*, 2:87. On the fraught relations between Caylus and Winckelmann, see Pucci, *Il passato prossimo*, pp. 80–84.

47. Justi, *Winckelmann*, 2:95.

48. Buffon's famous dictum "Le style c'est l'homme même" has often been understood (or misunderstood: see L. Spitzer, "Linguistics and Literary History," in *Representative Essays*, ed. A. K. Forcione et al. [Stanford, 1988], pp. 13, 34) as meaning that style is an expression of the idiosyncratic individuality of the writer. Hegel is among those who have taken it in this sense (G. W. F. Hegel, *Vorlesungen über die Aesthetik* [Frankfurt am Main, 1970], 1:379: Hegel refers to a "well-known French dictum," without mentioning Buffon). Other explanations have been given by Géruzez (see Buffon, *Morceaux choisis*, ed. J. Labbé [Paris, 1903], pp. 11 f.: "Buffon's remark 'Le style est l'homme même,'" so often quoted and sometimes altered, means that style displays the true nature of the intelligence that produces it. Thought is, so to speak, general and impersonal; it depends upon humanity; style depends upon and expresses the man alone") and by the editors of the American edition of Spitzer's essays (p. 453, n. 40): "In context, Buffon's phrase . . . suggests that by means of good writing style man achieves his essential humanity and assures his immortality"). Both these explanations are erroneous. The text reads thus: "Ces choses [les connaissances, les faits et les découvertes] sont hors de l'homme, le style c'est l'homme même" (These things [knowledge, facts and discoveries] are external to man; style is man himself). Buffon means that scientific discoveries are external in relation to the human species ("l'homme" in the generic sense, not the individual writer); they may become truly the property of the human species, and thus immortal, only by virtue of style (a few lines earlier, Buffon says: "Les ouvrages bien écrits seront les seuls qui passeront à la postérité" [Only well-written works will go down to posterity]). This interpretation is consistent with the emphatic praise for the impersonal style that is expressed in the *Discours*—an aspect that is misunderstood in Pucci's otherwise valuable *Il passato prossimo*.

49. P. Junod, "Future in the Past," *Oppositions* 26 (1984): 49.

50. See D. Irwin, *John Flaxman* (New York, 1979), pp. 204–215.

51. See M. Praz, *Gusto neoclassico* (Milan, 1990), p. 67. More generally, see the published version of S. Symonds's Ph.D. dissertation, *Flaxman and Europe: The Outline Illustrations and Their Influence* (New York and London, 1984).

52. D. and E. Panofsky, *Pandora's Box* (New York, 1962), pp. 92 f.; G. Pre-

vitali, *La fortuna dei primitivi: dal Vasari ai neoclassici*, new ed. (Turin, 1989), pp. 169 f.

53. See J. Flaxman, *Lectures on Sculpture . . . as Delivered by Him Before the President and Members of the Royal Academy* (London, 1829). References are to the reprint edition published by Bell and Daldy (London, 1865); see Lecture 7, "Style," pp. 168–197. In addition to those cited in the body of the text, the following passage (p. 172) is also worth noting:

> In our pursuit of this subject we are aware of the propensity to imitation common in all, by which our knowledge of surrounding objects is increased, and our intellectual faculties are elevated; and we consequently find in most countries attempts to copy the human figure, in early times, equally barbarous, whether they were the production of India, Babylon, Germany, Mexico, or Otaheite. They equally partake in the common deformities of great heads, monstrous faces, diminutive and mis-shapen bodies and limbs. We shall, however, say no more of these abortions, as they really have no nearer connection with style, than the child's first attempts to write the alphabet can claim with the poet's inspiration, or the argument and description of the orator.

54. For this and the preceding three quoted passages, see Flaxman, *Lectures on Sculpture* (1865 reprint), pp. 168–170. E. H. Gombrich has not failed to note this passage: see "From Archaeology to Art History: Some Stages in the Rediscovery of the Romanesque," in *Icon to Cartoon: A Tribute to Sixten Ringbom*, ed. M. Terttu Knapas and Å. Ringbom (Helsinki, 1995), pp. 91–108, esp. p. 96.

55. *Choice Examples of Wedgwood Art: A Selection of Plaques, Cameos, Medallions, Vases, etc., from the Designs of Flaxman and Others. Reproduced in Permanent Photography by the Autotype Process, with Descriptions by Eliza Meteyard, Author of the "Life of Wedgwood," etc.* (London, 1879); and see the catalog of the exhibition *John Flaxman: Mythologie und Industrie*, Hamburg, 1979.

56. Irwin, *John Flaxman*, p. 207.

57. G. W. F. Hegel, *Vorlesungen über die Aesthetik* (Frankfurt am Main, 1970), 1:105 f. These lectures, published for the first time in 1836–1838, were based on notes taken by students in 1817 and 1829.

58. H. Heine, *Französische Maler: Gemäldeausstellung in Paris 1831*, in Heine, *Historisch-kritisch Gesamtausgabe*, 12/1, ed. J.-R. Derré and C. Giesen (Hamburg, 1980), p. 24 (S. Zantop, ed., *Painting on the Move: Heinrich Heine and the Visual Arts* [Lincoln and London, 1989], pp. 133–134). R. Bianchi Bandinelli quotes this passage as a reference to Friedrich Schlegel (*Introduzione all'archeologia* [Bari, 1975], p. 100, n. 4). See also W. Rasch, "Die Pariser Kunstkritik Heinrich Heines," in Hager and Knopp, *Beiträge zum Problem des Stilpluralismus*, pp. 230–244.

59. E. Delacroix, *Oeuvres Littéraires* (Paris, 1923), 1:23–36 ("Questions sur le Beau"). See also pp. 37–54, "Des variations du Beau" (1857).

60. C. Baudelaire, *Curiosités esthétiques: L'Art romantique et autres oeuvres critiques*, ed. H. Lemaître (Paris, 1962), pp. 215 f.: "Or, comment cette bizarrerie, nécessaire, incompressible, variée à l'infini, dépendante des milieux, des climats, des moeurs, de la race, de la religion et du tempérament de l'artiste, pourra-t-elle jamais être gouvernée, redressée, par les règles utopiques conçues dans un petit temple scientifique quelconque de la planète, sans danger de mort pour l'art lui même?"

61. Ibid., p. 213. "Que dirait, qu'écrirait—je répète—en face de ces phénomènes insolites un de ces *professeurs-jurés* d'esthétique, comme les appelle Henri Heine, ce charmant esprit qui serait un génie s'il se tournait plus souvent vers le divin?" On Baudelaire and Heine, see C. Pichois, "La littérature française à la lumière du surnaturalisme," in *Le surnaturalisme français: Actes du colloque* . . . (Neuchâtel, 1979), p. 27. See also the comment in Heine, *Historisch-kritisch Gesamtausgabe*, p. 566.

62. Baudelaire, *Curiosités esthétiques*, p. 217. "Il est encore une erreur forte à la mode, de laquelle je veux me garder comme de l'enfer . . . —Je veux parler de l'idée du progrès. Ce fanal obscur, invention du philosophisme actuel . . . Qui veut y voir clair dans l'histoire doit avant tout éteindre ce fanal perfide."

63. Ibid., p. 238, n. 1; p. 904, note to p. 217 (incorrectly given as p. 219).

64. Ibid., p. 219. "Toute floraison est spontanée, individuelle. Signorelli était-il vraiment le générateur de Michel-Ange? Est-ce que Pérugin contenait Raphaël? L'artiste ne rélève que de lui-même. Il ne promet aux siècles que ses propres oeuvres. Il ne cautionne que lui-même. Il meurt sans enfants."

65. The letter was published as a flyer attached to Semper's *Wissenschaft, Industrie, und Kunst* (Brunswick, 1852) (see H. F. Mallgrave, *Gottfried Semper: Architect of the Nineteenth Century* [New Haven and London, 1996], pp. 156 f.).

66. G. Semper, "London Lecture of November 11, 1853," published in *Res* 6 (Fall 1983): 5–31, with a commentary by H. F. Mallgrave and a prefatory note by J. Rykwert.

67. Ibid., p. 8.

68. Ibid., pp. 26 f.

69. In the afterword ("Postfazione") to G. Morelli, *Della pittura italiana. Studii storico-critici. Le gallerie Borghese e Doria-Pamphili in Roma* (Milan, 1991), pp. 494–503, J. Anderson criticizes my essay "Clues" and insists on the importance of Cuvier. However, see my references to Cuvier, and associated comments, in *Miti emblemi spie* (Turin, 1986), pp. 183 f. (The essay is available in English, in *Clues, Myths, and the Historical Method*, trans. J. and A. Tedeschi [Baltimore and London, 1989], pp. 96–125.)

70. Semper, "London Lecture," pp. 11 f.

71. G. G. Scott, *Remarks on Secular and Domestic Architecture, Present and Future,* 2d ed. (London, 1858), pp. 11, 16, 263 (italics in original).

72. Gustav Klemm's racial theories (on which see H. F. Mallgrave, "Gustav Klemm and Gottfried Semper: The Meeting of Ethnological and Architectural Theory," *Res* 9 [Spring 1985]: 68–79) had no influence on Semper.

73. G. Semper, *Der Stil in der technischen und tektonischen Künsten* (Munich, 1879), 2:1–5. Semper used the same example in his first London lecture: see *Res* (Fall 1983): 9 f.

74. See C. Schorske, *Fin-de-siècle Vienna* (New York, 1980), pp. 101–104.

75. See Riegl, *Stilfragen* (1893); and on *Kunstwollen,* see M. Olin, *Forms of Representation in Alois Riegl's Theory of Art* (University Park, Pa., 1992), p. 72.

76. See W. Hoffmann, *Gustav Klimt und die Wiener Jahrhundertswende* (Salzburg, 1970).

77. See Olin, *Forms of Representation,* and M. Iversen, *Alois Riegl: Art History and Theory* (Cambridge, Mass., 1993).

78. See Riegl's *Spätrömische Kunstindustrie,* p. 86 of the Italian translation (*Industria artistica tardoromana* [Florence, 1981]), where he speaks of the "necessary last phase of transition of the art of antiquity."

79. See W. Sauerländer, "Alois Riegl und die Entstehung der autonomen Kunstgeschichte am Fin-de-Siècle," in *Fin de Siècle: Zu Literatur und Kunst der Jahrhundertswende* (Frankfurt am Main, 1977), pp. 125–139.

80. A. Riegl, *Historische Grammatik der bildende Künste,* ed. K. M. Swoboda and O. Pächt (Graz, 1966); see p. 288 of the Italian translation (*Grammatica storica delle arti figurative,* ed. F. Diano [Bologna, 1983]).

81. Ibid. (Italian ed.), p. 261, n. 21. On Lüger, see Schorske, *Fin-de-Siècle Vienna,* pp. 133–146.

82. See M. Olin, "The Cult of Monuments as a State Religion in Late Nineteenth Century Austria," *Wiener Jahrbuch für Kunstgeschichte* 33 (1985): 199–218. Olin, who quotes without comment a letter sent to the art historian Franz Wickhoff written—by a reader who uses a pseudonym to conceal his identity—in an aggressively anti-Semitic tone, emphasizes that we should probably make a distinction between Riegl's mild and universalistic approach and the racist politics of the Christian Socialists (see pp. 196 f.).

83. Riegl, *Historische Grammatik,* Italian ed. (*Grammatica storica*), p. 77; Riegl, *Spätrömische Kunstindustrie,* Italian ed. (*Industria artistica*), p. 149n. J. von Schlosser shows his unease about the racial implications of Riegl's categories in his remarks in "La scuola viennese" (1934; see Schlosser, *La storia dell'arte nell'esperienze e nei ricordi di un suo cultore* [Bari, 1936]). Gombrich's tone is more detached: "As a child of his time, Riegl never doubted the influence of racial factors on artistic development" (see Gombrich, *The Sense of Order* [London, 1979], p. 184).

84. The theoretical incoherence of the opposition between "abstrac-

tion" and "empathy" that Worringer developed in a book of that title (*Abstraktion und Einfühlung*, 1907) was critically analyzed by E. Panofsky in *Der Begriff des Kunstwollens* (see p. 175, n. 7, of the Italian translation, *La prospettiva come "forma simbolica"* [Milan, 1961]). However, Worringer's distinction amounts only to a rather simplistic development of an opposition already suggested by Riegl: see, for instance, the latter's remark that certain forms of art—for example, the art of Egypt—are closely tied to "the objective and material vision of things" (Riegl, *Industria artistica*, p. 113).

85. W. Worringer, *Formprobleme der Gotik* (1911; second ed., Munich, 1912), p. 97. See p. 142 of the English translation by Herbert Read, *Form in Gothic* (London, 1964); the first edition of this translation was published in 1927. See also N. H. Donahue, *Forms of Disruption: Abstraction in Modern German Prose* (Ann Arbor, 1993), pp. 13–33.

86. Worringer, *Form in Gothic*, pp. 180 f. (The translation has been slightly modified.)

87. The German text of the essay is "Wissenschaft als Kunst: Eine diskussion der Rieglschen Kunsttheorie verbunden mit dem Versuch, sie auf die Wissenschaft anzuwenden," in *Sehnsucht nach dem Ursprung: Festschrift für Mircea Eliade*, ed. H. P. Duerr (Frankfurt am Main, 1983). See "Science as Art: An Attempt to Apply Riegl's Theory of Art to the Sciences," in *Art + Text* 12–13 (1983): 16–46 (a shortened version), and also the Italian translation, *Scienza come arte* (Rome and Bari, 1984), pp. 93–161. References here are to this Italian text.

88. Feyerabend's *Against Method* first appeared in English in 1975; a revised edition appeared in 1988 and a third edition in 1993 (all published by Verso, in London). The footnote in question is n. 219, p. 197, in the Italian version (*Contro il metodo* [Milan, 1973]).

89. Feyerabend, *Scienza come arte*, p. 118.

90. Ibid., p. 156.

91. Ibid., p. 51, n. 29. The list includes (as well as Riegl) E. Panofsky, B. Snell, H. Schäfer, and V. Ronchi. Riegl and Panofsky are added in a postscript; the other three are mentioned, in connection with *Against Method* (1970), in P. Feyerabend, *Killing Time* (Chicago 1995), p. 140.

92. See the essay "Quantitativer und qualitativer Fortschritt in Kunst, Philosophie, und Wissenschaft," in *Kunst und Wissenschaft*, ed. P. Feyerabend and C. Thomas (Zurich, 1984), pp. 217–230. Here Vasari is interpreted as in a way a precursor of Riegl; the latter is not mentioned, presumably because Feyerabend was not yet acquainted with his work.

93. Much is revealed by the way in which Feyerabend recounts his reaction to the news of the German surrender: "I was relieved, but I also had a sense of loss. I had not accepted the aims of Nazism—I hardly knew what they were—and I was much too contrary to be loyal to anything" (*Killing*

Time, p. 55). Not one of these statements seems credible in the light of what the author has told us earlier—that he used to read *Mein Kampf* out, in a loud voice, to his associates; that his attitude toward the Nazis had been ambivalent; that he had wanted to belong to the SS, and so on.

94. Ibid., p. 45.

95. Ibid., pp. 47–50. "I still have the complete text of the lectures—forty pages of a six-by-eight-inch notebook. This is truly miraculous, for I am not in the habit of assembling memorabilia" (p. 47).

96. See also J. Agassi, "Wie es Euch gefällt," in *Versuchungen: Aufsätze zur Philosophie Paul Feyerabends*, ed. H. P. Duerr (Frankfurt am Main), pp. 147–157, and Feyerabend's reply (*Scienza come arte*, pp. 83–85). I found Feyerabend's comments on Auschwitz very disturbing.

97. See the catalog of the exhibition "Degenerate Art" that took place at the Los Angeles County Museum in 1993. On Feyerabend's wish to become a painter, see *Killing Time*, p. 43.

98. This "aestheticization of history" is noted in W. Sauerländer, *Alois Riegl*, p. 432.

99. H. F. K. Günther, *Rasse und Stil: Gedanken über die Beziehungen im Leben und in der Geistesgeschichte der europäischen Völker, insbesondere des deutschen Volkes* (Munich, 1926) (Worringer's *Formprobleme der Gotik* is referred to on p. 56). A long article in praise of Günther, by L. Stenel von Rutowski, appeared in the *Nationalsozialistische Monatshefte*: see Heft 68 (November 1935): 962–998, and Heft 69 (December 1935): 1099–1114.

100. A. Hitler, "Die deutschen Kunst als stolzeste Verteidigung des deuschen Volkes," in *Nationalsozialistische Monatshefte* 4, no. 34 (October 1933): 437. The passage is quoted in part by S. Friedländer, *Nazi Germany and the Jews* (New York, 1997), 1:71. The issue in which Hitler's views were published was largely devoted to art in the Third Reich.

101. See Feyerabend, *Against Method*.

102. It is worth noting Feyerabend's embarrassed remarks in *Scienza come arte*, pp. 31–33.

103. Around 1840, T. L. Donaldson wrote that styles in architecture might be compared "to languages in literature. There is no style, as there is no language, which has not its particular beauties, its individual fitness and power—there is not one which can be safely rejected . . . so the architect is more fitted for the emergencies of his difficult career, who can command the majesty of the classic styles, the sublimity of the Gothic, the grace of the Revival or the brilliant fancies of Arabic" (quoted in H. F. Mallgrave, *The Idea of Style: Gottfried Semper in London* [1983 dissertation], p. 199). The parallel has a long history, going back at least to the passage from Castiglione's *Courtier* that we quoted earlier (Castiglione, *Il Cortegiano*, pp. 92 f.).

104. *The Notebooks of Simone Weil*, trans. A. Wills, 2 vols. (London, 1976),

1:244–245. See the Italian edition, *Quaderni*, ed. G. Gaeta (Milan, 1991), 2:152,
176. P. C. Bori has emphasized the importance of these passages in *Per un*

consenso etico tra culture (Genoa, 1991), p. 29.

105. T. Adorno, *Minima Moralia*, trans. E. F. N. Jephcott (London, 1974),
p. 75, aphorism 47, "De gustibus est disputandum" (which should be
referred to in its entirety).

106. See P. Holdengräber, " 'A Visible History of Art': The Forms and
Preoccupations of the Early Museum," *Studies in Eighteenth-Century Culture*
17 (1987): 115.

107. R. Longhi, "Critica d'arte e buongoverno," in Longhi, *Opere complete*
(Florence, 1985), 13:17 f.

108. Based on Aristotle, *Peri Hermeneias*, 18a.9–18, which was spread by
Boethius's translation; see chapter 2 above.

109. See E. Gombrich, *Art and Illusion* (London, 1960), pp. 5 f.

7. DISTANCE AND PERSPECTIVE: TWO METAPHORS

These pages are a slightly modified version of a lecture given at the Wissenschaftskolleg in Berlin on 12 June 1997. I thank Stephen Greenblatt for the critical comments he made, which I have taken account of here.

1. Paul Boghossian, "What the Sokal Hoax Ought to Teach Us," *Times Literary Supplement*, 13 December 1996, pp. 14 f.

2. See C. Guillén's notable essay "On the Concept of Metaphor and Perspective," in *Literature as System* (Princeton, 1971), pp. 283–371 (Christoph Lüthy kindly drew this to my attention).

3. Y. H. Yerushalmi, *Zakhor: Jewish History and Jewish Memory* (Seattle and London, 1982), p. 5. T. C. Römer makes no mention of Yerushalmi's book in his recent essay "Transformations in Deuteronomistic and Biblical Historiography," *Zeitschrift für die alttestamentliche Wissenschaft* 109 (1997): 1–11.

4. Yerushalmi, *Zakhor*, pp. 44, 26.

5. Ibid., p. 44.

6. A. Perry, "Thucydides' Historical Perspective," *Yale Classical Studies* 23 (1972): 47–61, esp. pp. 48 f.

7. In his famous essay "Die Perspektive als 'symbolische Form,'" in *Vorträge der Bibliothek Warburg, 1924–25* (Berlin and Leipzig, 1927), pp. 258–330, Erwin Panofsky argues that we can identify in Greek and Roman art a specific form of perspective, different from that developed in the Renaissance. (See E. Panofsky, *Perspective as Symbolic Form*, trans. C. Wood [New York, 1991].)

8. [Translators' note: Here and below, biblical quotations are from the text of the New English Bible. Here, we add the phrases "which is given for me; do this as a memorial of me," which are given in a footnote.] See G. Tel-

lenbach, "Die historische Dimension der liturgischen Commemoratio im Mittelalter," in K. Schmid and J. Wallasch, eds., *Memoria: Der geschichtliche Zeugniswert der liturgischen Gedenkens im Mittelalter* (Munich, 1984), pp. 200–214, esp. pp. 201 f.; the author refers to J. Jeremias, *Die Abendsmahlworte Jesu* (Göttingen, 1960), pp. 229 ff., 239 ff., where the Jewish connotations of the passage are emphasized.

9. Galatians 3:28.

10. Quoted in J. Pelikan, *The Mystery of Continuity: Time and History, Memory and Eternity in the Thought of Saint Augustine* (Charlottesville, 1986), pp. 36 f. The Latin text (*Patrologia Latina*, 42:1045) reads thus:

Trinitas quae imago Dei, jam quarenda in principali mentis parte. . . . Unde quae sciuntur, velut adventitia sunt in animo, sive cognitione historica illata, ut sunt facta et dicta, quae tempore peraguntur et transeunt, vel in natura rerum suis locis et regionibus constituta sunt, sive in ipso homine quae non erant oriuntur, aut aliis docentibus aut cogitationibus propriis. . . . Sunt autem vel in locis suis, vel quae tempore praeterierunt: quamvis quae praeterierunt, non ipsa sint, sed eorum quaedam signa praeteritorum, quibus visis vel auditis cognoscantur fuisse atque transisse. Quae signa vel in locis sita sunt, sicut monumenta mortuorum, et quaecumque similia; vel in litteris fide dignis, sicut est omnis gravis et approbandae auctoritatis historia; vel in animis eorum qui ea jam noverunt.

(See Augustine, *The Trinity*, trans. S. McKenna [Washington, 1963], p. 627). See also *De Trinitate* 15.12.21.

11. See V. Saxer, *Morts martyrs reliques en Afrique chrétienne aux premiers siècles* (Paris, 1980), pp. 125–133 (on monuments), 197 f. (on liturgical commemorations), 261 f. (on relics), 298 ff. (on reliquaries).

12. Cited in Pelikan, *Mystery of Continuity*, pp. 107 f. [Translators' note: Our rendering here is from the text in *Esposizioni sui Salmi*, ed. V. Tarulli (Rome, 1977), p. 901; see *Patrologia Latina*, 37:1951.]

13. See S. Benko, "The Meaning of Sanctorum Communio," in *Studies in Historical Theology* (London, 1964), 3:98 ff. (from which the translation is quoted) (on Nicetas of Aquileia's *Explanatio Symboli*).

14. See E. Auerbach, "Figura," in Auerbach, *Scenes from the Drama of European Literature* (New York, 1959), pp. 11–76; R. W. Bernard, "The Rhetoric of God in the Figurative Exegesis of Augustine," in M. S. Burrows and P. Rorem, eds., *Biblical Hermeneutics in Historical Perspective: Studies in Honor of Karl Fröhlich on His Sixtieth Birthday* (Grand Rapids, Mich., 1991), pp. 88–99 (where there is no mention, oddly, of Auerbach).

15. Saint Augustine, *De doctrina Christiana* 3.16.24; *Christian Instruction*, trans. J. Gavigan, in vol. 4 of Augustine's *Writings*, 2d ed. (Washington, 1950; reprint, 1966), p. 136.

16. *De doctrina Christiana* 3.10.15 (*Christian Instruction*, trans. Gavigan, pp. 129 f.):

Sed quoniam proclive est humanum genus non ex momentis ipsius libidinis sed potius suae consuetudinis aestimare peccata, fit plerumque ut quisque hominum ea tantum culpanda arbitretur, quae suae regionis et temporis homines vituperare atque damnare consuerunt, et ea tantum probanda atque laudanda, quae consuetudo eorum cum quibus vivit admittit, eoque contingit ut, si quid scriptura vel praeceperit quod abhorret a consuetudine audientium vel quod non abhorret culpaverit, si animum eorum iam verbi vinxit auctoritas, figuratam locutionem putent. Non autem praecipit scriptura nisi caritatem.

17. Ibid. 3.12.19: "Quod igitur locis et temporibus et personis conveniat, diligenter attendendum est, ne temere flagitia reprehendamus" (*Christian Instruction*, trans. Gavigan, p. 133).

18. Ibid. 3.12.20 (*Christian Instruction*, trans. Gavigan, pp. 133 f.).

19. See A. Funkenstein, *Theology and the Scientific Imagination* (Princeton, 1986), pp. 202–289, esp. p. 222.

20. Ibid., pp. 223 f. It is probable that Augustine's reply refers to manna or the sacrifice of Melchisedek: see Augustine, *In Johannis Evangelium, tractatus* 26, 12 (*Patrologia Latina*, 35:1612): "Hunc panem significat manna, hunc panem significavit altare Dei. Sacramenta illa fuerunt; in signis diversa sunt, in re quae significantur paria sunt" (quoted by W. Gessel, *Eucharistische Gemeinschaft bei Augustinus* [Würzburg, 1966], p. 179). More generally, see J. Lecuyer, "Le sacrifice selon Saint-Augustin," in *Augustinus Magister* (Paris, 1954), 2:905–914; G. de Broglie, "La notion augustinienne de sacrifice 'invisible' et 'vrai,'" *Recherches de science religieuse* 47 (1960): 135–165 (not a convincing essay).

21. S. Aurelii Augustini . . . , *Epistulae*, ed. A. Goldbacher (Vindobonae–Lipsiae, 1904), CSEL, 44:3, letter 138, "Ad Marcellinum," 1.5, p. 130: "Haec quaestio quam late pateat, profecto videt, quisquis pulchri aptique distantiam sparsam quodam modo in universitate rerum valet neque neglegit intueri. Pulchrum enim per se ipsum consideratur atque laudatur, cui turpe ac deforme contrarium est. Aptum vero, cui ex adverso est ineptum, quasi religatum pendet aliunde, nec ex semet ipso sed ex eo cui connectitur, judicatur; nimirum etiam decens atque indecens vel hoc idem est vel perinde habetur. Age nunc ea, quae diximus, refer ad illud, unde agitur. Aptum fuit primis temporibus sacrificium, quod praeceperat Deus, nunc vero non ita est. Aliud enim praecepit, quod huic tempori aptum esset, qui multo magis quam homo novit, quid cuique tempori accommodate adhibeatur, quid quando impertiat, addat, auferat, detrahat, augeat minuatve inmutabilis mutabilium sicut creator ita moderator, donec universi saeculi pulchritudo, cuius particulae sunt,

quae suis quibusque temporibus apta sunt, velut magnum carmen cuius-
dam ineffabilis modulatoris excurrat atque inde transeant in aeternam
contemplationem speciei, qui Deum rite colunt, etiam cum tempus est
fidei." The passage is quoted in part in Funkenstein, *Theology*, p. 223.
[Here the translation used is that by Sister Wilfrid Parsons, *Saint Augustine: Letters* (Washington, 1953), 3:38 f.] On the figurative interpretation of
Jewish sacrifices in Augustine's *Contra Faustum*, see S. D. Benin, *The Footprints of God: Divine Accommodation in Jewish and Christian Thought*
(Albany, 1993), pp. 102 ff.

22. "Et animadvertebam et videbam in ipsis corporibus aliud esse quasi
totum et ideo pulchrum, aliud autem, quod ideo deceret, quoniam apte
accommodaretur alicui, sicut pars corporis ad universum suum aut calcia-
mentum ad pedem et similia" (*Confessions* 4.13.20); "et pulchrum, quod per
se ipsum, aptum autem, quod ad aliquid accommodatum deceret,
definiebam et distinguebam et exemplis corporis adstruebam" (*Confessions*
4.15.4). Benin, *Footprints*, pp. 99 ff., sees the importance of these passages but
does not develop their implications.

23. See H.-I. Marrou, *Saint-Augustin et la fin de la culture antique* (Paris,
1958), "Retractatio" [1949], pp. 631–637; P. Brown, *Augustine of Hippo* (Berkeley and Los Angeles, 1969), p. 57; A. Solignac's note on *Confessions*, books
1–7, *Bibliothèque augustinienne*, 2d ser. (Paris, 1963), 13:671–673; T. Katô,
"Melodia interior: Sur le traité 'De Pulchro et apto,'" *Revue des études augus-
tiniennes* 12 (1966): 229–240.

24. M. Testard puts forward convincing arguments in favor of the idea
that the treatise *De pulchro et apto* was inspired by Cicero rather than directly
by Plato in *Saint-Augustin et Cicéron* (Paris, 1958), 1:49–66. He quotes various
passages from Cicero, but these do not include the one I discuss here.

25. Cicero, *De oratore*, Loeb series, trans. H. Rackham.

26. On this whole topic, see also chapter 6 above.

27. See M. Pohlenz, "*To prepon*. Ein Beitrag zur Geschichte des griechis-
chen Geistes," in *Nachrichten von der Gesellschaft der Wissenschaften zu Göttin-
gen aus dem Jahre 1933*, Phil.–Hist. Kl., n. 16, pp. 53–92. The importance of
Augustine's rhetorical education is emphasized by M. Simonetti in the
introduction to the Italian translation of *De doctrine Christiana*: see
L'istruzione cristiana, ed. M. Simonetti (Milan, 1994), pp. xxxii ff. See also
G. Strauss, *Schriftgebrauch, Schriftauslegung und Schriftbeweis bei Augustin*
(Tübingen, 1959).

28. *The Works of Aurelius Augustinus*, ed. M. Dods (Edinburgh, 1875), 12, 2,
197 ff.

29. H.-I. Marrou comments on this passage, from a viewpoint different
from the one taken here, in *L'ambivalence du temps de l'histoire chez Saint-
Augustin* (Paris, 1950), pp. 82–84.

30. "Sicut enim talares et manicatas tunicas habere apud Romanos veteres flagitium erat, nunc autem honesto loco natis, cum tunicati sunt, non eas habere flagitium est" (*Christian Instruction*, trans. Gavigan, p. 134).

31. Cf. *Tractatus adversus Judaeos*, 3 (*Patrologia Latina*, 42:53): "Ut populus Dei, qui nunc est populus christianus, jam non cogatur observare quae propheticis temporibus observabantur: non quia damnata, sed quia mutata sunt; non ut res ipsae quae significabantur perirent, sed ut rerum signa suis quaeque temporibus convenirent."

32. Yerushalmi, *Zakhor*, p. 8.

33. In his "Epilogemena zu *Mimesis*," *Romanische Forschungen* 65 (1954): 1–18, esp. p. 3, E. Auerbach writes that the modern perspectivist and "historicist" point of view has been fully developed only during the last century and a half. However, Auerbach's own essay "Figura" suggests that this "modern vision" has far older roots. Here, as elsewhere in this book, I seek to establish a dialogue between various aspects of Auerbach's work, drawing out their implications in ways that their author might not have accepted. In the footnote (p. 106, n. 7) that concludes his essay "Linguistic Perspectivism in the *Don Quixote*," in his *Linguistics and Literary History* (Princeton, 1948), pp. 41–85, L. Spitzer emphasizes that " 'perspectivism' is inherent in Christian thought," according to which "the common man has access to wisdom, as well as the learned man; . . . the spirit, if not the letter, of the law can be understood by anyone." This same idea is central to Auerbach's work—criticized by Spitzer, in the preceding footnote, for its excessively sociological approach. Neither Auerbach nor Spitzer observes that Christian perspectivism (often accompanied by the opposition maintained between the "spirit" and the "letter") was crystallized in the ambivalent relationship of Christianity to Judaism: a blind spot that was perhaps partly related to the fact that both men were assimilated Jews. I examined a similar case in connection with another great scholar, Fritz Saxl, who like Spitzer came from a Viennese Jewish family, in my essay "Die Venus von Giorgiane: Ikonographische Innovationen und ihre Folgen," *Vortage aus den Warburg-Haus* 2 (1998): 3–88.

34. This double point of view provides the starting point for Guillén's investigations in his essay "On the Concept of Metaphor and Perspective" (cited in n. 2 above). He rightly observes that the metaphor of perspective "is derived from a European, *historically* conditioned discovery in the visual arts" (p. 366). However, as we shall see, the metaphor articulates a notion that had already been formulated in a different sensory language.

35. *De vera religione* 22.44: "Totum autem ordinem saeculorum sentire nullus hominum potest."

36. *Patrologia Latina*, 33:527: "Atque inde transeant in aeternam contemplationem speciei qui Deum rite colunt, etiam cum tempus est fidei."

37. M. Jay, "The Scopic Regime of Modernity," in *Vision and Visuality*, ed.
H. Foster (Seattle, 1988), pp. 3–23; and see also the same author's *Downcast
Eyes: The Denigration of Vision in Twentieth-Century French Thought* (Berkeley,
1993) (useful as a survey but ultimately not very illuminating).

PERSPECTIVE
Two Metaphors

38. See the present author's *Miti emblemi spie* (Turin, 1985), pp. 59 ff.
(*Clues, Myths, and the Historical Method*, trans. J. and A. Tedeschi [Baltimore
and London, 1989]).

39. G. Bock, "Machiavelli als Geschichtsschreiber," *Quellen und Forschungen aus italienischen Archiven und Bibliotheken* 66 (1986): 153–190, esp. pp. 175 f.

40. See C. Dionisotti, *Machiavelleri*, (Turin, 1980), pp. 122 f.

41. N. Machiavelli, dedicatory letter to *The Prince*, in the translation by
George Bull (Harmondsworth, 1961), p. 30. Further quotations from *The
Prince* are from this translation.

42. See E. Solmi, "Leonardo e Machiavelli" [1912], in *Scritti Vinciani*
(Florence, 1976), pp. 535–571, esp. p. 569 (where it is implied rather than
stated that the dedication to *The Prince* may allude to Leonardo). The
alleged affinities between Machiavelli and Galileo have distracted attention from the former's possible links with Leonardo: though G. Sasso, in
Studi sul Machiavelli (Naples, 1967), pp. 318 ff., rejects both lines of argument. However, E. Garin, in *Rinascite e rivoluzioni* (Bari, 1975), p. 253, suggests it may be opportune to consider once more the old claim that
Machiavelli and Leonardo were in contact, a suggestion noted by Dionisotti (*Machiavellerie*, p. 28, n. 6). R. Masters, in *Machiavelli, Leonardo and the
Science of Power* (Notre Dame, Ind., 1996), enthusiastically takes up this
theme (though he shows no knowledge of much of the earlier work,
including the contributions of Solmi and Bock). See also the volume
Leonardo: Il codice Hammer e la mappa di Imola, ed. C. Pedretti (Bologna,
1985).

43. Solmi, "Leonardo e Machiavelli," p. 569; and see also C. Luporini, *La
mente di Leonardo* (Florence, 1953), p. 174, n. 63.

44. Leo Strauss argues in *Thoughts on Machiavelli* (Glencoe, Ill., 1958), that
Machiavelli's "modern" attitude toward human reality implied a discontinuity with the "ancient" (Greek and Jewish) tradition of antiquity. Karl
Löwith (*Meaning in History* [Chicago, 1949]) sees the decisive discontinuity
as lying in the opposition between Christianity and the ancient world. Probably they are both right and both wrong, inasmuch as they are pointing out
two radical discontinuities (Christian and "modern," respectively), which
Hegel inherited and combined together.

45. *The Prince*, p. 29.

46. See G. Bock, "Civil Discord in Machiavelli's *Istorie Fiorentine*," in
Machiavelli and Republicanism, ed. G. Bock, M. Viroli, and Q. Skinner (Cambridge, 1990), pp. 181–201.

47. See G. Procacci, *Machiavelli nella cultura europea dell'età moderna* (Bari, 1995).

48. R. Descartes, *Correspondance*, in *Oeuvres*, ed. C. Adam and P. Tannery (Paris, 1976), 4:406.

49. Descartes, *Correspondance*, 4:485–496.

50. Ibid., 4:492: "Car le crayon ne represente que les choses qui se voyent de loin; mais les principaux motifs des actions des Princes sont souvent des circonstances si particulières, que, si ce n'est qu'on soit Prince soy-mesme, ou bien qu'on ait esté fort longtemps participant de leurs secrets, on ne les sçauroit imaginer."

51. J. J. Goux might have drawn further support from this passage for the rather hasty remarks in his "Descartes et la perspective," *L'Esprit Créateur* 25, no. 1 (Spring 1985): 10–20. See also G. Boehm, *Studien zur Perspektivität: Philosophie und Kunst in der frühen Neuzeit* (Heidelberg, 1969), pp. 172–184.

52. While he was in Paris in 1675 and 1676, Leibniz transcribed and translated several manuscripts by Descartes. See E. Garin, introduction to the Italian ed. of Descartes' *Works* (*Opere* [Bari, 1967], 1:xxxv); and O. Klopp, ed., *Correspondance de Leibniz avec l'électrice Sophie de Brunswick-Lunebourg*, 3 vols. (Hanover, 1874), 1:158.

53. See Procacci, *Machiavelli*, p. 264.

54. G. W. Leibniz, *Monadology*, trans. with an introduction and notes by R. Latta (Oxford, 1898), no. 57, p. 248; see *Monadologia*, in Leibniz, *Opera philosophica*, ed. J. E. Erdmann (Aalen, 1959), p. 709: "Et comme une même ville regardée de différens côtés paroît tout autre et est comme multipliée perspectivement, il arrive de même, que par la multitude infinie de substances simples, il y a comme autant de différens univers, qui ne sont pourtant que les perspectives d'un seul selon les différens points de vue de chaque Monade." The connections we are examining provide the basis for a fresh look at the comparison between Descartes' perspectivism and that of Leibniz, as this has been set forth (for instance) by U. J. Wenzel, "Descartes in die Perspektive des Perspektivismus: Eine Skizze," in *Perspektiven des Perspektivismus: Gedenkschrift zum Tode Friedrich Kaulbachs*, ed. V. Gerhardt and N. Herold (Berlin, 1992), pp. 59–73, esp. p. 59. See also Guillén, "Concept of Metaphor," pp. 318–325 (on Leibniz's visual metaphors).

55. G. W. Leibniz, *Théodicée*, in *Opera Philosophica*, p. 548: Dieu, par un art merveilleux, tourne les défauts de ces petits Mondes au plus grand ornement de son grand Monde. C'est comme dans ces inventions de perspective, où certains beaux desseins ne paroissent que confusion, jusqu'à ce qu'on les rapporte à leur vrai point de vue, ou qu'on les regarde par le moyen d'un certain verre ou miroir. C'est en les plaçant et s'en servant comme il faut, qu'on les fait devenir l'ornement d'un cabinet. Ainsi les déformités apparentes de nos petits Mondes se

réunissent en beauté dans le grand, et n'ont rien qui s'oppose à l'unité d'un Principe universel infiniment parfait: au contraire, ils augmentent l'admiration de sa sagesse, qui fait servir le mal au plus grand bien. [Translators' note: We translate from the French. For an abridged English translation, see Leibniz, *Theodicy*, ed. D. Allen (Ontario, 1966).] In a letter to des Bosses of 1712, Leibniz counterposes "scenographiae diversae," which are different and depend on the spectator's viewpoint, to the "iconographia seu geometrica representatio," which is single and unique, and corresponds to the vision of things enjoyed by God (quoted in A. Funkenstein, *Theology and the Scientific Imagination* [Princeton, 1986], p. 112, n. 9).

56. See R. Koselleck, "Standortbindung und Zeitlichkeit: Ein Betrag zur historiographischen Erschliessung der geschichtlichen Welt," in Koselleck, *Vergangene Zukunft: Zur Semantik geschichtlicher Zeiten* (Frankfurt am Main, 1979), pp. 176–207.

57. J. M. Chladenius, *Einleitung zur richtigen Auslegung: Vernünftiger Reden und Schriften*, with an introduction by L. Geldsetzer (Düsseldorf, 1969), pp. 181–189, esp. p. 188. See also H. Müller, *Johann Martin Chladenius (1710–1759): Ein Betrag zur Geschichte der Geisteswissenschaften, besonders der historischen Methodik* (Berlin, 1917); P. H. Reill, *The German Enlightenment and the Rise of Historicism* (Berkeley, 1975), pp. 104–112 (see p. 110 on visual metaphors); M. Ermarth, "Hermeneutics and History: The Fork in Hermes' Path Through the Eighteenth Century," in *Aufklärung und Geschichte: Studien zur deutschen Geschichtswissenschaft im 18. Jahrhundert*, ed. H. E. Boedeker et al. (Göttingen, 1987), pp. 193–221.

58. Chladenius, *Einleitung*, p. 187. Koselleck also notes this passage (*Vergangene Zukunft*, p. 185).

59. See Procacci, *Machiavelli*, pp. 370–373, on Hegel's *Über die verfassung Deutschlands*, and on Fichte's important essay of 1807, "Über Machiavelli als Schriftsteller, und Stellen aus einer Schriften" (in *Fichtes Werke*, ed. I. H. Fichte (Berlin, 1971), 11:401–453). On pp. 430–433, Fichte transcribes and comments on the passage on the depiction of landscape from the dedication to *The Prince*.

60. B. Kaiser and I. Werchan, eds., *Ex libris Karl Marx und Friedrich Engels* (Berlin, 1967), p. 134, no. 286. In a letter to Engels of 25 September 1857, Marx refers to Machiavelli's *Istorie fiorentine* as a "masterpiece" (see Marx-Engels, *Collected Works* [Moscow: Progress Publishers], 40:187). This evidence may be added to that analyzed in Procacci, *Machiavelli*. B. Croce's well-known comment on Marx and Machiavelli is in *Materialismo storico ed economia marxista* (1899; reprint, Bari, 1951), p. 161, n. 1.

61. See F. Nietzsche, *Die fröhliche Wissenschaft*, 354 ("Vom Genius der Gattung"), in *Kritische Gesamtausgabe* [KGW], V/2, ed. G. Colli and M. Monti-

nari (Berlin and New York, 1973), pp. 272–275; Nietzsche, *Zur Genealogie der Moral*, 3:12. KGW, 6/2 (Berlin, 1968), pp. 382 f.; "Nachgelassene Fragmente, Anfang 1888 bis Anfang Januar 1889," KGW, 8/3 (Berlin and New York, 1972), pp. 165 f. See also F. Kaulbach, "Nietzsche und der monadologische Gedanke," *Nietzsche-Studien* 8 (1979): 127–156; V. Gerhardt and N. Herold, eds., *Perspektiven des Perspektivismus: Gedenkschrift zum Tode Freidrich Kaulbachs* (Würzburg, 1992).

62. See Justinus, *Dialogues* 11:3, ed. G. Archambault (Paris, 1909). On the theological implications of the terms *"verus"* and *"verissimus"* in Augustine's writings, see Lecuyer, "Le sacrifice"; de Broglie, "La notion de sacrifice." M. Simon, *Verus Israel* (Paris, 1983), is of fundamental importance as regards this whole question (see p. 93 for a note of the now-lost work against Marcion written by Justinus). Justinus refers back to Romans 9:6 ("for not all descendants of Israel are truly Israel"), and more generally to the Pauline understanding of the relations between Jews and Christians in terms of the opposition between letter (or flesh) and spirit, and between Esau and Jacob (see chapter 9, below).

63. It may also be the case, looking at it from another point of view, that the need to hold together, in a material sense, the Torah, the prophetic books and the Gospels was one factor that led the Christians to prefer the codex to the less manageable scroll: a hypothesis put forward in E. Bickerman, "Some Notes on the Transmission of the Septuagint" (1950), in Bickerman, *Studies in Jewish and Christian History* (Leiden, 1976), 1:137–166, esp. pp. 138 f.

64. See W. Kamlah, *Christentum und Geschichtlichkeit: Untersuchungen zur Entstehung des Christentums und zu Augustins "Bürgerschaft Gottes,"* 2d (rev.) ed. (Stuttgart and Cologne, 1951), p. 17. It would be quite interesting to compare this with the first edition of this notable study (*Christentum und Selbstbehauptung: Historische und philosophische Untersuchungen zur Entstehung des Christentums und zu Augustins "Bürgerschaft Gottes,"* [Frankfurt am Main, 1940])—see also the comment of J. Taubes, in a note to F. Overbeck, *Selbstbekenntnisse* [Frankfurt am Main, 1966], p. 152). The afterword to the second edition draws attention to a number of changes, which include a new introduction (to which I refer above). One notes that the epithet *"philosophisch,"* inspired by Heidegger (who is gratefully acknowledged on pp. xii–xiii), figures in the subtitle of the first edition but has disappeared from the second, where it is stated at the outset that the inquiry to be conducted will be "historical" (p. 7).

65. E. Gellner, *Postmodernism, Reason, and Religion* (London, 1992). F. Fukuyama's book *The End of History and the Last Man* (New York, 1992) is discussed, and set in a broad intellectual context, in P. Anderson, "The Ends of History," in *A Zone of Engagement* (London, 1992), pp. 279–335.

66. M. Iversen, "Warburg—neu gelesen," in Baumgart (ed.), *Denkräume zwischen Kunst und Wissenschaft*, ed. S. Baumgart (which I read at the suggestion of Karen Michels). Cf. also G. Bock, "Der Platz der Frauen in der Geschichte," in *Neue Aufsätze in der Geschichtswissenschaft* (Vienna, 1984), pp. 108–127; D. Haraway, "Situated Knowledge: The Science Question in Feminism and the Privilege of Partial Perspective," *Feminist Studies* 14 (1988): 575–599, esp. pp. 581 and 583 (which I read at the suggestion of Nadine Tanio).

67. See my "Just One Witness," in S. Friedlanger, ed., *Probing the Limits of Representation: Nazism and the "Final Solution,"* Cambridge, Mass. 1992, pp. 82–96; *History, Rhetoric, and Proof,* London and Hanover 1999.

243

8. TO KILL A CHINESE MANDARIN The Moral Implications of Distance

8. TO KILL A CHINESE MANDARIN: THE MORAL IMPLICATIONS OF ᴅISTANCE

This essay was given as a lecture in 1994 as part of the series of Oxford Amnesty Lectures on the theme "Human Rights and History." For their help and criticism, my thanks go to Perry Anderson, Pier Cesare Bori, Alberto Gajano, Samuel R. Gilbert, Stefano Levi Della Torre, Francesco Orlando, and Adriano Prosperi. The version printed here is slightly longer than the lecture as originally given.

1. Aristotle, *Rhetoric*, trans. with introduction and notes by G. A. Kennedy (New York and Oxford, 1991), pp. 102 f. George Steiner offers an analysis of the various images of Antigone, from Sophocles to the present, in *Antigones* (Oxford, 1986).

2. Aristotle, *Rhetoric*, trans. Kennedy, pp. 153 ff.

3. See P. Vidal-Naquet, "L'Atlantide et les nations," in Vidal-Naquet, *La démocratie grecque vue d'ailleurs* (Paris, 1990), pp. 139 ff.

4. Aristotle, *On the Art of Poetry*, in *Aristotle, Horace, Longinus: Classical Literary Criticism*, trans. and ed. T. S. Dorsch (Harmondsworth, 1965), p. 50.

5. Diderot, *Oeuvres*, ed. A. Billy (Paris, 1951), pp. 759–781.

6. See W. E. Edmiston, *Diderot and the Family: A Conflict of Nature and Law* (Saratoga, Calif., 1985), pp. 75 ff.

7. Diderot, *Oeuvres*, p. 772.

8. Diderot, *Oeuvres Esthétiques*, ed. P. Vernière (Paris, 1988), p. 206.

9. However, when Diderot refers to a "text" ("ce texte épuisé," p. 742), he does not necessarily mean a written text; cf. p. 817 (*Lettre sur les aveugles*).

10. Diderot, *Oeuvres*, ed. Billy, p. 820.

11. See the insightful comments in F. Venturi, *Jeunesse de Diderot* (Paris, 1939), pp. 142–167, esp. pp. 163–166.

12. Diderot, *Oeuvres*, ed. Billy, p. 820.

13. D. Diderot, *Paradoxe sur le comédien*, in *Diderot's Writings on the The-*

atre, ed. F. C. Green (Cambridge, 1936), p. 284. [Translators' note: This anthology contains Diderot's text in French, which we translate here.]

244

8. TO KILL A
CHINESE MANDARIN
*The Moral
Implications
of Distance*

14. Venturi, *Jeunesse de Diderot*, pp. 159 f.

15. In reference to Diderot's observation that to a blind person there is no difference between a man urinating and a man bleeding, Venturi remarks on the "characteristic cruelty often associated with the vision of nature in the eighteenth century" (*Jeunesse de Diderot*, p. 165).

16. D. A. F. de Sade, *La philosophie dans le boudoir*, in *Oeuvres Complètes* (Paris, 1966), pp. 514 f.

17. See the passage quoted by M. Delon in the introduction to de Sade, *Oeuvres* (Paris, 1990), p. xxiv.

18. F.-R. de Chateaubriand, *Génie du Christianisme* (Paris, 1930), 1:166 f.

19. P. Rönai was the first to point out the connection between Chateaubriand and Balzac in "Tuer le mandarin," *Revue de littérature comparée* 10 (1930): 520–523. Despite the article's subtitle, L. W. Keates does not consider eighteenth-century precedents in "Mysterious Miraculous Mandarin: Origins, Literary Paternity, Implications in Ethics," *Revue de littérature comparée* 40 (1966): 497–525. A. Coimbra Martíns explicitly denies that the two passages in Diderot are significant in "O Mandarim assassinado," in *Ensaios Queirosianos* (Lisbon, 1967), pp. 11–266, 381–383, 387–395; see esp. pp. 27 f. See also R. Trousson, *Balzac disciple et juge de Jean-Jacques Rousseau* (Geneva, 1983), p. 243 and n. 11.

20. H. de Balzac, *Old Goriot*, trans. M. A. Crawford, (1951; reprint, Harmondsworth, 1979), p. 157; see also p. 176. On the mistaken attribution to Rousseau, see Coimbra Martíns, "O Mandarim assassinado," pp. 38–40.

21. Balzac, *La comédie humaine* (Paris, 1976), 1:593. P. Rönai remarks on the passage (see Coimbra Martíns, "O Mandarim assassinado," pp. 38–40).

22. D. Hume, *A Treatise of Human Nature*, introduction by A. D. Lindsay (1911; reprint, London, 1936), 2:139.

23. Diderot, too, alludes to a text supposedly by Rousseau (*Oeuvres*, ed. Billy, p. 1418, n. 7), citing *Emile* but giving no precise reference. That the reference is erroneous can be rapidly confirmed by checking in E. Brunet, *Index-Concordance d'Emile ou de l'éducation*, 2 vols. (Geneva and Paris, 1980).

24. C. Browning, *Ordinary Men: Reserve Police Battalion 101 and the Final Solution in Poland* (New York, 1992).

25. A. Smith, *The Theory of Moral Sentiments*, ed. D. Raphael and A. Mac-Fie (Oxford, 1979; reprint, Indianapolis, 1982) pp. 136 f. This passage was drawn to my attention by Perry Anderson.

26. Hume, *Treatise*, p. 140, italics in original. The text reads "superior," not "inferior"; but the entire logic of the following passage requires "inferior," and I amend accordingly.

27. Hume, *Treatise*, p. 143.

28. W. Benjamin, "Theses on the Philosophy of History," in Benjamin, ed. H. Arendt, trans. H. Zohn, *Illuminations* (London, 1970), p. 257 (Thesis VI).

29. H. Lotze, *Microcosmus: An Essay Concerning Man and his Relation to the World*, trans. E. Constance Jones (Edinburgh, 1894), pp. 172, 173 f.

30. On Benjamin's intellectual debt to Lotze, see S. Mosés, *L'Ange de l'histoire: Rosenzweig, Benjamin, Scholem* (Paris, 1992), p. 166. And see also H. D. Kittsteiner, "Walter Benjamin's Historicism," *New German Critique* 39 (Fall 1986): pp. 179 f. (brought to my attention by Dan Sherer).

31. Benjamin, "Theses," p. 256 (Thesis II).

9. POPE WOJTYLA'S SLIP

I acknowledge with thanks the critical comments of Pier Cesare Bori, Gianni Cova, and Stefano Levi Della Torre.

1. M. Politi, *"In ginocchio davanti agli ebrei"* (On his knees before the Jews), *La Repubblica*, 24 September 1997 (on some remarks made by Cardinal Martini).

INDEX

Illustrations are indicated by plate number in italics (for example: 1 pl.)

EUROPEAN PERSPECTIVES

A Series in Social Thought and Cultural Criticism

Lawrence D. Kritzman, Editor

Norbert Elias — *The Germans*

Louis Althusser — *Writings on Psychoanalysis: Freud and Lacan*

Elisabeth Roudinesco — *Jacques Lacan: His Life and Work*

Ross Guberman — *Julia Kristeva Interviews*

Kelly Oliver — *The Portable Kristeva*

Pierra Nora — *Realms of Memory: The Construction of the French Past*

vol. 1: *Conflicts and Divisions*

vol. 2: *Traditions*

vol. 3: *Symbols*

Claudine Fabre-Vassas — *The Singular Beast: Jews, Christians, and the Pig*

Paul Ricoeur — *Critique and Conviction: Conversations with François Azouvi and Marc de Launay*

Theodor W. Adorno — *Critical Models: Interventions and Catchwords*

Alain Corbin — *Village Bells: Sound and Meaning in the Nineteenth-Century French Countryside*

Zygmunt Bauman — *Globalization: The Human Consequences*

Emmanuel Levinas — *Entre Nous*

Jean-Louis Flandrin and Massimo Montanari — *Food: A Culinary History*

Alain Finkielkraut — *In the Name of Humanity: Reflections on the Twentieth Century*

Julia Kristeva — *The Sense and Non-Sense of Revolt: The Powers and Limits of Psychoanalysis*

Régis Debray — *Transmitting Culture*

Sylviane Agacinski — *The Politics of the Sexes*

Alain Corbin — *The Life of an Unknown: The Rediscovered World of a Clog Maker in Nineteenth-Century France*

Michel Pastoureau — *The Devil's Cloth: A History of Stripes and Striped Fabric*

Elisabeth Roudinesco — *Why Psychoanalysis?*